9/00

D0945504

WITHDRAWN

CHINA ON THE BRINK

CHINA ON THE BRINK

The Myths and Realities of the World's Largest Market

CALLUM HENDERSON

McGRAW-HILL

New York   San Francisco   Washington, D.C.   Auckland   Bogotá
Caracas   Lisbon   London   Madrid   Mexico City   Milan
Montreal   New Delhi   San Juan   Singapore
Sydney   Tokyo   Toronto

Library of Congress Cataloging-in-Publication Data

Henderson, Callum.
  China on the brink / by Callum Henderson.
      p.   cm.
  ISBN 0-07-134515-9
  1. China—Economic conditions—1976-   I. Title.
HC427.92.H455   1999
330.951'059—dc21   99-11274
                                                                CIP

McGraw-Hill

*A Division of The **McGraw·Hill** Companies*

1 2 3 4 5 6 7 8 9 0 DOC/DOC 9 0 4 3 2 1 0 9

ISBN 0-07-134515-9

Printed and bound by R. R. Donnelley & Sons Company.

McGraw-Hill books are available at special quantity discounts to use as premiums and sales promotions, or for use in corporate training programs. For more information, please write to the Director of Special Sales, McGraw-Hill, 11 West 19th Street, New York, NY 10011. Or contact your local bookstore.

 This book is printed on recycled, acid-free paper containing a minimum of 50% recycled de-inked fiber.

Contents

To Ken H. and John Lilley

do-je

Acknowledgments

There are countless books on the history of China, and similarly countless ones that describe China's recent ascent from economic obscurity. This book, at its most ambitious, seeks to offer something different, a critical analysis of the quality of China's economic performance which lies beneath the headline figures. In short, it offers the contrarian perspective that all is not necessarily well with China's economy, despite the undoubted and impressive successes it has achieved; that China has fundamental weaknesses, just as did its Asian counterparts; and that tough policy decisions have to be taken if the Asian crisis is not to be played out once more in China itself. The aim is not to deny the progress made to date. It is instead to sound an alarm, to seek to address issues while they are still manageable.

With regard to this endeavor, I am profoundly grateful for the advice and encouragement I have had from my friends, colleagues, and counterparts within the financial industry, and to those individuals who were gracious enough to give of their time and their thoughts. Necessity dictates that some of these remain anonymous. Of those who can be mentioned, particular thanks must again go to Meryl Phang and Tony Ngan, of Standard & Poor's MMS in Hong Kong. My gratitude must one more be expressed to my two teachers during my time in Asia, Ken Ho and John Lilley.

Callum Henderson is an Emerging Market Currency Strategist at a global investment bank in London. The views expressed in this book are his own personal views and are not necessarily shared by his employer.

Introduction

The crack and whine of bullets, the buzz-soar roar of automatic
fire filled the air. Some people ran in blind panic, desperately trying to get away from the advancing soldiers. Others stood their
ground, screaming, hurling abuse, only to be cut down where they
stood . . . the morning hours of June 4, 1989 . . . the day China
butchered its young, its own people.

November 1998, some nine years later . . . and the crowds are
surging again on Tiananmen Square, some on foot, some on bicycles, pressing, pushing against a wall of police which bars their
way, cursing, shouting, their outrage no less heartfelt, no less im-
passioned. Yet this time their cause is not political, but financial,
for the crowd is a sea of angry investors, demanding their money
back after the commercial failure of a company. This time, the authorities, well aware of the political dangers of economic distress,
seek to play down the incident, merely shepherding away the
demonstrators from the government buildings where they had
been trying to make their case.

Two incidents that show how far China has come, how far it
must go. Two incidents that demonstrate the different allegiances
and passions that have been felt by the ordinary person in
China—and how those seem to have changed radically over such
a relatively short period of time. Despite the occasional bout of
political dissidence, China—at least for now—is no longer so en-
flamed by political and radical ideas and ideologies. The focus
now for most people is much more on the economic rather than
the militant. There is a deep irony with regard to the protest of

November 1998, however humble that was compared with its predecessor. The people who took to the streets in 1998 to voice their discontent were precisely those whom Deng Xiaoping had exhorted to drive the economy forward, precisely those whom China's late paramount leader had told in his revolutionary statement of the 1980s that "to get rich is glorious." These were the very inheritors of his vision for a commercially viable and prosperous China. That they were on the streets, protesting their financial losses, again demonstrates how far China has come; yet it also shows the dangers inherent with that progress.

China's government has done much to promote the "socialist market economy" as the way forward, as the ultimate compromise between the egalitarianism of communism and the economic benefits of a free-market economy. However, this too has its economic victims. Indeed, its victims are all too visible, most notably on the outskirts of all the main cities in China. And with the gathering economic slowdown in China which we continue to witness—with some trepidation—the number of these victims is rising. There will come a time in the not too distant future when, if that number continues to rise unchecked, a situation of economic distress could once again become political. Most in the West see the events of June 4, 1989, as specifically a rejection of the political status quo. Yet in reality the roots of June 4 were economic just as much as, if not more than, they were ever political. Indeed, to a great extent, they started out as a protest against the excesses brought on by inflation, most notably official corruption. This interlinking of economics and politics, however much the authorities might officially deny it, is a lesson not lost on the leaders of the Chinese Communist Party, lodged in their fortresslike headquarters of the Zhongnanhai. Indeed, this is most probably why the latest outpourings of economic discontent have been treated with relative care.

Stability lies at the very epicenter of what passes nowadays for ideology in China. While the need for substantial economic advancement remains, despite the successes to date, such advancement cannot be achieved without stability, so thought Deng Xiaoping. Given how he himself, and others in the upper echelons of the Party, suffered during the madness that became known as the Cultural Revolution, it is hardly surprising that he came to such a view. Indeed, as we shall see, stability and the paramount need to avoid any repetition of the chaos of the Cultural Revolution constitute a central theme of all prevailing official thought, including economics and finance, which are the main subjects of this book. Deng's economic philosophy of "feeling for rocks underfoot while crossing the river"—or *"Mo zhe shi tou guo he,"* in Putonghua (Mandarin Chinese)—was specifically aimed at adopting a cautious approach to reform, avoiding the type of chaos that China has so often suffered from, in both the political and economic spheres.

The differences present between the China of 1989 and 1998 are starkly clear in the two incidents mentioned above; yet there are also similarities, recurring themes. Of these, the most profound is the most obvious—that they both took place on or near Tiananmen Square. To the West, Tiananmen—the Gate of Heavenly Peace—is synonymous with the brutal events of June 4, 1989. Yet it is steeped in history. Indeed to a great extent, it is the very font of Chinese history, from which all expression and change have come. The history of Tiananmen is the history of China. In the time of the emperors, Tiananmen was the central symbol of unity, a unifying place from which edicts were issued and complaints heard. Tiananmen was the locus of power, the center of the center of the world. In the twentieth century, while still playing a leading part in Chinese history and politics, Tiananmen has taken on a slightly different role, as a focal point for Chinese popular dissent, initially against foreign and then latterly against domestic oppression. The events of May 4, 1919, caused a sea change in Chinese popular thinking when some 3,000 students protested against the terms of the Versailles Treaty, which granted German concessions in China to the Japanese. Thus, Tiananmen became the focus of protest rather than of obedience, the focus of dissent, of rebellion. In 1925, it was again the scene of protest when Beijing locals demonstrated against the killing of demonstrators in Shanghai by British troops. And again in 1926 and 1935, it was the stage for anti-

Japanese demonstrations, first against the government's capitulation and then as a rallying cry for national resistance against Japan. After the war, on October 1, 1949, Chairman Mao stood on the reviewing platform of the Gate, facing the masses crowded into the square, and declared that the Chinese people had finally "stood up." In 1966, it was where the Cultural Revolution began, where hundreds of thousands of Red Guards were exhorted to purge the nation of cultural and ideological impurity. Again, in 1976, there were mass demonstrations in the square following the death of Zhou Enlai, the brutal suppression of which marked the beginning of the end for the Gang of Four. In the early 1980s, people gathered to discuss previously heretical ideas of democracy, writing their thoughts on what became known as the Democracy Wall on the edge of the Forbidden City.

The brutal crackdown on June 4, 1989, was, as Zhao Ziyang, the sacked Party general secretary who sided with students, said many times, a "mistake," though to the authorities at the time, seemingly an unavoidable one. Given China's history, however, and given the history of Tiananmen Square, it was predictable, and it is not inconceivable that it could happen again. China is not a democracy, whatever its merits, and the authorities that govern it will not go quietly—if go they do. For the West to think otherwise is merely wishful thinking, and indeed the new rapprochement between Western governments and China suggests a new realism—or at least a desire not to antagonize China and to get at its markets! China's more recent history has—thankfully— been more peaceful, with both the authorities and the people focusing on economic success rather than political conflict. This success was brought about as a result of the economic revolution launched by Deng Xiaoping at the 11th Party Congress in 1978. It is a paradox that the man who gave the orders for the Tiananmen Square crackdown in 1989 was also responsible for what is arguably one of the greatest economic successes of all time, a paradox that is a reflection both of China's past and of the difficulties and challenges it will face going forward, attempting to balance the requirements of rapid economic liberalization with an official desire to limit political development. All the same, the results of Deng's economic revolution were unquestionably astounding. China averaged over 10% annual GDP growth from the mid-1980s through the early 1990s, and Western commentators fell over themselves to herald it as the new economic superpower. "The giant had awakened," as Napoleon Bonaparte so famously predicted, and in economic circles (and no doubt political ones as well), the world did indeed tremble. Coinciding with the economic ascent of Southeast and other parts of North Asia, China's progress seemed unstoppable, its ultimate supremacy as the world's leading economy inevitable. The events of 1989 notwithstanding, the world resolved itself to adapting to a new and potentially dominant player on the world economic stage.

Growth boomed. It was led initially by the agricultural sector, freed from the restrictions of the collective system as a result of deregulation in 1979. Subsequently it was fueled by the township and village enterprises (TVEs), the first transmission mechanism from a socialist command economy to a market economy. Then the first truly private enterprises emerged in their own right, followed by heavy industry itself. Gradual liberalization of selective economic regulations, sectors and areas, such as the special economic zones (SEZs), gave the population renewed purpose and opportunity. With the rise in growth came side effects, both positive and negative. On the positive side, indicators of economic advancement, such as infant mortality, life expectancy, and diet composition, showed the requisite improvements for a nation that was seeking to attain a new and higher level of economic development. The proportion of the population that lived in a state of "absolute poverty," as defined by international organizations such as the World Bank and the Asian Development Bank, fell from around 25% in 1978 to 10% by the mid-1980s. The general standard of living, as seen both by the data and anecdotally, was clearly improving, and as throughout the world, the Chinese people sought to take advantage of their improved situation.

Consumption patterns changed radically, becoming more aggressive. And business, whether state-owned, private, or foreign, sought to change with them. The national savings' rate stayed extraordinarily high, with gross national savings as a percentage of GNP averaging 34.3% from 1981 to 1990—three times that of Western Europe or the U.S. Yet consumption as a percentage of total income also rose as the people felt the economic benefits of the reform process. A visitor returning to Beijing or Shanghai today, or even the likes of Shenzhen or Guangzhou, would be stunned by the enormity of change, of advancement, that China has experienced in the last two decades. To be sure, China still has the hallmarks of an "emerging market," both socially and economically. Yet the trappings of economic prosperity that the West takes for granted, indeed almost as a defining characteristic of the West and the Western way of life, are increasingly to be found in abundance in modern-day China. From neon-fronted bars, to cabaret shows, discos, and chic restaurants, it is clear that the Chinese consumer has also awakened. Leisure pursuits once frowned upon or banned outright by the Maoisu are in ever-increasing abundance. China is in part proof that the world is indeed becoming a smaller place. There are parts of the Bund in Shanghai or Wangfujing in Beijing, which are the same the world over, full of the young, the eager, and the commercial.

Yet just around the corner from that Irish bar in Shanghai, that Jamaican restaurant in Beijing, remain stark, painful reminders that China, whatever its remarkable triumphs, still has a long way to go. Large economic disparities still exist, and the reform process itself has resulted in a significant number of social and economic casualties. For along with the positive side effects of growth, there have also been negative ones, the first notable example of which was rampant inflation. Aside from endangering the cause of long-term economic stability and growth, inflation clearly threatened China's fledgling banking system, and was duly dealt with necessary ruthlessness through fiscal austerity from 1993 to 1994. Since the beginnings of the economic reform process in 1978, China has gone through a series of increasingly harsh economic cycles, characterized most notably by excessive credit expansion and deteriorating national

budget accounts. Offsetting the budget deficit has been a booming trade surplus. However, as Chapter 1 of this book describes,
the Asian crisis could well hit Chinese export growth, reducing
China's total current account surplus. As the ASEAN nations
now know to their cost, deterioration in both the budget and the
current account is a potentially lethal combination.

Growing unemployment has also been a negative side effect of
the drive toward a market economy. The restructuring of the
state-owned enterprises (SOEs), announced at the 15th Party
Congress in September 1997, will itself put a further 25–30 million people out of work. Given that the SOEs effectively act as
mini welfare states for their workforce rather than just businesses, losing one's job could mean losing one's flat and whatever meager benefits the company offers. The social ramifications
of rising unemployment and little or no safety net are all too
clear, particularly against a backdrop where the Party's only legitimacy nowadays is to make people better off. In sum, China's
economic success story of the last two decades, as stunning as it
has been, is flawed, at both the macroeconomic and the microeconomic level—just as with the ASEAN and other parts of Asia
which were devastated by the Asian crisis of 1997 and continue
to suffer from the aftereffects.

China's economic flaws are serious, fundamental not only to
its own future economic health, but also to that of the global
economy as a whole. Not so long ago—and even in some cases
still to this day—renowned economic commentators were describing China as "number one," as inevitably and inexorably
becoming the largest economy in the world. Today it is clear that
China is undergoing a significant and wrenching economic
slowdown—a process that Chapter 2 addresses in detail, at both
the macroeconomic and the microeconomic level—while simultaneously attempting to complete in record time one of the
largest industrial restructurings in world economic history. Yet
most of what we hear and read about China's economy remains
remarkably bullish, seemingly overlooking the fundamental
negatives within the economy which at the least have yet to be
ironed out and at the worst are potentially life-threatening.

There are clear reasons why the U.S. is the world's largest and most powerful economy, and there are equally clear and fundamental reasons why China is not and will not be for a considerable time—if ever. Just as there were those who argued that Asia was "different," and did not necessarily have to obey the same fundamental economic rules prevalent in the West—the folly of this thesis being proved conclusively in 1997–1998—there are those who stubbornly argue that China also is somehow "different." Interestingly, China's economic leaders themselves are not among the advocates of this argument, instead portraying China's development as typically characteristic of an emerging nation, albeit one with the world's largest population.

China on the Brink: The Myths and Realities of the World's Largest Market is meant as an antidote to the many books and commentaries that unquestioningly lavish praise on China's economic progress but that do not ask why China's slowdown—which began in 1992–1993—is accelerating, potentially threatening the global economy if it cannot avoid a crash landing. At its most ambitious, this book is offered as an attempt, amid all the hype, at a higher degree of realism, an evenhanded response to the arguments of the China bulls. It is not intended as a snapshot of China or indeed as a static view of how China works or where it has come from. There are plenty of such works already, many by authors with considerably more expertise in the fields of Chinese history and social development than this author has achieved. Instead, *China on the Brink* is an attempt to show where China's economy is heading, an attempt to discover and analyze the fissures and fault lines that lie beneath the surface of economic history's most stunning recent success. Amid the aftermath of the Asian currency and debt crisis of 1997, many still see China unscathed, safe behind its self-imposed regulatory barriers. Yet just as the bricks of the Great Wall were not able to hide the Middle Kingdom from the gathering hordes of old, so its regulatory and legal walls will not completely save it from what some see as their modern equivalent, the unfettered forces of free-market capitalism. Thus, the answer to China's present economic problems must not be to rely merely on such regulatory defenses. Nor is the answer to revert to past economic and political practices, reversing free-market reforms and moving back to a more command-oriented model of economic and political freedom, a tempting move in times of difficulty which would in reality return a great nation to the dark ages. Rather, the answer lies in increasing and broadening the reforms from within, improving the internal structure and making it more able to deal with free-market forces, while maintaining at least some defenses until such time as that structure is strong enough to fully withstand such forces.

This may seem surprising from a purely capitalist viewpoint. In our modern world of freely-floating exchange rates, the prevailing doctrine is that only the markets can decide and arbitrate and thus currency pegs of all types must eventually go (to be sure, Europe appears to be taking a different view on this). However, were it not for the fact that the renminbi is not yet convertible on the capital account, China's banking system would have melted down, gone the way of Indonesia and Thailand amid a mountain of bad debts and overleverage, the result of decades of politically driven credit policies. Were it not for these very restrictions on capitalism within China, much if not all of the progress that China has made in the past two decades would have been wiped out. In short, those in the West who call for full, immediate, and unfettered liberalization of the financial markets in China do not know what they are talking about. That said, the reform process still has a considerable way to go if China is ever to become the global economic leader anticipated by so many. The restructuring of the SOEs, as hazardous as that is, comes not a minute too soon. Equally, the decades of politically directed credit from state banks to the SOEs has resulted in a national banking system that is technically bankrupt, though, to be sure, still supported by the state. The solution to this must be to cut even more jobs; yet this will inevitably, as Chapter 3 seeks to demonstrate, cause increasing social tensions, leading to clashes with the authorities and potentially, as Chapter 4 elucidates, a political backlash against the prevailing forces of reform. The outskirts of Beijing, Shanghai, and Guangzhou are already clogged with the human casualties of the reform process, the homeless, the jobless. It would not take much for the "left"—those few in the Party who remain opposed to the central doctrines within the reform process—to mount a spirited campaign of support for these "dispossessed," thus potentially destabilizing President Jiang Zemin's hold on the reins of power and thus the reform process itself.

From a Western perspective, many saw China's opening as a new opportunity for plunder—to be sure, not the same type of plunder as practiced by the Western powers in the nineteenth century, but economic plunder nonetheless. At the start of the 1990s, Western manufacturers regarded China as a gold mine. Companies "had to be in China," and set about creating joint ventures and manufacturing plants—and in the process ignoring the fundamental tenets of business. Who, after all, was going to buy their products? Who was wealthy enough to do so? What about their cost base? And meanwhile, just down the road, a Chinese company was copying their production technology. These modern-day plunderers found a new and infinitely more skilled host, wise through experience, a host that extracted its full pound of flesh and more for any potential return the Western companies might make. When I first went to Asia, there was a disquieting and embarrassing murmur among economic and business circles— no one was making money in China. Indeed, most Western manufacturers were losing a lot of money. How could this be so? Because they had not done their homework. For sellers of products, there have to be buyers. Yet the majority of China's population when the first Western companies arrived were still startlingly poor. In addition, China was rightly determined not to allow itself to be exploited again in an imperialistic fashion.

Western manufacturers' near-term expectations for the China market are now considerably more sanguine than previously, and the same is gradually becoming the case with regard to Western fund managers' expectations for returns in the Chinese capital markets. This is no bad thing. However, it is the fundamental argument of this book that in the short term these expectations will have to be ratcheted down even further. Indeed, there remains the potential in China for complete financial and economic collapse. This could in turn pressure the Chinese government into allowing a devaluation of the renminbi in an attempt to provide relief for the ailing economy. China's exporters would potentially benefit from such a devaluation, as it would regain them lost trade competitiveness resulting from Asian currency devaluations of 1997 and 1998. Chapters 5 and 6 seek to address the crucial question of how much economic pain China is prepared to tolerate before it considers letting go its currency. The stakes over the next 2 or 3 years could not be higher—for China and for the global economy as a whole. Naturally, such issues will have a profound impact on Hong Kong, China's prodigal son returned to the fold. Fundamentally, there is no reason why Hong Kong should suffer from a renminbi devaluation. Indeed, as most of its exports are in fact reexports from Guangdong Province, its trade account should benefit considerably. So much for theory. It could be an entirely different matter in practice as speculative forces would seek to force the Hong Kong Monetary Authority to depeg the Hong Kong dollar and allow it to devalue.

Chapter 7 examines China's changing role in the world—its increasing economic and political importance, the danger and the opportunity that it represents, for both the world as a whole and its own people. China has never in its history been more important than it is today, never had such an impact on world affairs as it does right now. One could never have imagined even 5 years ago that world financial markets—and thus real economies —would hang on the every word of Chinese economic officials, and yet that is indeed the present situation. The global economy is being profoundly affected by the inclusion of the Chinese workforce, the rising Chinese trade surplus, and the stability or otherwise of the renminbi. China itself is seeking to be a force of stability amid the carnage of the Asian crisis; yet it is uncertain that China will be able to maintain this position. The consequences of it not being able to do so could be catastrophic—and not just for China.

While all this may seem extremely bearish, in the final analysis there remains much to be optimistic about—optimistic in a hard-headed, realistic manner as opposed to being "maximum bullish." For one thing, in the long traverse of the "stream," as Deng Xiaoping put it, China's leaders have seen, by the mistakes of others, where *not* to tread, where the eddies and strong currents are, the dangers that lurk beneath. The crucial weakness of external overreliance, noted in my book *Asia Falling: Making Sense of the Asian Currency Crisis and Its Aftermath*, which led to explosive C/A deficits and external debt mountains, will be avoided. Indeed, China's Ministry of Finance has already made very clear that it will maintain an extremely cautious approach to borrowing. China has come a long way and that is largely the result of a combination of the ingenuity and industriousness of the Chinese people and the quality of China's economic leaders. The challenges of 1978 were substantial, and yet China managed to cope with them and even excel. Chapter 8 looks at the likely strategies that will be undertaken to cope this time with the economic slowdown and the individuals who will lead them. The last two chapters examine the fundamental need to streamline capacity and build institutional and "real" (bricks and mortar) infrastructure, and finally make some personal forecasts about how I expect China to fare in the coming decades.

In the next few years, China will continue to experience considerable economic and social pain, pain that cannot be avoided if real and meaningful economic development and progress are to be achieved, pain that will pose fundamental social and political questions as well as economic ones. With their economic successes of the past two decades, China's leaders have shown they are fully capable of reaching the other side of the stream. The challenges, in this context, are manageable; yet they should not be underestimated either. Time and again, following the initial phase of the Asian currency crisis, I saw economists and journalists say that China was "safe," that China was a "different case." It is partly because of such snake-oil scholarship that the Asian currency crisis happened in the first place.

Economics is not (as some would have it) a science, but there are some fundamental tenets that hold true. The fact that Asian current account deficits and large external debt loads caused a currency collapse was nothing new in terms of economic history. Such an event has been seen many times before in other parts of the world. Equally, many of those who now say China is different are the same ones who initially said Asia was different—that Asia lived by different rules and did not have to abide by the same economic and social (and even political) tenets as did the West. Asia was and is no different, and China is and will be no different. The Asian currency crisis of 1997 was a typical macroeconomic response to previous imbalances. To use the subject of Asian values to claim some special exception to the central tenets of economics is not only unjustified but untenable. Asia is learning its lesson—a very painful one to be sure, but a necessary one. China will have to do the same. Having seen the examples of the bubble economies of Japan and the ASEAN, it starts with a considerable advantage; yet failure will have ramifications for more than just the Middle Kingdom.

As the title of this book suggests, China is once more at a pivotal stage in its history—"on the brink" either of continued economic slowdown or even potential collapse or, alternatively, of rebirth, of moving on to a new and higher stage of development. Observers will look back and see the next few years as having been fundamentally crucial to China's future—and potentially the future of the world itself—for if one thing is certain, it is that China will continue to play an ever-increasing role in global matters. An economically weak China, with the resulting social and political implications of that, will present a very real threat to global stability. Conversely, should these pivotal years of restructuring produce a China whose economic fundamentals are sound, healthy, and improving, the world will be a much better place for it. There are still elements in the West which see China as a "frontier" state, as the last "gold rush," ripe for plunder. It would befit Western leaders to look beyond such superficial—and easily countered—analysis and see China for what it could be, for the benefit of all—a leading source of world growth for the global economy in the twenty-first century. There has been much talk of constructive engagement with China, but as yet there has been little action and one might say little sincerity. It is time the West treated China with the respect and dignity that it deserves; yet as someone who believes profoundly in the principles of freedom and democracy, I am bound to say that it is equally time for China to admit that the events of 1989 were indeed a mistake and that, however cautious and gradual, the path to eventual universal suffrage has been taken. Only when both sides take up their responsibilities will mutual suspicion and distrust start to wane and the potential for prosperity and growth truly open up.

Those who have not merely studied China but have been there have their favorite anecdote, their favorite memory. Mine, however insignificant and humble, is unquestionably the time I went to Beijing in the summer of 1996. More specifically, it is of taking a taxi at 3 o'clock in the morning to Tiananmen Square, of the driver shaking with fear as he snatched my renminbi as the Public Security Bureau and People's Liberation Army (PLA) were checking cars behind us. It is of standing by the outer railing in Tiananmen Square, closing my eyes, and breathing in history. For those who have not been to Tiananmen, it is difficult to sufficiently describe the sense of awe one has at the sight of what is surely the greatest square in the world. Standing with the towering Great Hall of the People behind me, the Museum of the Revolution before me, on the other side of the square, I pondered—not for the first time or the last—the paradox that is China. China has come so very far, its ascent a meteoric escape from the tyranny of the Maoist regime. In both economic and political terms (and also military), the rise of China poses profound questions for global stability and prosperity, reshaping the "balance of power." Yet China still has a considerable way to go if it is to succeed in a meaningful way to empower its own people in an economic sense, let alone a political one. Its successes, while momentous, remain alarmingly fragile, and the current economic slowdown is testimony to that fragility. The taxi driver's fear is equally symbolic of the costs of political repression—and potentially a portent of a time when the frightened will empower themselves to, as Mao described, "stand up." For stand up they will if they feel the authorities, who have in all but name abandoned the credo of communism for the benefits of the "socialist market economy"—thus tying their own fate to that of economic success—are not doing the job. More than anyone else, China's leaders should be aware of the rule that those who ignore the "mistakes" and lessons of history are condemned to repeat them. The events of June 4, 1989, after all, began because of economic slowdown and perceived corruption. The paradox is thus that politics and the economy, despite the best efforts of the authorities to separate the two, remain inextricably linked, that the sense of schizophrenia of economic development and lack of political development will have a judgment day if it is not addressed. Perhaps with this in mind, China's leaders will strive even harder, no doubt, to boost the economy from the slowdown which continues to this day.

Callum Henderson
London
March 1999

1

Asia Falling—

The Competitive Threat

THE INITIAL STAGES of the Asian crisis were viewed with deep concern by China, but subsequently China seemed to emerge unscathed. Indeed, such was its headline economic performance in the second half of 1997, particularly in relation to the chaos all around it, that China's leaders allowed themselves the luxury of some self-congratulation. This was surely proof of the wisdom of slow and gradual economic reform rather than great leaps forward, proof of the wisdom of caution rather than risking chaos, a central theme in the modern-day Chinese ideology (officially known as the "socialist market economy") which has replaced orthodox Maoism or Marxist-Leninism. China's economy remained relatively buoyant, and while the Asian crisis represented unwarranted and unpleasant turbulence in the country's economic journey, it would sail through such squalls—so this thinking went.

During the Asian crisis, a clear "winner" appeared to have emerged, in both the diplomatic and the economic sense—China. While other Asian nations lost their cool, lashing out at perceived speculative forces for their role in the crisis, China's government not only unveiled a series of revolutionary economic reforms at the 15th Party Congress in September 1997, which were every bit as visionary as the initial reform ideas in

1978, but sought to emphasize China's role as a source of stability, a safe haven amid the financial *"dai foong"* (typhoon) that continued to lash other parts of Asia. China even went so far as to repeatedly and confidently predict that the economy could achieve an impressive 8% growth for full-year 1998 despite the region's problems. China, so it seemed, appeared to have pulled away from the pack of competing Asian nations and looked to be closing in on Japan for the status of most dominant nation in Asia, in both the economic and the diplomatic sense.

Today, most people take a slightly different view, partly because the Asian crisis has gone on for longer and affected Asia more profoundly than many expected and partly because we are increasingly seeing the effects of the Asian crisis on China's economy. In any case, the previous euphoria about China was dangerously misplaced and naive. Far from escaping the effects of the Asian crisis or being a safe haven, China's economy and markets have already been hit hard. In addition, prior to the crisis there were already dangerous domestic signs aplenty, notably increasing deflationary pressures given the significant overcapacity in the domestic economy. By the end of 1997, retail prices in China were actually falling rather than just showing reduced growth. The Asian crisis has significantly exacerbated these domestic pressures and is likely to continue to do so over the next few years. There will be no escape. There is now little doubt that China will be profoundly affected by the Asian crisis. But in order to say by how much and why, one has to go back to the Asian crisis itself, to how it happened and what are its specific implications for China. There are many reasons why the Asian crisis took place in 1997, why it subsequently carried on into 1998, and finally why a currency crisis turned into a debt crisis, and a debt crisis into an economic and social crisis. It is not for this book to repeat the arguments of my previous work, *Asia Falling: Making Sense of the Asian Currency Crisis and Its Aftermath.* However, I summarize my views here on the key reasons for the crisis, both those represented in that work and more up-to-date thoughts.

The most obvious lesson from the Asian crisis is—yet again—that sizable current account deficits if left unchecked will inevitably come home to roost. Thailand, seen as the catalyst for the Asian crisis or at least where it began, was running a current account deficit of above 8% of GDP heading into 1997. Such an imbalance puts a significant burden on three other areas of the economy to offset this: the fiscal account, monetary policy, and foreign portfolio and direct investment. Indeed, alarm bells were first sounded when Thailand posted a budget deficit for the first time in most people's memory for the fourth quarter of 1996. This quite correctly reminded financial markets of the Mexican 1994 situation, which had witnessed the classic economic curse of twin deficits on both the current and fiscal accounts. Foreign portfolio investment, somewhat quicker to react than its direct investment counterpart, started to slow, and in some cases reverse, with some institutional investor accounts actually cutting their exposure to the Thai asset markets. Most stayed put, however—only to panic later, again, just as in the case of Mexico. With the fiscal account under pressure and foreign portfolio investment slowing, monetary policy had to take the strain in order to offset the burden of the large and growing current account deficit, and so it did. Interest rates went up, simultaneously protecting the Thai baht while seeking to offer attractive interest rates to entice further foreign investment or at the least to stop existing foreign investors in Thailand from leaving. Meanwhile, real GDP growth had been slowing, largely due to a decline in gross domestic investment growth (5.4% in 1996 versus 12.3% in 1995). The key warning flag, however, was the collapse in nominal export growth, to a stunningly low 0.1% in 1996 versus 24.7% in 1995. This poor performance in 1996 export growth was mirrored across Asia, not just in the ASEAN but also in Taiwan and Korea (and even China, but more on that later). Taiwan's export growth fell to 8.2% versus 20%, and that of Korea to 4.1% versus 31.5%. It was a similar story in the rest of the ASEAN; the only exception was the Philippines, whose export base continued to outperform in 1998 due to wage cost advantage. Why did Asian exports collapse in 1996? The U.S. economy, the main importer of such goods, remained relatively strong, while Japan had yet to fall back into the recession that began after the April 1997 consumption tax hike. If there was an external culprit, it was the dollar-yen (USD-JPY) exchange rate.

Following the April 1995 G7 statement, which called for an "orderly reversal" of the dollar's decline and subsequent policy changes and bouts of joint intervention, the USD-JPY started to recover. First it broke back above the 100 level from its low of 79.85; then it accelerated higher in the latter part of 1996 and 1997; finally it broke back above 130. Asian exporters, which had during 1993–1995 benefited enormously from the dollar's collapse, did very little in the face of this apparent competitive threat. Their counterparts in Japan, however, had been somewhat busier. Having been forced to restructure productive capacity and their cost base significantly when the USD-JPY fell to 80, they were now in a much stronger position to take advantage of the yen's decline from late 1995 onward. They regained significant market share in the export markets of the U.S. and Europe from their Asian counterparts as a result of the yen depreciation's dampening effect on Japanese export prices. This coincided with a collapse in the price of semiconductors—the price of some chips falling 95% in a year—due to significant oversupply and slowing demand. This last was extremely important to the likes of Thailand, Taiwan, Korea, Malaysia, and Singapore, which had made the export of low-price (and low technological value-added relative to Japan) electronics components a key aspect of their modernization plan. Thus, looking again at the example of Thailand, going into 1997, you can see that there was a fiscal account under mounting pressure, a huge current account deficit, and a collapse in export growth. This in turn was a significant burden on economic growth, slowing foreign portfolio inflow and prompting the Bank of Thailand to tighten monetary policy in a vain attempt to offset all these fndamental weaknesses.

There were two more key elements that finally brought down the whole house of cards. First, there was external debt. At the time, the deregulation and liberalization of the Thai financial markets was hailed domestically and internationally as a clear sign of Thailand's economic advancement. However, that liberalization process was only partial, missing some vital elements that otherwise might have helped avoid the crisis that ensued. For instance, the capital account was opened up, attracting significant foreign portfolio inflow. Yet sufficient regulatory "infrastructure"—an important theme that we will return to later in the book with regard to China—was not developed. Hence there was no effective way to monitor, regulate, and channel these flows. In addition, a key feature of Thailand's liberalization was the Bangkok International Banking Facility (BIBF), whose very purpose was to entice the domestic corporate base to borrow through the BIBF at significantly lower dollar-based interest rates than were available in baht in the onshore market, thus encouraging Thai companies to take on potential foreign exchange risk. Of course, at the time, the Thai baht remained exceptionally stable against the dollar, and thus there was no perceived foreign exchange risk. Subsequent events were to prove this view tragically misguided. In any case, as a result of the general financial liberalization process and more specifically the creation of the BIBF, the size of Thailand's total external debt continued to grow through the 1990s as domestic companies and investors sought cheap financing in order to fund the domestic economic boom, more than doubling from USD33.266 billion in 1991 to 78.500 billion in 1996. This was 43% of the country's entire GDP.

Second, the Thai baht was pegged to the dollar via a basket mechanism whereby the Bank of Thailand every day set the reference rate for the dollar-baht (USD-THB) to a basket of currencies and tried to allow that rate to deviate plus or minus only 2 satang, during market trading. For over a decade, this had enormously beneficial effects, the stable exchange rate helping to attract considerable foreign portfolio investment. However, with economic fundamentals clearly deteriorating, a more flexible exchange rate mechanism was needed. Not only did this *not* happen, but the Bank of Thailand stubbornly defended the peg to the last (the financial equivalent of France's ignominious defeat at the hands of the Viet Minh at the Battle of Dien Bien Phu, fought in a valley, surrounded by hills, an impossible place to defend). By the start of 1997, it was probably too late in any case. Fundamental pressure and belated speculator interest to attack the Thai baht proved too much, and on July 2, 1997, the Bank of Thailand, its foreign exchange reserves severely depleted (we were only to learn the true nature of that catastrophic depletion some time later), allowed the Thai baht to float against the dollar. The rest, as they say, is history. The baht was smashed, and the speculators, having found relatively easy prey by the time they got on the scene, looked for other meals. There were plenty to be had, as the fundamental weaknesses that had brought low Thailand were prevalent elsewhere, nowhere more so of course than Indonesia. There, economic mismanagement was combined with widespread corruption at the highest levels, a lethal brew for the economy when Indonesia was itself forced to depeg the rupiah.

Yet why did the Asian currency crisis become a debt crisis? As I explained in *Asia Falling,* the Asian corporate base not only had *not* taken account of the rise in USD-JPY and the potential threat that represented to its trade competitiveness, but also had for the most part completely ignored the issue of foreign exchange risk altogether. The age of these exchange rate peg mechanisms and the fact that no major problems had occurred up to that point—the warning of the Mexican crisis also having been firmly and resolutely ignored—coupled with the significant benefits of exchange rate stability had lulled Asian governments and companies alike into a false sense of security, that the pegs could and would hold no matter what the fundamentals, that the good times were here and they would stay. Sadly, the history of exchange rate pegs is, to misquote somewhat, "paved with good intentions." Ultimately, there has to be an adjustment mechanism within the peg system. Otherwise a significant change in economic fundamentals will prove an unsustainable burden on the peg and the peg will fail. There are countless examples of this, and not only with regard to the strict definition of exchange rate pegs but with all manner of artificial mechanisms forced on the market by governments, only to be eventually thrown off.

The reason the baht was forced to devalue and the Hong Kong dollar (HKD) peg remains in place is first because a currency board system works in a different way, but more generally and more fundamentally because implicit in the Hong Kong dollar peg is an adjustment mechanism. In actuality, the Hong Kong peg is not a peg but a currency board, just as the Hong Kong Monetary Authority is not a central bank, though it thinks of itself as such. The Hong Kong dollar does not devalue because the strain is taken elsewhere—selling of HKD drains liquidity from the system, which forces interest rates higher, which eventually attracts back interest to the HKD, which adds liquidity to the system, which forces interest rates back down again. This is a somewhat simplistic explanation granted, but that is the nuts and bolts of it. The Hong Kong asset markets thus explicitly take the adjustment to a change in economic fundamentals. In Thailand, there was no such relieving or adjusting mechanism for the baht. The currency was to be defended to the death—and it was. This is not to say that in this instance Hong Kong does not have its own problems, nor that there might not come a time, hypothetically, when the government might deem the pain of asset price adjustment too great. However, it will in this case not have been the currency board that failed, but the government's willingness to allow the currency board to do exactly what it was designed for.

Having belatedly woken up to the fact that they faced massive foreign exchange rate risk given the baht's devaluation, Thai companies panicked and bought dollars by the truckload, forcing the value of the baht lower in an accelerating decline. The speculators—the hedge funds which were vilified by certain Asian governments for causing the crisis but which in fact came on the scene rather late—were happy to ride the coattails of this move. With the government and the Bank of Thailand having thus lost control of the currency, the decline of the baht accelerated, forcing companies to buy more dollars, not only for import purposes but for purposes of repaying their massive—and growing—dollar debt outstanding. This was a chicken and egg situation. Thai companies and banks bought dollars en masse to belatedly hedge their foreign exchange risk to dollar debt, thus forcing the USD-THB significantly higher, and in turn forcing them to buy even more. There was no countervailing force because by this time the foreign investment community had also woken up and was heading for the hills—also selling baht to do so.

The Bank of Thailand occasionally tried to intervene to smooth out the move, but its efforts were contemptuously swept aside. With the baht seemingly a one-way bet, the interbank market was increasingly only willing to make wide prices given the inherent risk implied by buying baht. Thus overall liquidity dried up, further hurting the ability of the Thai corporate base to cover its dollar debt risk. Unable to do so, and with the baht's devaluation meaning greatly increased debt repayments when translated into baht, many Thai corporates were staring default in the face. It was not long before this actually started to happen. In turn, with Thai companies starting to go under, Thai bank exposure to the corporate base in the form of nonperforming and unrecoverable loans rose exponentially. Meanwhile, on the domestic side, the high interest rates to defend the currency accelerated the downturn in economic growth. Tightened external liquidity conditions fed through to the domestic side and exposed the hitherto largely ignored fact that Thailand had massive overcapacity, notably in the finance and property sectors, which were strongly interlinked. Finance and property companies faced with a downturn on the domestic side and greatly reduced external financing ability also started to go under. Eventually, the credit rating agencies woke up to all this and downgraded Thailand— one major rating agency did not do this until 3 full months after the Thai baht devaluation. The currency crisis had become a debt crisis. It had become a credit crunch where the level of nominal interest rates was no longer so important and where perceived credit risk ruled supreme, the benchmark of whether a company or finance house would get a loan or not. In this world, both the sick and the healthy found getting credit extremely difficult if not impossible.

What relevance has this to China? If one looks back at the above example of Thailand, it all stemmed from the exchange rate peg mechanism. The lack of flexibility, a deterioration in real economic fundamentals, and a significant and growing external debt burden were together too much for such an artificial and inflexible exchange rate regime. China also has an effective exchange rate peg system, keeping the value of the renminbi pegged to the dollar within a defined range. (The yuan is actually the exchange rate value, whereas the renminbi—or "people's money"—is the domestic unit of value. For the purpose of clarity, I will refer exclusively to the renminbi in both the domestic and external contexts.) The likelihood or not of the renminbi being devalued will be looked at in considerably greater detail in Chapter 5. For now, looking at the available economic data, one can say that China has a number of similarities with Thailand and there are justifiable grounds for concern. That said, China does not have a current account deficit, a notable difference.

Leaving the currency issue aside for the moment, what is the threat to China and the Chinese economy from the Asian crisis? I would argue that the "threat" can be subdivided into two principal components. The first results from the Asian currency devaluations of 1997 and 1998, and the second from Japan and the USD-JPY exchange rate. Regarding the first, in many ways, up until October 1997, when the full impact of the Asian currency crisis was first felt in Hong Kong—and thus China—1997, the Year of the Ox, had been China's year. As a result of fiscal austerity measures put in place in 1994, inflation had been brought sharply under control. The economy continued to perform well with growth just short of 10%. Foreign exchange reserves continued to rise toward the year-end goal of USD140 billion—a crucial defense against financial turbulence. Foreign direct investment (FDI), which had been USD42.3 billion in 1996, hit yet another annual record at 43 billion in 1997, and 45 billion in 1998!

So much for the economy. On the political side, President Jiang Zemin had skillfully and clearly stamped his authority as leader at the 15th Chinese Communist Party Congress in mid-September. At the meeting he unveiled the next stage of China's economic revolution, which called for the wholesale restructuring of the state-owned enterprises (SOEs). At the same time he removed powerful opposition in the form of Qiao Shi, who was ousted from his positions as chairman of the National Peoples' Congress and member of the Politburo Standing Committee. The events of the 15th Party Congress secured Jiang Zemin's domestic legitimacy and gained him the requisite power base from which he was now able to delegate policy in much freer fashion. Amid the turmoil in other parts of Asia, China initially stood aloof, expressing sympathy and diplomatic support, lambasting speculators, and offering financial aid. While the market ravaged the ASEAN currencies and economists hastily downgraded their economic forecasts, China stood out as the exception. It had managed to steer its way through the potentially troubled political waters of the death of leader Deng Xiaoping, the British handover of Hong Kong, and the 15th Party Congress. Its economy was strong and its currency safe from currency speculators. Not a question was raised about its near-term future—until the crisis hit Hong Kong, causing asset markets to collapse. In their wake, falling Hong Kong stock prices dragged down the stock indexes of Shanghai and Shenzhen, as well as Hong Kong's own red chip stock sector. The message was clear—no one was totally immune.

While no doubt distressing, China weathered the storm of October 1997 with relative ease compared with its Southeast Asian counterparts, remaining publicly confident in Hong Kong's ability to deal with the speculative pressures. However, within the sell-off in Hong Kong, an important message was becoming clear. In terms of exports, Hong Kong's economy would not be that badly affected by the turbulence given its modest presence in domestic exports as a percentage of GDP, but the same was not true for Guangdong Province in China, where most of Hong Kong's reexports were actually manufactured. And if exports from southern China could be hit, why not those from the whole of China? Had not the devaluation of the renminbi in 1994, unifying the swap and official rates, been a key factor in the ASEAN losing economic competitiveness in subsequent years, particularly in relatively low-tech products such as textiles, garments, shoes, and home appliances where China competed directly against Thailand, Indonesia, and the Philippines? In that move, Chinese products had regained around 26% price competitiveness, even taking account of domestic inflation—which at the time was soaring. The currencies of the ASEAN had just lost some 40% or more against the dollar. Could not the same thing now happen to China? At the time, to ask such a question was tantamount to near heresy. It was to question the unquestionable, that China's fundamentals were sound, that China was different from the rest of Asia and did not (and more importantly would not) suffer the same financial and economic ills as had the ASEAN and Korea.

Let us look at China's export sector in greater detail. Exports, or rather trade as a whole, have been a leading light in the overall Chinese economic reform process, one of the greatest of its many success stories. Before the economic reform process got under way in 1978, trade played but a tiny part in China's economy. By 1994, however, things had changed dramatically. Indeed China's total exports in 1978 were not much more than the 1994 trade surplus (USD7.3 billion), with 1994 exports at USD102.6 billion. By the following year, China's trade surplus had grown to USD18 billion. By 1997, that figure was over USD40 billion and for full year 1998 some USD 43.6 billion. China has clearly had great success, first for its initial strategic initiative for import substitution and its drive for export growth, and second, on a microeconomic level, for tinkering with the domestic regulation system in order to micromanage the trade balance.

Yet, equally clearly, given the extent of the Asian currency devaluations, the competitive threat remains. From July 2, 1997, to July 2, 1998, while the renminbi stayed relatively steady, the Thai baht lost 38.55% of its value against the dollar (note this is the percentage in value lost of the currency against the dollar, not the percentage rise in dollar-baht, which was of course substantially higher). For its part, the Malaysian ringgit lost 38.54% of its value against the dollar, the Philippine peso some 36.30%, the Korean won 38.13%, and the Indonesian rupiah a stunning 83.29%. Meanwhile, the USD-JPY went from 127 after the massive Bank of Japan intervention in April 1997 (totaling around

USD20 billion) to 147. With the USD–RMB rate remaining stable, this implied a significant further depreciation in the value of the yen against the RMB. This is important because while 60% of China's exports go to Asia as a whole (as measured by 1997 data, and including Hong Kong and Japan), of that number, some 20% go to Japan alone. With Japan's economy mired in recession, China's exports faced the double whammy of a collapse in domestic demand and a depreciation of the yen that made those exports more expensive. The same is of course true for the rest of Asia that has been affected by the Asian crisis. Some 14% of China's exports went to the new industrialized economies of Korea, Hong Kong, Taiwan, and Singapore. Korea and Hong Kong are facing the prospect of a recession in 1998, an actual contraction in the economy, while Singapore and Taiwan are likely to see sharply lower growth. To be sure, there remains strong growth in the U.S. and thus strong demand for China's exports to the U.S., while Europe is starting to pick up after years of stagnation. However, the combination of the collapse in Asian domestic demand and the effective competitive devaluations by the Asian currencies against the RMB will bite hard into China's export growth in 1998 and 1999. Indeed, as of the May 1998 report, China's exports had actually started to decline on a year-on-year basis. For full year 1998, China's exports grew only 0.5% and they could well contract on a year-on-year basis in 1999. Thus the export base could act as a burden on the economy as a whole rather than the boost it has usually been in the 1990s. For China's actual export performance in the first half of 1998, which shows the start of the deterioration process, see Table 1.

The total value of Chinese trade (exports and imports combined) in this period was USD151.4 billion, a 5.2% increase on a year-on-year basis. Yet this actually reflects a slowdown compared with the value of trade in the first half of 1997, which grew at 13% year-on-year. China's first-half exports saw growth of 7.6% year-on-year, a relatively respectable performance until one compares it with full-year 1997 export growth which was just over 21%. China's State Information Centre, a respected

Table 1
First Half 1998 Trade Data for China (USD Billions)

	June	May	April	March	February	January	Full-year 1997
Trade balance	3.75 (–8.6% Y/Y)	3.64 (+6.4%)	4.26 (+19.7%)	3.39 (+13.4%)	3.15 (+41.2%)	3.99 (+87.3%)	40.34
Exports	15.61 (+1.6% YY)	14.93 (–1.5%)	15.95 (+7.9%)	15.27 (+8.1%)	12.15 (+21.4%)	12.68 (+8.5%)	182.70
Imports	11.86 (+5.3% Y/Y)	11.29 (–3.8%)	11.69 (+6.3%)	11.88 (+6.7%)	9.00 (+15.4%)	8.69 (–13.9%)	142.36

Source: Official data releases.

economic think tank within the powerful State Development Planning Commission, forecast full-year 1998 export growth of 5%, suggesting it believed that second-half export growth would be an extension of the deteriorating performance in the first half. Yet even this 5% full-year target was too high given the current economic environment. In reality, Chinese exports actually contracted in the second half. As a result, the government is coming up with various measures to help exporters.

For a start, the government is seeking a relaxation in the issuance of export licenses. Theoretically this beefs up the export ability of the economy. But in China, since this represents a policy reversal, some complications are encountered. For instance, the Ministry of Foreign Trade and Economic Co-operation decided to issue more export licenses for base metals in a bid to increase base metal exports, whose growth had slowed to just 2.5% in the first 5 months of 1998 from 30.1% in the same period in 1997. This represents a reversal of the past decision to issue limited licenses, a strategy adopted to ensure profitability. Exporters who bid for the licenses in January expecting to be the only exporters now have to compete with several others and accept lower prices and profits. With demand limited, this measure will only result in a sharing of export orders among different exporters and not necessarily more exports. Worse, exporters may face overcapacity, and overall they run a risk of accumulating stockpiles that will depress earnings further. In addition, the

People's Bank of China has urged banks to lend more readily to exporters. What the extra credits can do is help the exporters to produce more and perhaps enable them to cut prices and compete with the cheaper options offered by the beleaguered Asian nations and their exporter bases. Value-added tax rebates for exports of ships have been increased to 14% from 9%, iron and steel to 11% from 9%, cement to 11% from 9%, and coal to 9% from 3%. Textiles exports get a full 17% rebate from 9%. Certainly in theory, this increase in rebates is equivalent to a currency devaluation in that it enables exporters to gain cost advantage and cut costs. For instance, textile exporters enjoy an 8% devaluation now that they are entitled to 8% more rebate. However, though textile exports make up 20% of overall exports, iron and steel account for only 7%, and cement, ships, and coal all account for less than 1% each. The reimbursement of rebates takes a long time. As of April 1998, only 11% of rebate claims were reimbursed. Any effect of the increase in rebates not only will be limited, but will be delayed as well.

The issue of the export sector and the currency should be looked at not only in terms of nominal value, but also in terms of the real effective exchange rate—the trade-weighted exchange rate adjusted for inflation. On this basis, if one looks at China's REER with 1990 as the base year and a value of 100, the RMB's REER rose to 107.0 in 1991, climbed to 111.1 in 1992, jumped to 130.7 in 1993, and went into orbit in 1994, almost doubling to 231.3.[1] A high REER reflects a high degree of trade competitiveness—as a result of trade and/or capital and FDI inflow—and at the same time the gradual loss of competitiveness. The more the REER increases, the harder it is to compete on a relative basis. This is exactly what happened to many of the ASEAN countries as a result of the peg systems. There is, however, a further variable, which is domestic price competitiveness—as in if wages in one country are a fraction of those in another, the first's REER has to rise that much further against the currency of the second before it starts to lose trade competitiveness. In 1995, China's REER fell back to around 214 and fell again in 1996 to just above the 200 level. In 1997 it rose as a direct result of the Asian currency devaluations. Logically, one might assume Chinese exporters have as a result lost 40% of their trade competitiveness and that Chinese exports will collapse. It is not as simple as that. China has a far greater labor surplus than its Asian competitors. In addition, that labor surplus is growing and this growth will accelerate as a result of the rationalization program, further dampening wage costs and driving down the exporters' cost base. Based on mid-1997 levels, average hourly wages in China (Shanghai) were USD0.90 relative to 1.80 in Jakarta, 4.60 in Kuala Lumpur, and 3.00 in Bangkok.

The Asian currency devaluations will reduce China's wage cost advantage but will in most cases not eliminate it. The exceptions are Indonesia (where wage costs are not so much the immediate issue as being able to feed oneself and avoiding riots) and the Philippines, now a substantially more potent competitor to Chinese low-tech exports to the U.S. and Europe. That said, the devaluations will have a significant impact, regaining for China's main Asian trade competitors some of their lost market share of the strong growth markets of the U.S. and Europe. In 1989, China and Hong Kong (through which a significant amount of Chinese exports are reexported, which does not show up under the China export data) had a market share of 24% of Asian exports to the U.S. By 1993, after a period of RMB depreciation, that had grown to 33% and then to 34% in 1996 (before skyrocketing in 1997).[2] During that same period, the share of Asian exports to the U.S. of the New Industrialized Economies (NIEs) (Korea, Singapore, and Taiwan) fell from 59% to 44% and then 41%, with Korea and Taiwan significantly affected. That of the ASEAN rose from 17% to 23% and finally 25% (before plunging in 1997). The data thus confirm anecdotal suggestion that there is a high degree of competition between Chinese exports to the U.S. and those from its Asian competitors, in particular from the likes of Korea in heavy industry and Thailand and the Philippines in low-tech exports such as textiles, garments, and household products.

The key external element in all this is the USD-JPY. It was the USD-JPY that finally drove the USD-THB substantially higher, along with a plethora of domestic Thai fundamental reasons.

The fact that the USD-RMB has not adjusted to this new environment, or rather not been allowed to adjust, suggests that some of the inroads China made into the market share of Asian exports to the U.S. will eventually be lost. In this same period (1989–1996), the share of China and Hong Kong exports to Japan rose from 23% to 35%, while that of the NIEs fell from 40% to 31%. Here too China will suffer, given the depreciation of the yen and the fact that Japanese domestic demand remains mired in recession. The negative effects of collapsing Asian domestic demand and Asian currency devaluations will deal Chinese exports a hammer blow in 1998 and 1999. China's exporters have been in a pitched battle with their Asian counterparts in other countries for the lucrative markets of the U.S. and Europe for quite some time now. During the early 1990s, exporters in China made inroads at the expense of these competitors, given Asian currency REER appreciation relative to the value of the renminbi. For a more detailed look at how the battle has fared so far between China and its most important competitors in the ASEAN and the NIEs, see Table 2.

Table 2
Export Share of Selected Asian
Countries in the U.S. Market, 1989–1996

Country	1989	1993	1996
Greater China	24%	33%	34%
China	13	25	29
Hong Kong	11	8	5
NIEs	59	44	41
South Korea	22	14	13
Singapore	10	10	11
Taiwan	27	20	17
ASEAN-4	17	23	25
Indonesia	4	4	5
Malaysia	5	8	10
Philippines	3	4	4
Thailand	5	7	6
Total	100%	100%	100%

Source: IMF Direction of Trade Statistics.

Much of China's earlier competitive gains will be lost. Yet China will at least get a grace period, albeit a brief one. The Asian currency devaluations have resulted in rising import costs. That, together with the inability of many Asian corporates to get export finance because of the perception of greatly increased credit risk, will at least give China some breathing room. That is the good news. The bad news is that once the Asian economies recover, 1999 could hypothetically be even worse for Chinese export growth and market share. Ahead of that, China has some time at the microeconomic level to tinker with and boost incentives for its export base. A major way of doing that is to seek to further reduce the cost base for exporters by reducing import tariffs, raising export rebates for existing exporters, and encouraging those companies and sectors that do not overtly target export markets to do so. As a result of China's pledge to enter the WTO, China has reduced its tariffs to an average of 17% from 23% and said it will cut them to 10% by 2005. This specific measure lowers the cost to the exporters of imported goods and services, which can then be reexported at a more competitive price. The government put a further measure in place in order to ensure that the RMB did not actually appreciate too much in 1997. The measure allowed certain mainland trading companies to keep 15% of their export earnings in foreign exchange rather than RMB. This is one way of avoiding a devaluation while seeking to keep the RMB at a more realistic and competitive exchange rate level relative to trade demand and supply. Of course, if Asian export sectors recover, given the dynamics of the Asian crisis where the exporter base remains under pressure due to rising import costs, this should mean that inflationary pressures have been tamed and that consequently monetary policy has been eased. Although increased credit risk in Asian banking systems will limit the ability of banks to pass on the benefits of lower nominal interest rates, domestic demand should also have found a bottom by this time, with the result that imports also will start picking up—including imports from China. On balance, this should offset the loss of market share in the U.S. export market to its Asian counterparts.

A further caveat to those who see Chinese export growth potential in purely bearish terms is the fact that over 50% of Chinese annual export volume consists of partially assembled goods being imported into China and then reassembled in labor-intensive factories. The RMB's relative appreciation against its Asian counterparts reduces the imported cost of these goods and thus of their export price. This is a point not lost on foreign companies, which make up over half of China's annual export volume.

That said, the Asian crisis will not just impact Chinese exports directly. It will also have an indirect impact, slowing or even reversing the rise in foreign direct investment into China. China is the world's second largest recipient of FDI and the largest among the emerging markets. Yet, contracted FDI started to slow in the second half of 1997 as two things became evident to potential foreign investors: the Asian crisis as a whole and the fact that China's economy was starting to slow in any case due to overcapacity relative to demand. Despite China's advantages over those parts of Asia that were being ravaged by the currency crisis, a notable advantage being that its capital account remained largely closed and not convertible, financial and corporate investors clearly demanded a higher-risk premium on China in the wake of the Asian crisis, as measured by slowing contracted FDI, the widening of credit spreads on China's dollar-denominated debt, and the increase in renminbi nondeliverable forward (like a forward contract but denominated and settled in dollars to avoid capital account restrictions) premia. That higher overall risk premium will have a sobering effect on future foreign investor interest. With over 80% of China's capital inflows due to FDI given that the renminbi remains inconvertible on the capital account, the pace of FDI growth will clearly be hit. A further factor to consider is that while initial FDI into China was for the purpose of using it as a low-cost export base, by the mid-1990s a new wave of FDI was specifically targeting the rapidly rising domestic market, in recognition of what one management consultancy has called the "consumer revolution." With China's economy clearly in a period of economic slowdown, this shift in emphasis should in turn accelerate the slowdown in FDI.

In addition, over 80% of FDI into China comes from Asia (1996 and 1997 data), with Hong Kong by far and away leading the pack, followed by Taiwan and Japan. Hong Kong and Japan in particular are not in any position to expand that FDI base given the financial and economic problems they themselves are suffering from. The signs of slowdown in FDI are already here— the value of new FDI contracts fell almost 30% in 1997 year-on-year. Granted, it is significantly harder and more laborious to actually reverse FDI (i.e., take a factory apart, brick by brick, and then ship it somewhere else). Thus, China will again have some breathing space to work with. However, the decline in FDI growth will have important repercussions for the domestic economy. That said, that breathing space should not be wasted. Time is of the essence, and China has little to waste. Contracted FDI actually fell fractionally year-on-year in the first half of 1998, though it was still around USD20 billion. This in turn feeds into the export issue since FDI and the resulting factories and reexports easily make up a majority of Chinese manufactured exports.

As dictated by the 15th Party Congress, China is undergoing a massive restructuring of its manufacturing base, more specifically of 300,000 state-owned enterprises, under the guiding principle of "grab the large and free the small"—consolidating the larger SOEs into Korean chaebol-like industrial conglomerates, while freeing up the smaller businesses to either sink or swim by restructuring themselves through Western-style capitalist methods. This restructuring process will greatly add to the level of unemployment. Officially, this is around 4%; however, this only includes urban populations and of these only those who actually register and who have not been paid part-time wages to stay home (however meager). The SOE restructuring process alone will add a further 25–30 million to the ranks of the unemployed. The 4% figure is clearly conservative. Say one remains conservative, even in realistic terms, and doubles it. That still represents 70 million people unemployed out of the total workforce. A more realistic figure, including underemployed and unemployed rural people, is probably double that again. In order to offset the negative economic effects of the restructuring process, China needs foreign capital inflow, whether in the form of export growth or FDI in order to create jobs and reduce the overall job losses. In 1998, it seems highly unlikely that such job funding will be there. Thus, the slowdown in export growth and FDI could have important consequences for the restructuring program itself—it could stop it dead in its tracks, or more realistically slow it down.

In social terms (looked at in more detail in Chapter 3), the restructuring process could have important ramifications as well. Put simply, the peasants are rebelling. There were numerous instances of low-paid urban and rural workers protesting against cutbacks resulting from the restructuring process before the SOE reforms were even tabled. The latter can only increase this. To a political party that has in reality replaced its ideological *raison d'être* with the idea of making people better off, this is extremely dangerous. The temptation will clearly be to avoid such economic, social, and political risks by slowing down the reform process—continuing the "feeling for rocks underfoot while crossing the river approach." While this may again gain it some time, China is left with the existing problem of a sharp slowdown in the domestic economy. In addition, any reluctance to restructure the economic and financial system could cause the economy not only to continue to slow but actually to stagnate. This has been the case with other economies, developed and developing alike, which have failed to grasp the immediacy of the need for real structural reform. It is to this that we turn next.

2

Slowdown at Home—
Not Rich and Not Glorious

IN COMPARISON WITH many of its Asian neighbors that
were devastated by the events of 1997, China remains (for now)
a bulwark of stability. Yet despite that, the Asian crisis could not
have come at a worse time, exacerbating the domestic economic
slowdown that was already taking place. Rising unemployment,
declining prices, slowing growth, and bouts of social unrest had
increasingly become key characteristics of China's economy.
The Asian crisis and more specifically the Asian currency devaluations—against the renminbi as well as the dollar—have
merely added to China's problems. GDP growth slipped again in
1997 to 8.8% from 9.6% in 1996, dragged down by declining
industrial output growth and the first signs of deflationary pressures in the fourth quarter of that year.

It was all so different in the 1980s and early 1990s, encapsulated by Deng Xiaoping's remark that "to get rich is glorious."
China went from being an inward-looking nation, focused on
self-reliance and hostile to all but a few, to economic rebirth and
the Open Door policy. These were very much the initial boom
years, where individuals and companies, cautiously at first, tested
the boundaries of the reforms that Deng and his faction within
the Chinese Communist Party had brought about. In the 1980s,
encouraged by Deng's emphasis within the Party itself of

"thought liberalization" and his bold statement that "poverty was not socialism," the idea of a Chinese consumer society was first born. Western fashions began to emerge in line with their gradual availability. A sea change in mind-set took place when the Mao jacket was shed for the likes of Yves Saint Laurent and Pierre Cardin, though it was not necessarily realized at the time. The accoutrements, the clothes of the individual, replaced the drab signature of the collective; color and light replaced gray. The reforms of the 1980s were extended to the 1990s, where private business—heretical under Mao—was revitalized and a new middle class, numbering in the tens of millions, began to (re)emerge. It was a time when the first mainland Chinese bought a Ferrari, when Western restaurants and clubs opened and boomed to the latest Western music, where the new elites posed, so like their Western counterparts. It was a time when it was fashionable to "*xia hai*," literally to jump into the sea (of business). Not that this temptation has gone, but at least a peak was seen in the early and mid-1990s when China boomed. It was a stunningly exciting time to be in China, when the only way to go was up, when easy money was supposedly to be made everywhere, when Party cadres, army officers, university lecturers, and students alike dropped out of their usual roles and started up businesses. China's fledgling stock markets in Shanghai and Shenzhen were a graphic expression of this. Few understood the concept of stock markets, but people were crushed to death in the stampede to get lottery tickets for the right to get share certificates when the bourses opened. Prices, whether consumer goods or stocks, roared. Books on stocks sold out in minutes. It was the Eastern equivalent of the gold rush, when fortunes were to be made by a variety of means that had never been dreamed of before—when fortunes were indeed made, encouraging others to follow suit. Heady times indeed. The Chinese consumer at least had "stood up" and was beginning to like the feeling. As ever, the market responded, whether through legal or illicit means. Anything was available for a price. Anything was possible.

Shanghai in particular changed from being a relatively insular and unwelcoming city to at least a resemblance of its former glorious (and infamous) past. The core of the revolution, however, was in the south, in Guangdong, which had in any case been a mercantilist province since the times of the emperors. Led by the special economic zones in Shenzhen, Zhuhai, and Hainan (which was itself to become a separate province), and encircling the colony of Hong Kong (which was due to be returned to the mainland at midnight June 30–July 1, 1997), Guangdong, or Canton as it was known in colonial times, exploded—to an extent that greatly troubled even the most ardent advocates of the reform process, let alone the hard-liners. Along with the expansion in the economy came more dubious aspects—rising crime and corruption, prostitution, and gambling. For most people, however, either these aspects were irrelevant to their everyday life or they simply ignored them in the rush to achieve what Deng had predicted for his country, a better standard of living. Walking the streets of Beijing, I still found immense curiosity, vibrancy, and interest in what the West might have to offer China. To see a people truly wake up (from what was surely a nightmare of monumental proportions, considering the Cultural Revolution alone) was an astounding and exhilarating experience. My dismal inadequacy in the *"Putonghua"* language did not seem to matter. Communication has certain basic aspects in any language, and the people I met, whether on the streets or in the night clubs and restaurants, were more than eager to try their English. This is not meant to sound patronizing. I do not mean this in the slightest. It is simply what I felt and saw and experienced—not unique in the slightest, simply like the countless millions of Westerners who have journeyed to see China. The difference for me was in the timing and also in the dramatic contrast between one's expectations as a Westerner of a Communist moonscape and the stunning reality. In addition, I viewed it not simply as a tourist, but as an economist, as someone who analyzes human behavior from the specific viewpoint of production and activity—again, by no means unique. But to experience it oneself, to see that reality, was like a scientist hearing of a great invention and then actually witnessing it. There was an unquestionable sense of awe at witnessing the rebirth of capitalism—or rather its teenage years! At least in the cities, the people I met were optimistic, excited, wanting to take part, to be a part of this new and strange experiment.

In pure economic terms, it was a time that was characterized by year after year of double-digit GDP growth. Indeed, from 1981 to 1990, China achieved an average annual GDP growth of 10.3%.[1] Annual GDP per capita also averaged double-digit growth throughout that period, and Deng Xiaoping set what in most developed countries would be an impossible target of quadrupling the size of the economy by the year 2000 to meet the standards of what he deemed an "affluent society." Commentators have likened this transformation in China to the industrial revolution in the U.S. and Europe, but in truth what happened in China from 1978 to 1990 far surpassed even those events. For one thing, it took China 12 years to accomplish what it took many nations in the West almost a century to do. For another, China had to face a largely hostile world while attempting this. Relations with the U.S. had barely thawed despite the efforts of Nixon, Kissinger, and Carter; and the Soviet Union remained a thinly veiled enemy on China's northern border. In addition, the U.S., the world's most successful nation, had a fraction of the population China presently has when its economic reform process started to take hold in the nineteenth century. China's economic rebirth ranked as the most incredible economic feat in the history of man. It was particularly remarkable because it represented the regaining of lost ground—that which was lost as a result of imperialist meddling and intrusion. The lives of ordinary people had been clearly and unequivocally improved. Over 150 million people were rescued from below the poverty line, housing space increased, and consumption exploded, all the result of the economic revolution that Deng set in motion.

So what went wrong? How did China come to the point where its economy was rapidly slowing down going into the Asian crisis? There are two aspects to this, the internal /domestic reasons for the slowdown and the external factor, more specifically, the dollar-yen (USD-JPY) exchange rate. On the domestic side, such was the success of Deng's economic revolution, led by the guiding principles of the "Four Modernizations" (agriculture, industry, science and technology, and national defense), in the 1980s that it had some very Western-style nefarious economic side effects, most notably inflation. At the heart of the Open Door policy was the expansion of trade. The growth in trade itself brought with it a dramatic expansion in China's foreign exchange reserves, which boomed to the hitherto unheard of heights of USD15 billion as of 1987 (compared with just over USD140 billion a decade later!). The combination of the expansion of the money supply which accompanied this growth phase in the 1980s, booming foreign exchange reserves, and the effort to decentralize the power base, theoretically freeing up the provinces to boost the economy, in practice allowed the monetary supply-demand equation to get out of hand. Like Germany, China is particularly sensitive to memories of inflation. Indeed, it could well be argued that rampant inflation in the late 1940s played a key role in the Communist Revolution of 1949, further undermining the support of an already unpopular government. The government's response to an explosion in consumer prices in the mid- to late-1980s, resulting from too much money chasing too few goods, was to recentralize, to put a tight squeeze on credit growth. While the medicine worked, it did not do so quickly enough to avoid political consequences. Inflation and the corrupt practices of bureaucrats to bypass rising prices were key reasons why there was substantial support from ordinary workers throughout the country for the student demonstrations in Tiananmen Square in 1989.

Needless to say, the events of that year resulted in China becoming an international pariah. Thus the country faced a liquidity squeeze, with foreign direct investment and tourism falling sharply and its access to the international capital markets all but cut off. China was unable to meet its existing external liability payments on principal and interest through new credits. It had no choice but to draw down on its foreign exchange reserves, in effect further reducing the money supply in addition to domestic efforts at credit constraint. The result was a brief period of austerity. This was partly imposed as a reaction to Tiananmen, but the severity of the slowdown in monetary indicators from 1988 to 1991 showed clearly the government's eagerness to avoid inflationary excesses, an omen for the kind of fiscal and monetary austerity Zhu Rongji was prepared to put in place in 1994 to tame price pressures. It wasn't long before the economy was picking up again. Where the West had stopped investing in China, others in Asia itself took up the opportunity. Soon, trade and foreign exchange reserves were booming, and prices once again reacted to the reexpansion of domestic money supply, with the consumer price index (CPI) averaging an annual growth of 11.5% during 1990–1995, peaking at 21.7% in 1994. This again resulted in a government clampdown on credit control and the fiscal deficit. Ironically, the rebound in inflation in 1993 and 1994 was largely due to the government overcompensating for the slowdown from 1989 onward. After 3 years of austerity and with consumer sentiment slumping, the government was anxious to keep the economic slowdown from becoming something much more serious. Hence, credit controls were relaxed, and with consumer goods in short supply, producers greatly increased supply to meet the shortfall. In 1994, it was a case of producers sprinting to keep up with consumers. Inflation once again got out of hand. The genie had again been let out of the bottle.

Modern macroeconomic policy, while it has been phenomenally successful in the last two decades, remains very much in its infancy in China in historical terms. Government bodies continue to experiment with economic policy, very much in line with Deng Xiaoping's mantra that one must "look for rocks underfoot in order to cross the river." To Zhu Rongji, the then economic "tsar," as the Western press called him, and vice premier, the lesson was clear that greater care must be taken in avoiding a reoccurrence of inflationary pressure, that inflation was the enemy, the scourge of economic development. In 1988–89, clearly the government had not been ruthless enough since inflation was quick to reemerge. This time the government must be unflinching in its aim of stamping out excessive price pressures to ensure future prosperity and stability.

Nicknamed *"Lao ban,"*—"the boss"—Zhu was indeed ruthless and unflinching in practice. The property and stock markets, which up to then had been on fire, were choked of the lifeblood of credit and went into a slump. In terms of consumer goods inflation, as opposed to its asset equivalent, Zhu's imposition of credit controls and quotas also starved the state enterprises and newly founded collectives of the capital to continue at their heady pace of growth and expansion. Zhu's war with inflation seemed at times almost obsessive; however, the need to tame price pressures was clearly of paramount importance if long-term economic stability was to be assured. That said, it could be argued that he stamped on the brake too hard. In addition, the Asian crisis has clearly added to this, with the demand side being hit hard, further reducing consumption growth. See Table 3 for a comparison of GDP, CPI, and M2 growth from 1991 on.

Table 3
China GDP, CPI, and M2 (Money Supply) Growth, 1991–1997

China	1991	1992	1993	1994	1995	1996	1997
GDP growth rate	9.3%	14.2%	13.5%	11.8%	10.2%	9.7%	8.8%
CPI	2.9	5.4	13.2	21.7	14.8	6.1	2.8%
M2	26.5	31.3	36.8	35.1	29.5	26.8	20.8%

Source: Official data releases.

As you can see from the table, inflation was tamed, price pressures in terms of both assets and consumer goods began to recede, and money supply growth slowed, albeit off a high base. All was well, or so it seemed for a time. However, far from stabilizing the situation, the slowdown that followed this period of austerity began to accelerate, as Table 3 shows. Granted, everything is relative. We are now talking about high single-digit growth instead of the double-digit growth rates of the past, in comparison to 3–4% growth in the U.S. or Europe, which is just beginning to recover from an extended period of stagnation. However, it was—and is—the pace of the slowdown that was the chief concern for Beijing. Zhu and his allies believed that so long as exports remained the chief engine of growth, in line with the Open Door policy that specifically aimed at expanding China's trade sector, this could offset the slowdown on the domestic side. This brings into play, however, the second, external, factor in the slowdown—the dollar-yen exchange rate.

From 1993 to 1995, everything was fine as far as China's exporters were concerned. The USD-JPY fell to a new postwar low of 79.85 in April 1995, and China's exports boomed, both to Japan and the rest of Asia and also to the U.S. and Europe. China was outcompeting its rivals through lower wage costs and the effects of the decline in the USD-JPY, which reduced Japan's trade competitiveness. Needless to say, from late 1995 onward, it was a different story, with the USD-JPY reversing course and heading higher in the wake of the G7 Accord. This helped recover Japan's lost trade competitiveness, and the result was the Asian slump in exports in 1996. The Asian crisis of 1997 exacerbated this situation, given the collapse in domestic demand throughout Asia. Around 60% of China's exports went to these countries. Exports were no longer the engine of growth.

The slowdown continues to this day. Indeed, there are signs that it is accelerating. An economic slowdown is of course not just a question of lower real gross domestic product growth on a year-on-year basis. It involves significant changes at the micro-economic level, changes in consumer patterns, in production and investment plans, in the availability of credit. Above all, it involves a dramatic reduction in consumer confidence. People become more cautious in their spending habits and save a higher percentage of their income. There are side effects. The reduced ability to get new credit causes some companies to go under, thus putting pressure on banks, causing their percentage of nonperforming loans (NPLs) to rise. The resulting increased credit risk hurts their own funding ability, further reducing available credit in the system. Not handled carefully, a slowdown can turn into a recession, a recession into a depression. Anyone who doubts this should just take a look at Japan.

In China's case, why is the economic slowdown continuing? We have seen that it is not just a case of the Asian crisis at work. China's economy was already slowing down before the crisis. In order to answer the question, and indeed attempt an answer to the further question of how long it will last, one has to look at the specific dynamics of the economic slowdown in China, at its main characteristics. The most obvious of these is overcapacity, oversupply relative to demand. Theoretically, this can be reached in one of two ways. One is that demand chases supply, thus creating inflation until such a point where despite shortages people are no longer prepared to pay such high prices, in which case supply follows demand on a sharply downward track. The other is that demand can be artificially deflated—such as by tighter credit conditions through interest rate hikes by a central bank. In China's case, the austerity measures put in place in 1994 have almost worked too well. Demand has received a body blow. Looking at the demand side in greater detail, there are two sorts of demand, fundamental and speculative. The first is concerned with buying essential goods and services needed for everyday life; the second, usually on margin credit, is instead focused on buying luxuries. Speculative demand, needless to say, is usually the first victim of tighter fiscal or monetary conditions. It is when fundamental demand starts to be affected that the slowdown becomes a recession or even a depression.

In the case of China, however, another variable distorts the usually market-oriented and market-sensitive supply-demand equation: state-directed credit. This artificially inflates the supply side. As long as the combination of state credit and speculative demand can offset this apparent overcapacity, the equation remains balanced for a time. Yet, both in theory and practice, this is unsustainable. This is particularly the case when the government decides to change the game. And this is exactly what China did in 1994, and more recently in 1997 at the 15th Party Congress. President Jiang Zemin made clear in his reform program that the credit practices of old could not and would not be continued and that a wholesale restructuring of the state-owned en-

terprises would take place. The implication of this was that
state-directed credit would no longer be available, or at least not
in such quantity. In truth, however, the process had already begun. The SOEs were already throwing people out of work in an
attempt to become more efficient, and the state banks, up until
then absolutely profligate with credit, were, for their standards,
becoming decidedly more circumspect about new loans. The
idea was that less state credit and a slowing of speculative demand, given the tighter monetary and fiscal conditions following the 1994 austerity move, would lead to lower returns at the
least and more likely companies starting to actually go under. In
addition, the result was in theory rampant overcapacity.

Theory is nothing, however, to real life. In a way very much
reminiscent of the skyline of Bangkok, Shanghai's vista is testimony to overindulgence, to excess supply. Finished and half-fin-
ished office and residential apartment blocks fill the horizon.
Trucks full of cement clog the streets. The deafening noise of the
buildings being put up is something to behold, all encompass-
ing, nonstop, ear splitting. Aside from being decidedly unpleasant, it suggests that something is deeply wrong, that there is a
deepening malaise within the supply side. In 1994, Shanghai had
total office space of just about 500,000 square meters. In 1997,
this had risen to 3.5 million square meters. To give some context
to this, Shanghai is achieving in one decade what it took Hong
Kong the best part of four decades to do. Nowhere is this "irra-
tional exuberance" more evident than just across the Huangpu
River in Pudong, where the central and municipal governments
have transformed the area into the city's main financial district.
It is the same story in Beijing and Guangzhou. China's three
leading cities are becoming clogged with offices, apartments, and
shopping malls. This malaise is to be found in other sectors of
the economy as well, indeed in almost every sector of industry.
Inventories are rising across the board. By the end of 1996,
China had stockpiled 20 million bicycles and over 100,000 cars.
It is the same situation for heavy industry, for steelmaking and
petrochemicals that have been hit by declining export growth
and cannot sell their products domestically because of reduced

demand. Shopping malls are full of inexpensive consumer goods that have not been, and it would appear cannot be, sold at current prices. Where is the demand going to come from?

Overcapacity relative to demand traditionally leads to first declining price growth, then to actual price declines, to deflation. This is indeed what we are seeing in China's economy. The CPI annual rate in 1996 was 6.1%, down substantially from 14.8% in 1995. Zhu's reforms and austerity measures from 1994 were clearly working, but in the fourth quarter of 1997 we saw the first signs of actual price declines on a year-on-year basis in the retail price index (RPI), which is the more widely used indicator of price direction and velocity. This was the first time deflationary pressures had been experienced in China for over a decade. Since then, they have accelerated. The RPI for 1997 was up only 0.8%. For 1998, it fell 2.8% year-on-year.

Once again, the gravity of the situation is shown more clearly by real life than by macroeconomic data. Since 1995, residential condominiums have halved in price, and they are still falling. This should theoretically lead to a surge in rental values—a greater demand to rent given the inability or unwillingness to buy. Yet this is not the case. Rental values are falling too. In Beijing, around 40% of the office space is unused and office blocks are still being put up. Just across the border from my former home in Hong Kong, gleaming new towers ascend to pierce the sky with regularity in Shenzhen. This is sure confirmation at a time when Guangdong Province's economy is slowing down from its heady growth rates of the early 1990s that there is something deeply wrong with the supply side of the equation. China is experiencing a property crisis, and there is every chance that it will be just as nasty and prolonged as that currently being seen in Hong Kong or other parts of Asia. June RPI was –3.0% year-on-year, as against –2.7% in May. Thus, by mid-1998, there was yet no sign that deflationary pressures were abating despite two interest rate cuts, one in March and the other at the start of July. Indeed, deflation appeared to be picking up pace. Given the extent of existing overcapacity in China and the fact that the supply side has yet to stop (new buildings are still being built), this would appear to suggest that prices still have some way to fall, in terms of both assets and consumer goods.

Overcapacity and falling prices result in diminishing returns. In the corporate sense, the meaning is obvious. Lower revenues and higher costs mean substantially lower profits. In the West, this would mean companies cutting costs, laying off workers, and reducing investment to meet shareholder requirements. In China, given the restructuring process already under way, it does indeed mean increasing the ranks of the unemployed in order to make the SOEs more efficient. However, wages are understandably a politically sensitive issue. Still, left alone from government interference, market forces will inevitably drive wages lower. At the very least, SOEs and township and village enterprises that have been hurt by the slowdown will seek to relocate to cheaper parts of China, notably middle China or the western parts where wage costs are a fraction of the coastal areas and Guangdong.

Of course, that's fine in theory, but in practice municipal governments would seek to stop this process, frightened of the economic and social impact of companies leaving their area. China has come a long way, but it has not quite got to the stage where at the local level government officials unhesitatingly accept the full implications of the market. Estimates abound, but it is safe to say that half the SOEs don't make money. The slowdown will mean that more of them face an increasingly grim future, which in turn means more economic pain for their workers, thus extending the slowdown as consumer spending is cut back, and so on down the line.

In the government sense, diminishing returns mean larger budget deficits—less immediate return on government investment and spending and reduced tax revenue. In China, the latter is not necessarily the case since enforceability is less of an issue. However, the budget deficit is already a major problem, and this will merely exacerbate it. Despite the austerity measures devised by Zhu Rongji in 1994, the budget deficit has continued to represent a strain on the economy. In 1996, the official figure was 0.2% of GDP. However, as the Asian Development Bank itself states, this does not include SOE deficits financed by the

People's Bank of China. Including the latter, the budget deficit is around 6%, a major concern by any standard. It is exactly for this reason that the government has sought to restructure the SOEs, thus relieving to a great degree the budgetary burden of financing them through the PBOC. In the short term, though, such action merely adds to the casualties of the reform process and exacerbates the economic slowdown as a whole.

Finally, when dealing with the characteristics of the slowdown, there is the issue of the state banks themselves. (This sector is dealt with in more detail in Chapters 8 and 9 when examining the fundamentals of the banks and the leaders who will seek to revive them.) China's four main state banks represent a massive burden to the economy as a whole. They have been the lifelines to the SOEs, funneling 75% of total bank credit to this sector. While this has kept the SOEs afloat, in contrast to the decimation of state industry in the former Soviet Union after the fall of the Communist system, it has drained much needed credit away from faster-growing and more profitable sectors, the TVEs, the newly founded fully private enterprises, which are a small but flourishing part of the economy.

Credit rating agencies have determined that as a result of the state-directed credit to the SOEs, up to 30% of the banks' total loans, around RMB2 trillion, are now nonperforming. Technically, the state banks are insolvent several times over; their financial state is every bit as bad as if not worse than that of their counterparts in Thailand, Indonesia, or Korea. In the past decade, their return on assets has fallen by over 80%, even as lending has soared (the diminishing return on assets noted earlier). They make inadequate provisions for bad loans, and they have the highest cost structure of any banking system in the world as measured by assets per employee. What keeps the state banks afloat is the fact that the renminbi is not convertible on the capital account, and therefore depositors are not readily able to put their funds in other currencies. The stock and bond markets are in their infancy, and any time the stock market is seen to be getting out of hand, the government clamps down and imposes draconian antispeculative measures. There is thus little alternative but to simply park one's savings at the state banks, despite the fact that paltry returns are available. In addition, depositors believe that ultimately the government and the PBOC will keep the state banks afloat. The day of reckoning for the banking system has been delayed as a result of these artificial tactics and measures, but it will come.

In the meantime, attempts to make the economy more efficient—to restructure the SOEs and to clean up the banking system by increasing credit risk worthiness measures and tightening controls on credit to specific sectors—have only exacerbated the slowdown. The government has shown it is prepared to sacrifice present growth rates to ensure a better foundation for the future, but it will not forsake growth entirely. To do so would not only be economically imprudent; it could threaten a social explosion. While seeking to continue the reforms, the government has equally sought to alleviate the pain through macroeconomic and microeconomic measures. These can be divided into monetary easing, fiscal easing, export promotion, and encouragement of foreign investment. On the first, the PBOC, while remaining cautious in the speed of implementation, is clearly trying to do its part to reignite economic growth. The PBOC interest rate cuts at the end of June 1998 in the 1-year deposit and lending rates were the fifth such since 1996, as Table 4 shows.

Table 4
Renminbi-Denominated Deposit Rates

Deposit rate	Savings	3-month	6-month	1-year	2-year	3-year
1995	3.15%	6.66%	9.00%	10.98%	11.70%	12.24%
1996	2.62	4.82	7.05	9.07	9.68	10.23
1996	1.91	3.22	5.08	7.02	7.42	7.76
Oct. 1997	1.71	2.88	4.14	5.67	5.94	6.21
Mar. 1998	1.71	2.88	4.14	5.22	5.58	6.21
July 1998	1.44	2.79	3.96	4.77	4.86	4.95

Source: Standard & Poor's MMS Emerging Asia Insight product.

In addition, in a somewhat desperate bid to stop further deterioration in the economy, the PBOC did a complete U-turn in late June 1998 by issuing an edict calling on the state banks to restart their lending to loss-making SOEs. This was a complete reversal from the policy ordered by the PBOC and the government earlier in the year which had been in line with restructuring and reform plans set out at the 15th Party Congress to enforce stricter credit checks for new loans. This reversal clearly shows how worried Beijing is by the continuing slowdown in the economy and the side effects this is having. In June the PBOC and the State Economic and Trade Commission called on the state banks to increase lending to loss-making SOEs in order to keep them afloat, to help them to find guarantors for their borrowings, and to reduce administrative fees.

On the fiscal side, the government announced plans to dramatically increase fixed-asset investment and public works expenditure. The State Information Centre, an economic think tank within the government, forecasts full-year 1998 fixed-asset investment growth at 15%, compared with around 10% in 1997. While the government in China has considerably more say in the degree of corporate investment than governments in many countries, this forecast seems overoptimistic. On the spending side, the government is planning a 20% increase, amounting to USD60–70 billion, in public works' spending. Yet, at the same time, it has publicly stated that it is looking to cut the budget deficit in line with its attempts at prudent fiscal and monetary practice. Clearly, something has to give. The only way it can finance this increased expenditure without allowing the budget deficit to increase is to increase taxes or to recycle the money through increased state-directed credit through the state banks—thus increasing the banking sector's already massive problems. Despite this, the government has been undaunted in its task, injecting RMB270 billion (USD32 billion) into the state banks via government bond issues in an attempt to recapitalize the banking system. In addition, various departments within the government are debating how to expand the government and corporate bond markets in order to achieve a more efficient means of reallocating and transmitting savings into the economic development projects. At the moment, up to USD560 billion in private deposits is sitting in the state banks. This is clearly a wasted resource; yet the state banks fear that if fully efficient bond markets are developed, they will lose their deposit base or a portion of it, making it far harder for them to carry on sustaining the burden of their NPLs.

On the export side, the government announced in July 1998 measures to stimulate export growth by raising export rebates on specific industries (notably, textiles, coal, steel, and ships) and by encouraging the state banks to increase lending in particular to SOEs that exported marketable products. China is also seeking to boost foreign investment. This may seem strange given recent years when foreign direct investment was booming. However, it has slowed markedly of late. Realized FDI was down 1.5% year-on-year in January–May of 1998. In May it fell 6.9% year-on-year after slumping by 19% in April. Multinationals looking to be involved in major infrastructure projects are suddenly finding the negotiation process easier and more flexible. In addition, in a further attempt to encourage foreigners to invest in China, Beijing is suddenly starting to care about whether such investors actually make money or not, something it did not care much about in the past. There are signs the State Economic and Trade Commission could enact lower tax rates and low-interest loans for foreign joint venture projects involving infrastructure.

How long will the slowdown go on for? Will these measures work, or is China in store for a protracted slowdown going into the year 2000? In terms of monetary policy, Western economic sensitivity to cuts in nominal interest rates is inversely proportional to the degree of nonperforming loans in the banking system. The higher the NPL rate, the more time it takes for rate cuts to feed through to a boost to real economic activity. China is a slightly different case given that the government and the PBOC have a much greater degree of enforceability on bank lending and corporate investment. However, an ironic result of

the economic reform process and in particular of the decentralizing of the economy has been that this enforceability has in
practice been greatly reduced in the last few years. The PBOC
can of course be heavy-handed in its policy reversal of getting
the state banks to lend more to the SOEs. But even if it succeeds
in this—which is itself questionable—the feed-through effects
in terms of boosting economic activity would not be seen for
quite some time to come. In any case, with NPLs at around
25–30%, the ability of the state banks to pass on the effects of
the PBOC's interest rate cuts is limited. The PBOC also cut its
reserve requirements in an effort to free up more capital, theoretically allowing the state banks greater room to lend. However,
even in China there remains a conflict of interest between the
state banks, which only recently were directed to become more
efficient and are thus focusing on their bottom line (probably for
the first time), and the corporate base, both the SOEs and the
TVEs, which are seeking new or increased loans. In Korea and
Thailand, despite substantial cuts in nominal interest rates, this
did not automatically feed through to a resumption in economic
activity. That's because Thai and Korean banks used the surplus
funds resulting from the rate cuts to buy safe government and
central bank paper rather than lend to a risky corporate base. Although not to the same degree since there is greater enforceability, this phenomenon could also be seen in China.

On the fiscal side, the feed-through effect from public infrastructure projects could also take a considerable time from
implementation before they result in a pickup in domestic demand. Workers' pay from these projects does not immediately
cause a pickup in economic activity, even if one assumes that the
workers use their new-found salaries to consume rather than to
save. Quantifying this is extremely difficult and can depend very
heavily on the degree of prevailing consumer gloom in the economy. Given that the economy appears to be slowing down on all
counts except investment, it would appear safe to assume that
domestic demand has slowed rapidly. Falling asset prices and
rising unemployment add to this bearish and insecure view of
the world. This encourages individuals to save rather than

spend, thus limiting or even negating the benefit to the economy in terms of a near-term pickup in domestic demand as a result of the projects. Officially, despite the government's monetary, fiscal, export, and FDI efforts, export growth was expected to slow to 5% growth in full-year 1998, according to the State Information Center; however, as noted before, in reality it grew a mere 0.5%. Real consumption growth, for its part, should slow to around 6.5% in 1998 from 9% in 1997. Industrial output continued to slow down in the first half of 1998 but picked up in the second half given rising investment and output by the state sector, as mandated by the central government. The result of this, however is that inventories will continue to rise, testimony to overcapacity, to excessive supply and falling demand as speculative consumption dries up within the economy.

The official overall result for full-year 1998 is GDP growth of 7.8%. This is still an extremely good result, but remember that it comes off a 1997 level of 8.8% growth and continues the grind lower from the 1992 peak in the 1990s which saw growth of 14.2%. In addition, there is a possibility that some contributing provinces could have artificially inflated their data. Looking at the performance from 1992 to 1997, it could well be argued that this is symptomatic of diminishing returns—which would be somewhat ironic since it was Marx who said that capitalism would ultimately fail due to ever-diminishing returns. While capitalism as a whole has disproved Marx's theory, proving itself remarkably flexible and adaptable to new situations and conditions, this trend in China is cause for concern. It has nothing to do with the Asian crisis. It started long before that. In the immediate term, there appears little prospect for recovery. Indeed, on the export side, a major concern is the fact that in dollar terms Asian countries that were forced to devalue their currencies have yet to see any major pickup in exports. This is due to the combination of greatly increased credit risk that has reduced the availability of trade finance and the high import content of exported goods. The currency devaluation has greatly increased import costs and therefore has all but eliminated the exporters' ability to use the devaluation for price advantage. When these

Asian countries finally manage to get their export engines going, Chinese exporters are in for even fiercer competition. If the renminbi's value is to be maintained and not allowed to devalue, then the economic strain resulting from a loss of trade competitiveness must be taken elsewhere, in much the same way that the Hong Kong dollar peg works. That means that asset prices have to fall further, that the cost base must be further reduced in order to regain competitiveness. Yet to do this is bound, in the short term at least, to exacerbate the sense of economic gloom that is starting to pervade the country.

The reform and restructuring process and the ongoing economic slowdown, which are in themselves interlinked, have had serious economic and social side effects, most notably unemployment. The very reason the PBOC reversed course on state bank lending to the SOEs was because the SOEs were doing too good a job of following the restructuring plans set out at the 15th Party Congress, throwing thousands if not millions of workers out onto the street or sending them home on partial pay—the *"xia gang,"* those who have literally been "stood down." China's official unemployment rate is 3–4%. However, this grossly understates the true figure. For one thing, it only counts urban residents, thus missing out entirely unemployed or underemployed rural workers. In addition, it ignores the "floating" population—those in the rural community who leave the countryside to try and find work in the cities but do not manage to find full-time employment. And finally it also ignores the *"xia gang."* Including these categories, the true figure is around 20%, or 150 million people. The restructuring of the SOEs announced at the 15th Party Congress took into account the view that it alone would be responsible for a 20–30 million increase in the unemployed. It is unclear how much of this has already taken place. What is clear, however, is that the situation will continue to get worse before it gets better. This is true even if the government seeks to slow the pace of the restructuring in order to try and limit the degree of pain being felt in the economy. Despite the one-child policy—which was designed to encourage couples to only have one child and to punish those who defied the policy—every year some 6 million people enter the work-force. With growth slipping below the magic 8% figure, the economy will not be growing fast enough to absorb these work-ers and the casualties of the restructuring process.

Looking at individual industries, steel manufacturers are ex-pected to cut their workforce by up to 40% by the end of the century in order to become more self-sufficient and profitable, in line with the aims of the restructuring process. Textile manu-facturers are also being hit hard in their export markets, with the Philippines and Thailand now much fiercer competitors given the devaluations of their currencies. The textile industry could lose over half a million workers in the next couple of years if things are left as they are. Aside from the restructuring process, every percentage point decline in GDP growth results in an in-crease in the unemployed of 4 million. Thus should growth fall to 6% in 1999 from 8.8% in 1997, this by itself would result in an increase in the total number of unemployed of almost 12 mil-lion. In the U.S., workers who lose their jobs have the option of relocating to another part of the country where jobs are more plentiful and the economy is healthier. They have the option of retraining or choosing another career. Such options are for the most part not available in China (they have only been made partly available in Europe very recently, let alone in China). Most people in China—that is those who do not have the appropriate *"guanxi,"* or "contacts"—are condemned to remain in their city or rural location whether they have a job or not. Given rising unemployment and the inflexibility in the labor force and the economy as a whole, this has not surprisingly led to a resurgence in the black market, which, along with the small but growing private economy, provides some small relief from the burdens of state-induced restructuring.

Slowing growth, rising unemployment, increasing deflationary pressures, and foreign direct investors who are being more cau-tious with their money make for a potentially lethal mix when put in a social and political context. It is stating the obvious to say that China has had a turbulent history, that social discord and protest have been the norm rather than the exception, particularly this century. Those among China's leaders who made the Long March (a decreasing number as old age takes it toll), thus striking the spark for the Communist Revolution of 1949, and who subsequently lived through the chaos of the Cultural Revolution of the 1960s are particularly aware of the acute dangers that can result from social discontent. The flickering flame in a bush can turn into a brushfire that sweeps all before it; small provincial protests can turn into citywide rioting, into revolution itself. Aside from the drain on the economy and the waste of human resources represented by the rise in unemployment, the key issue now and going forward is one of social unrest.

In Indonesia, just under half the population, or 98.5 million, is expected to be below the poverty line this year by official estimates. In China, a country with 900 million rural people, unemployment is already over 100 million, and this figure does not count those who by the definition of international organizations live below the poverty line. Though there are obvious differences between the case of Indonesia and China—not least the fact that Indonesia's economy and social fabric lie in tatters in the wake of the Asian crisis and the May 1998 riots—this comparison clearly shows the potential gravity of the problem in China. Indeed, there are already growing signs of social unrest, and there have been for some time, as more and more people join the unemployed, as the gaps between rich and poor, between the countryside and the cities, continues to widen. While riots or worker demonstrations against poor conditions or unemployment have yet to touch the likes of Beijing or Shanghai, they are becoming more commonplace in middle and western China. There the slowdown bites the hardest, given the relative lack of wealth to start off with. The cities of Wuhan, Xian, and Kunming have been the scene of such rioting and demonstrations, while Shenyang in the north has also witnessed social protest against the costs of the restructuring process.

Increasing social discontent is aimed not only at the rise in the unemployment level but at the SOEs, which are further seeking to cut costs by reducing welfare costs. The SOEs act not like simple companies but welfare societies, providing pensions, health care, and housing in addition to employment. Some, just as in Russia, have not paid wages or pensions for months and cannot afford to pay health-care costs. The government has tried to alleviate the situation by building a social safety net. But this is a mammoth task and could take up to 5 years to be fully operational. Looking at the way social unrest appears to be growing in China, the country might not have that time to spare.

Granted, the government is trying other ways of reducing or at least controlling the unemployment rise. It has developed specific schemes to encourage laid-off workers to join other employment sectors such as the service sector, which it is eagerly seeking to promote. Infrastructure spending and increased public works spending will also take some of the burden. But such measures are not likely to be enough to stop the inexorable rise in the total level of unemployed. The government has a choice: either to reverse course in the restructuring process rather than merely slow it down or to risk the continued increase in casualties resulting from the restructuring and thus a corresponding popular backlash through social unrest and crime. Economic problems are becoming social problems. The danger is that eventually they could become major political problems.

3

Social Tensions—
Rising Discontent

THE SMASHING OF the Tiananmen Square protests with armed force and the growing benefits that the economic reform process brought about caused a sea change in social and political thought. The enthusiasm for political reform that had been a key undercurrent of political emotion and discourse in the late 1980s due to rising corruption, inflation, and inequality began to ebb. In effect, as Deng Xiaoping increasingly did away with the ideological focus of political and economic discourse, instead centering the Party's attention on pragmatic economic philosophy more akin to that in the West, China's leaders entered into a social contract with the people: Forget the ideology of the past. The ideology of the present and the future is that "We will make you better off and you will not clamor for increased political change and development." With China's economy slowing down, that social contract is in danger of unraveling (again). The social and political implications of this are clear. Tiananmen itself happened just after such a slowdown. It was not only a protest against corruption— for when everyone is making money, less people care about corruption. It was just as much a protest against economic pain.

While China's history is rife with examples of social dislocation and protest, a more modern example of the dire social and political ramifications of economic underperformance has been the case of Indonesia. Granted, this is a case where the economy and distribution network completely collapsed, which is not true of China. Yet the rioting in May 1998, when over a thousand people died in the fires in Jakarta and scores were beaten or raped, happened in a country that until then had been thought to epitomize social and political stability. Countless examples of social unrest in China, which we shall look at later in this chapter, show all too clearly that the Middle Kingdom is far from immune from this phenomenon. Indeed, taking both these increasingly frequent incidents and China's troubled history into account, it is evident that China is a potential powder keg. In addition, the type of social unrest that is being seen nowadays is more dangerous than its antecedent, which focused largely on ethnic or national issues—the rioting in Tibet and the bombings by ethnic Turkic people in Xinjiang Province, for example. Such forms of protest can be dismissed by the Chinese central authorities (and were) as acts of "separatism" and "split-ism," or as terrorist attempts to undermine the stability and unity of the People's Republic of China. However, when people—more specifically the workers, the proletariat for whom the Communist Revolution was officially dedicated—take to the streets to demand jobs, housing, and even food, then Beijing has a different, infinitely more dangerous problem on its hands.

As well as boosting the lives of millions of ordinary Chinese, the economic reforms have also caused casualties, people who for one reason or another have either been sacrificed by the restructuring or been left behind as a result of it. I touched upon the issue of unemployment at the end of the previous chapter, given its inherent characteristic as a nefarious side effect of economic slowdown. Let us look at it in more detail.

In any country, no issue is more socially painful or more politically sensitive as that of unemployment. In China, it is an even more sensitive issue given the Party's leading role, both in the past to be the vanguard of the proletariat and in the present to improve people's financial well-being. Central to the economic reform movement in the 1990s has been the restructuring of the

Chinese corporate base. This initially took the form of allowing the TVEs and a small private sector to divert some capital away from the state sector, to act as an alternative source of growth and eventually an effective competitor, accelerating the restructuring within the state companies themselves by default. The plans announced at the 15th Party Congress were not only an extension but also an acceleration of this process. The announcements that 300,000 SOEs would have to restructure themselves within a 3-year time period, that SOEs would be floated on the Chinese stock markets, and finally that the larger ones—around 10,000—would be "grabbed" while the smaller ones would be "set free" (to sink or swim) amounted to nothing short of a revolution in itself.

It was officially acknowledged at the time that some 20–30 million workers within the SOEs were effectively underemployed, meaning they did nothing, and were superfluous to the needs of what the new, restructured SOEs would look like. This figure came about because the government calculated that around 55 million, or 36%, of the workers in SOEs were surplus labor. Of this, it was thought 36 million could be redeployed, hence the figure of 20 million people being without a job. Given the economic slowdown and consequently the reduced chance of redeployment as less jobs are being created, this figure could be overoptimistic—that is, if the restructuring process in the SOEs continues to go ahead.

So much for the SOEs. What of the workforce as a whole and especially the rural workers who still represent over 70% of the total? Official estimates are that of the 450 million rural workers, only around 150 million can be accommodated by the current agriculture business and available resources. Manufacturing plants can of course move to the countryside, where costs are substantially cheaper than in the leading cities. However, this by itself will not make up the substantial surplus in rural labor, which amounts to at least 100 million people by conservative estimates. This is obviously a key reason why unemployed or underemployed rural laborers continue to pour into the cities in search of work, or at the least in search of some sort of social safety net. Given that the cities can no longer cope with this excessive inflow, the result is that several cities are now ringed with shantytowns that house these people. In general, China is looking for ways to continue to trim surplus labor. However, it has a major problem if other parts of the economy are slowing down as well, as indeed they are. In the past, China has created an effective advance warning system to deal with the unemployment problem. Should the nominal level of unemployment reach a certain "crisis" level, the government uses executive powers to temporarily stop restructuring-related layoffs, halting acceptance of bankruptcy applications, controlling rural workforce access to cities, and allowing some personnel to retire ahead of schedule. Needless to say, this flies in the face of the reform process and has only a limited ability to reduce the economic pain. Such is the state of the economy that the reform process must be carried through in order to avoid future pain—which might involve even greater unemployment levels, with the predictable result in the form of a social backlash.

The restructuring of the SOEs not only means throwing people out of work, as grievous as that is. It also means changing the very nature of the SOEs, from effective welfare states to efficient state or semiprivate companies. It entails the smashing of the "iron rice bowl," the term commonly given to the job security, conditions, and welfare system which up until now have been provided as an inherent right of working in an SOE. Iron rice bowl subsidies in the SOEs in many cases actually exceed the wage bill. In addition to allowing access to company housing, they involve ration coupons for consumer durables such as clothes and coal, subsidized food, and the delivery of social services and health care. The SOE also administers state labor insurance welfare provisions and provides other subsidies such as supplementary payments and even loans. In the U.S., almost half the family budget goes to housing utilities, transportation, and medical care. In China, this figure is less than 10%—the SOEs provide the balance. Clearly going forward, this will change. The degree to which it changes will dramatically affect how SOE workers—those lucky enough to still have a job—view not only their workplace, but their very society and more specifically those who rule over them.

In addition, the smashing of the iron rice bowl, while necessary from an objective economic viewpoint in making the SOEs more efficient and less of a drain on the national budget, does not occur in a vacuum. Difficult working conditions, which were taken for granted in the past when Chinese society was in fact relatively egalitarian (in its misery if nothing else!), are now less tolerated in a time when the official mantra is "to get rich is glorious." The perception of widening income gaps reminds the "proletariat" first and foremost of their stifling working conditions on the factory floor, where advantage is gained by whom one knows rather than what. While the distribution of housing for SOE workers is no longer so openly manipulated by Party cadres in favor of themselves and their families, it has given way to a more subtle form where local Party and SOE management leaders often join forces to take the best in benefits for themselves. This leaves the "drippings for the poor" in a way that would bring a tear to the eye of recalcitrant feudalists. In addition, despite the overall improvement in living conditions and financial benefits in the wake of the reform process, the Party still attempts to control manufacturers at the factory-floor level through networks of activists, who along with the factory directors and group leaders—middlemen between the management and workers—seek to dominate not only the manufacturing process but social interaction. This is so, despite the fact that as an ideology, communism is becoming obsolescent for the majority of the population, let alone the "workers."

There is thus a natural inclination to view Party efforts to maintain a role for itself at the factory-floor level as almost revisionist, given the trend toward economic—if not political—openness and restructuring. In the township and village enterprises, an experiment that in purely economic terms has been astonishingly successful in offering an alternative source of growth and expansion for the economy, there are further potential sources of worker dissatisfaction. There is no effective union

representation to oversee even the most basic working conditions—irony piled on irony—and wages are decided on the
whim of the managers. Regulations for working hours and conditions are minimal, and in many cases workers do not get the
same welfare benefits as those working for SOEs—at least those
who still have such benefits. Officially, the All China Federation
of Trade Unions provides for the needs of the workers. However,
it has done little in practice to improve the plight of the ordinary
laborer. Thus, faced with the relative inactivity from the state-
imposed union, the attempt by the Party to maintain some degree of control on the factory floor, and rising income
disparities, workers who see no one as being on their side are,
not surprisingly, becoming increasingly frustrated with life. Various elements of the Party are clearly distressed with this situation for either humanitarian or ideological reasons. However,
there is unanimity in the view that only the leadership of the
Party, whether imposed directly or indirectly, can be allowed to
improve things. It was no accident that in the events of Tiananmen Square that took place on June 4, 1989, the Beijing Au-
tonomous Workers' Federation (BAWF), a spontaneous
grouping that specifically sought to address the grievances of the
workers rather than, as the students did, to focus on more
overtly political issues, came in for especially harsh treatment.
The reason was that the BAWF represented a threat to the
Party's domination in and of the working class. Such an approach by the Party may seem old-fashioned and indeed out of
place given the reforms that we have seen. Yet this in a nutshell
is the paradox that is China—change on the economic front, but
minimal if any change on the political front and the Party trying
to hang on to its dominant position despite the fact that its ideology has long since been condemned to the dustbin of political
discourse for all but a few sad utopians.

While conditions in China do not equate to any degree to the
rampant and almost institutionalized corruption that exists in,
say, Russia, the combination of local bureaucrats, the Party, and
enterprise management which now dominates society, in many
cases at the expense of the workers they are supposed to serve,

has increased the general feeling of unfairness. This is not only the case among those who have actually lost out through being made unemployed, being "stood down," or otherwise having lost their iron rice bowl benefits. The concept of the *"dakuan"*—the "fat cats"—is an overt, in-your-face reminder to the workers of the rising inequality in the new China. This is particularly the case in a time of economic slowdown when such inequality is further emphasized. While people remain in the workforce, they still have something to lose. Indeed, as we have seen, they have a lot to lose, including not only their job, but also their benefits and entitlements such as housing, pension, and health care. In addition, despite the inexorable decline in popular support or interest for the Party, the Party's attempt to maintain some degree of power at the factory floor limits the ability of the disgruntled—but still working—to mobilize themselves (though the events of Tiananmen show that even such efforts are not always successful).

However, the unemployed are freed on a relative basis from these constraints. They do not have much left to lose (apart from their lives), and the Party's ability to control their thoughts and actions is itself constrained by the inherently greater difficulty of trying to keep tabs on the unemployed. They are thus more able to join forces, to coalesce, to organize into social protests that are becoming an increasingly dangerous political threat. The constituents of those who have organized social protests are not simply ex-factory workers or peasants. They are also bureaucrats and intellectuals who either face retirement age or face the prospect of minimal or low pension benefits, and they are members of other parts of society—even within the PLA itself—who do not have the requisite support network of *"guanxi."*

The elimination of the benefits of the iron rice bowl, albeit for sound economic reasons, is presented by the Party as the natural, but unfortunate, extension of the reform process in allowing for competition and the Open Door policy. Indeed, in a somewhat two-faced approach, the Party publicly states that it should only exercise limited control over such elements of the reform process as reduction in benefits, whatever the consequences, while at the same time attempting to maintain some degree of control at the grassroots level. The focus of the Party's work now is to support management in order to achieve efficiency and dissipate whatever existing worker discontent there is. To those who maintain their Maoist ideological credentials, this is tantamount to treason, to a betrayal of the revolution itself. The benefits of the iron rice bowl were psychological just as much as they were real. Employment was for life, and one's children would inherit the job, an additional reform put in place only after 1978. They thus represented a force for maintaining the unity of the workforce. In modern times, that means the unity of the workforce of the state sector, which no longer represents the majority of annual industrial output. However, we are still talking about 100 million workers. With the smashing of the iron rice bowl, that force for unity is no longer there. As has been seen in Eastern Europe, to those who have been used to the psychological comfort of state aid for most of their lives, this is a deeply traumatic message, as well as representing a threat to their financial well-being. Finally, the effort by the government to make the banking system more efficient (it could hardly be less given that the banking system is technically bankrupt in a Western sense) necessitated that the four state banks reduce funding to the SOEs and explicitly eliminate funding to loss-making SOEs, which make up around half the total. As a result, many SOEs have been unable to pay wages, pensions, and iron rice bowl benefits even if they wanted to and even if such benefits were not immediately targeted for rationalization or elimination. Take this and combine it with rising unemployment and rising inequality and you get the fundamental reasons for rising social discontent and unrest at the worker level.

In China, source of the world's largest workforce, there has always been a fundamental conflict between the need to increase labor productivity and the requirement to continue to increase employment in order to maintain social stability. This has particularly been the case since the beginning of the reform process in 1978. The message of the 15th Party Congress was that growth and, if necessary, employment would be sacrificed to a degree in order to maintain and accelerate the reform process, no doubt for the purpose of ensuring long-term prosperity. For those who have lost out to this reform process in the present day, future rewards offer little comfort, and in any case it is questionable whether such people will be the beneficiaries of these rewards. The economic slowdown has exacerbated and exposed fundamental paradoxes within the reform process. Even the new role of the Party as the administrator of the economy rather than the vanguard of the proletariat is itself being challenged, for being both unjust and inadequate. So much for the reasons behind the phenomenon of rising worker social unrest in China. In what ways is it manifested? Looking at past demonstrations and examples of social discontent is a dangerous business in attempting to predict the future. It is equivalent to trying to forecast a revolution something that many revolutionaries have themselves failed to do.

Social unrest in the industrial workforce has been manifested in two main forms. The first is factory sit-ins and demonstrations against employers, and the second, overt protests against the authorities. In most cases, the latter have been directed against the provincial authorities, but on at least one occasion— shortly after the 15th Party Congress, in fact—it was directed explicitly against Beijing and the reform process itself. Examples of the first type number in the hundreds if not thousands and are certainly too numerous to list. A few examples are instructive, however, as to what the authorities, at both the provincial and the national levels, are indirectly faced with.

A fine example is that of the sit-in on New Year's Day 1997 in Acheng, a satellite town of Harbin City in the northeast province of Heilongjiang.[1] Acheng was the location for the setting of several large SOEs after the founding of the PRC and has historically been a major sugar beet and flax production base. However, since the beginning of the reform process, the government has consistently reduced the emphasis on buying from the state sector and has practiced survival of the fittest. Many of the industrial SOEs, which were used to getting state aid and were being overstaffed and inefficient, have found it extremely difficult to

compete in the new environment. This is precisely the point of
restructuring—to make the entire system more efficient and
profitable. Yet the downside was that these SOEs in Acheng, just
as elsewhere, faced with reduced available credit and state aid,
found it increasingly difficult to buy raw materials, sell their
products, repay loans, and even pay wages and welfare benefits.[2]
Eventually, they started laying off people and reducing production to more realistic levels. Most stopped short of declaring
outright bankruptcy to try and avoid a worker rebellion, instead
"standing down" workers, giving them at most a "livelihood subsidy" of between USD12 and 20 a month. Not surprisingly, the
workers eventually protested against this. The sit-in shocked local officials given the source of the protest, coming from the industrial base seen as a heartland of "loyalty"—as if to protest for
losing one's job or for not being paid for months was disloyal.

Elsewhere in Heilongjiang Province, in the industrial cities of
Shuangyashan, Jiamusi, and Mudanjiang, where up to 80% of
the SOE workers were laid off, there have also been sporadic
protests against the costs of the reform process. This reached the
level of open confrontation against the local authorities when on
October 22, 1996, hundreds of unpaid miners staged a sit-in in
front of the local Party headquarters.[3] Many of the miners made
redundant by the collapse of the local coal mining industry did
not have enough money even for winter clothing. In neighbor-
ing Liaoning Province, also part of the northeastern industrial
belt, there have also been widespread layoffs and closures as well
as worker protests.

Such demonstrations of worker anger are however not limited
to the industrial northeast. They have been witnessed in Wuhan,
Xian, Tianjin, Sichuan, and even Beijing and Shanghai themselves. In 1997, there were over 6,000 SOE bankruptcies. That
number continues to rise on an annual basis, with inevitable
consequences for employment, welfare benefits, and the likelihood of an increasing social backlash. Workers in the southern
city of Lianyungang, in Jiangsu Province, who had not been paid
for over 6 months staged a protest outside local government offices on December 20, 1997, to demand their money. Many

demonstrations by workers in the cities and peasants in the rural areas have involved several hundred people, some several thousand. In the southwestern city of Mianyang, thousands of workers demonstrated to protest the closure of their factories—and were met by an oppressive police crackdown.[4] In one of the most dramatic incidents, up to 20,000 workers in the city of Nanchong in Sichuan Province besieged city hall for 30 hours to demand back pay. Given the size of the protest, the authorities compromised, arranging loans and providing some workers with the first wages they had seen in over half a year. Worker discontent has on the odd occasion been aimed not only at local management, bureaucrats, or government officials but at Beijing itself, a development that the leaders in the Zhongnanhai must view with extreme alarm. Just after the 15th Party Congress took place, at the start of October 1997, there were a series of rallies in the central industrial city of Wuhan where workers not only petitioned the local government to help them out as a result of their having lost their jobs due to the SOE restructuring process, but also called on the national government to cease the restructuring process itself because of the economic casualties it was causing. In an even more overt example of worker anger, there were a series of bomb explosions across China, from Guangzhou to Beijing itself, several of which were allegedly planted by the Laid-Off Workers Committee.[5] In response, the government called on SOE managers to try and monitor the behavior of laid-off workers. However, this is clearly an impossible task given the size of the problem.

As a result of the restructuring process, the economic slowdown, and the casualties that have been created, a series of social fissures have developed within Chinese society, cutting across many plains and levels. In social and political terms, these fissures can be compared to tectonic plates, continuing to shift, occasionally creating sporadic disturbances on the surface, biding their time for the big one—a volcanic explosion that would threaten the very existence and nature of the PRC. The first of these tectonic plates is elementary—the "haves" and the "have-nots." In China, at least in more recent times, this is actually a relatively new phenomenon. While Mao did not escape the trap that has befallen all leading Communists (despite their ideological pretensions), of creating an elite within the supposed Party of the people, by the people, and for the people, Chinese society was relatively egalitarian under his reign—albeit miserable and extremely dangerous. The reforms created in 1978 changed all that. One of the most potent criticisms by the BAWF in 1989 was that the reform process had victimized the working class, essentially betraying the Party's supposed role of protecting the proletariat against capitalist profiteers. Indeed, the whole spirit of the reforms appeared to create the backdrop for inequality and rampant corruption. The spirit of "to get rich is glorious" meant not only attaining and having wealth, but no longer being inhibited in demonstrating it, flaunting it even. On a visit to Beijing or Shanghai in particular, this is most immediately visible in the fashions that the emerging middle and upper classes are wearing, in the wide variety of products and goods that are available in department stores, and above all in the numbers of cars on the road. It is unlikely that cars will ever outnumber bicycles in China (such an idea would of course be an automaker's dream). However, the rise in car ownership is striking compared with only a decade ago. In addition, it is not only the fact that new products are available to the Chinese consumer, but the type of product that is available, that demonstrates the dramatic and rapid change China has undergone. The sight of flashy Western cars in the streets of the major cities has long since stopped being a novelty. Trendy discos are now jammed with the progeny of the elite and also of the rising new elites. The "little emperors" want the best, and the best is seen as coming from Europe and the U.S., whether it is a bottle of Remi Martin or a new Mercedes.

Such ostentation does not go unnoticed. To those few who still deem themselves faithful to the Maoist branch of Marxist-Leninism, this development is tantamount to a reversal of the revolution, to a return to the pre-liberation days in Shanghai especially, when income disparities were monumental, when prostitutes and triads filled the streets where decent people walked, where corruption and greed were everywhere. Such ostentation is tantamount to a betrayal, with the animosity directed not only at the perpetrators of such "class crimes" but at the instigators of the reforms themselves. The poor in the cities and the surrounding suburbs probably see things in a simpler light: What they see creates either hatred and jealousy or, if hopes still exists, a desire to emulate.

Such hope is eliminated when corruption is perceived to be involved in the getting of the wealth, when it is thus deemed impossible to prosper through ordinary means. Of course, again, the hypothetical person can look at this two ways: The first is with disgust; the second takes the view that "if you can't beat them, join them." The rise of overt wealth has been paralleled by the rise of corruption, both overt and covert. At the highest levels, the Party now admits that it is no longer the vanguard of the proletariat. Down in the ranks, this implies that Party cadres no longer have to be bound by the same sense of morals and ideological vigilance and purity that once was the norm. To some in the Party, the reforms have brought with them a golden opportunity to loot and rape their own country. The government has periodically carried out extensive and severe crackdowns. Certainly the punishment can be severe. The penalty for financial fraud is death. However, it is doubtful that more than a few heads of the hydra have been cut off—only to grow back again. The body, the desire to make illicit gains, remains in place. The growing black market is testament and confirmation to this. It is a well-known fact that several leading Hong Kong triads achieved friendly relations with Beijing prior to the handover of Hong Kong to China. In return for their support of the handover process, the government effectively promised not to crack down on them. The result has been that the triads, thus free to move around without disturbance in the mainland, have joined forces with mainland secret societies, a further reminder of the Shanghai of the 1930s which the Party elders thought they had managed to eradicate. The rise in corruption will only be halted or reversed when the government manages to eliminate or severely reduce poverty. In China, that is a monumental, some would say impossible, task, not so much in the cities but in the countryside where the divide between the haves and the have-nots is especially evident, where the word "peasant" still, at the end of the twentieth century, has meaning.

For while the cities have boomed in the 1990s, the countryside, the rural areas that began the whole reform process through the decollectivization of farms, has lagged behind. Indeed, the issue of haves and have-nots is particularly important and particularly poignant in the rural areas. For a start, there are still very few haves in the countryside. These haves are either rural workers of TVEs or SOEs which are uncharacteristically successful and prosperous or leading local Party or government members. For the great majority of people in the countryside, even though their general level of lifestyle has been greatly improved since the 1970s, the advancement of other sections of society, notably the cities, is a painful reminder of just how far they, the "peasants," still have to go. This is a particularly ironic situation because, as just noted above, it was the countryside that led the reform process. The return of market principles—at least to a degree—to the farming process in China brought with it extraordinary initial returns. Farming incomes, and with them the general standard of rural living, rose almost 20% a year in the 1980s. However, once the government began to focus on urban reconstruction and development, the countryside was no longer a priority and began to lag behind. The spread of mass media communications, through television and radio, even to many rural areas in China has made the growing disparity between standards in the countryside and the cities increasingly visible and apparent.

Corruption is a further problem that exacerbates rural tensions and concerns. Indeed, it is a leading source of rural worker dissatisfaction and unrest and is even a cause of peasants migrating to the cities. Many migrate not only because they are out of work but because they are seeking to escape the clutches of oppressive and corrupt local officials. While many rural Chinese view their urban counterparts as snobbish, selfish, and individualistic, urban Chinese view the "peasants" as an echo of China's past, as backward. Those rural people who are forced to settle in shantytowns outside the cities—where crime is rampant —are viewed scarcely as more than criminals themselves.

For those rural people who stay on the land, there is a problem there too, as far as the government is concerned. The events of Renshou County in Sichuan Province in June 1993 when thousands of rural people protested against excessive local taxes on farms is a case in point. It is an example where the problems of rural poverty and local corruption and oppression merged, potentially leading to an explosive backlash. There is a clear link between corruption and unrest in the countryside, as of course there is between rural poverty and unrest—this is merely to state the obvious. That said, corruption is not the only problem. The desire of the national government, all else being equal, to increasingly reduce its role in the economy and become a national administrator rather than the guiding hand of a command economy, means in effect that farm prices have failed to keep up with those of manufactured products. Granted, a series of record harvests has clearly had a dampening effect on rural product prices in the 1990s. However, the reduction and in some cases the elimination of subsidies mean that rural incomes continue to underperform.

The logical solution is a free-market-based rural economy where rural enterprises and farms are forced to merge, thus creating efficient and prosperous businesses. To a degree this is indeed happening, though the pace is slow—and the patience of those who feel left behind is wearing extremely thin. The rural areas of China (the majority of the landmass) suffer greatly from a lack of infrastructure, particularly of efficient roads and highways, investment in which might dramatically promote the attractiveness of such regions. Again, Beijing and the local provincial governments are attempting to alleviate this problem, precisely through the building of highways and railroads. Time, though, is not on the side of the government. Rural poverty is of course nothing new in China in historical terms. However, the key factor now that is causing dissatisfaction and on occasions bouts of actual unrest is the fact that improved communications between the cities and the countryside mean that rural people now know how much better life could be. As the saying goes, revolutions happen not when times are extremely hard and there is no hope, but when standards have actually improved, when hope once forgotten is reborn. It is interesting to note that many villagers still hang pictures of the Great Helmsman, of Mao himself, in their house, as a reminder of someone who looked after the peasants, as indeed someone who made the peasants the heart and soul of the revolution.

Not only is that revolution dead—or at least on its last legs—but the priorities of the government appear to have changed. Many in the rural areas feel not only let down by the change in ideology, but abandoned by Beijing. At one time, all the main leaders of the Party, including Mao himself, came from the countryside and consequently understood the grievances of the peasants, the hardship of rural life. The same cannot be said today where most of the leaders were born in the cities, went to the leading universities in Beijing (Beishida, Beida) or Shanghai (Qinghua, Fudan), and have themselves received substantial material benefits resulting from the reform process. The leaders of the national government and Party are (rightly) now seen as a technocratic elite. Indeed, that appears to be their very aim. As such, they are generally not viewed as having any significant understanding of the grievances of the peasants—or caring. Grievances, jealousy, and a feeling of abandonment can turn to hatred, and hatred to a desire to do something about it. Mao himself wrote in the 1930s that the peasants would rise up like a whirlwind and sweep away the decadence and corruption that were most visibly demonstrated by the cities. It happened once. Who is to say it could not happen again? Going forward, unless the economic boom extends inland, to the heartland of China, to the provinces of middle China such as Hebei, Anhui, and Heinan, the government could have major social and political problems. Of course, the government knows this all too well. It has yet to come up with a convincing response, however.

Meanwhile, crime is on the increase in the countryside. Hijackings and kidnappings are becoming commonplace. Economic and social tensions between the city and the countryside, between industry and agriculture, continue to fuse into entrenched mutual intolerance and violence. It might sound alarmist to say, but there are signs that the side effects of the economic reform process, such as widening income disparity and city-countryside growing animosity, are starting to threaten the regime itself. The ethnic tensions that are most evident to Western viewers, such as those in Tibet and Xinjiang, are but the tip of the iceberg. In a global chemistry set, China is the social and economic experiment that is reaching the critical point. It could, if not cooled down, explode, with devastating consequences for Asia and the rest of the world.

The increasing divisions within China are evident along a further dimension—that between Beijing and the provinces. Granted, it was Beijing itself that first created this division, seeking to grant more localized power to the provinces in order to try to achieve greater economic efficiency. A fundamental aspect of the reform process and the move toward the socialist market economy was the emphasis on local initiative, on the provinces in effect competing against each other in order to drive growth forward. Deng Xiaoping, in his *"nanxun,"* or his "imperial visit to the South," in 1992 stressed this very point (that specific case was that Guangdong Province should be the spearhead of economic growth). As a result, the central government's share of national income, whether through taxes or income from the SOEs, has continued to decline throughout the 1990s, to the benefit of the provinces. A study by two Chinese authors, Wang Shaogang and Hu Angang in 1990, entitled "The Decline in the Extractive Capacity of the Chinese Government and Its Results," pointed to the historical dangers of decentralizing fiscal power. The authors stated that this was the key element behind the disintegration of Yugoslavia rather than ethnic hatred per se. In addition, they suggested that the late stages of the Ming and Qing dynasties in

China witnessed a similar decentralization process, allowing greater freedom to the regions which used this to set up competing and separate regimes.[6] The *People's Daily* has periodically criticized local provincial leaders for emulating the *"zhuhou,"* or the "petty prices," of feudal times. Some may see the rise of provincial bureaucrats, Party members, and businessmen—and the coalescing of those forces—as the inevitable and benign consequence of the drive for reform, more specifically for Beijing allowing those reforms to be led by the unleashing of the provinces. To a certain extent, Beijing sees it that way too. However, there is concern as well. Power corrupts, and absolute power corrupts absolutely. The local provincial leaders have in effect replaced the warlords of historical China as their economic successors. This equally inevitably strains the delicate balance between Beijing and the provinces, though to varying degrees in each case. It is not so much that the provinces are aimed at setting up independent states (the mere suggestion of which would bring an immediate and unequivocal response from Beijing), but that the provinces are happy with new-found wealth and power, want to keep them, and want to drive faster than Beijing necessarily wants. In other words, the most immediate tensions between the provinces and Beijing are centered on the idea of just how fast the reforms should be carried forward. Beijing, on occasion, appears to be an elderly adult, holding back its offspring. From Beijing's viewpoint, it is a similar analogy though the emotional response is not so much frustration at the adult as the idea of solemn responsibility to keep the economy in check at the local level and not let it run out of hand —for that could allow the reemergence of inflation, the main economic enemy to Beijing.

To see how this works in practice and how the economic reforms are proceeding at a local level, we have to examine the provinces individually. In terms of the most prosperous areas, when one thinks of the provinces in China one thinks immediately of Guangdong and Fujian. Deng Xiaoping's *"nanxun"* to Guangdong did indeed accelerate one of the most remarkable development stories in human history. Straddling the Pearl River, the main artery for sea trade, and bordering Hong Kong, which served as the main financial and service center for it, Guangdong exploded, recording annual growth rates of over 20%. Factories were in fact moved to Guangdong from Hong Kong because of the substantial cost differential. In effect, Guangdong became the manufacturing base of southern China and Hong Kong the service center, the two working in perfect harmony. Not content with this, Beijing set up Shenzhen as a special economic zone in its own right, with its own stock exchange and tax and trade benefits, further accelerating the reform process. Competition between Shenzhen and Hong Kong for mainland company listings, while seen as limited at the start in light of Hong Kong's historical and technical advantages, was seen as a likely catalyst for maintaining the speed deemed necessary for restructuring. Go to Guangdong and you will see how Western preconceptions of China are so massively off base. Friends in the U.S. and Europe asked me many times before the handover in Hong Kong whether I was not concerned at the impending domination of perhaps the world's most freewheeling capitalist society by "the reds." For those who have any experience with China, the question displays an alarming, though understandable, naivete. China is one of the most capitalistic countries in the world. Of course, Beijing does not view itself that way, preferring to focus on its concept of the socialist market economy, which embodies the rule of law, economic modernization, and decentralization. While there were sincere concerns among Hong Kong Chinese people about how Beijing would rule over its prodigal son, many told me that their principal concern was economic, not political. They were afraid that Hong Kong had become fat and lazy and could not compete openly with the more dynamic entrepreneurial spirit that existed just over the border in mainland China. This may completely dumbfound Westerners who view Hong Kong as the capitalist equivalent of the Wild West. My message, and that of the Hong Kong Chinese people who were kind enough to air their views, is this: That's nothing! Go to China itself.

Since the imperialist adventurers of the nineteenth century, Chinese development has been greatly affected by trade. The

history of Hong Kong and Guangdong since the start of the reform process in China has largely focused on trade, benefiting
from the establishment of the Shenzhen SEZ and the increasingly pragmatic approach between London and Beijing over
Hong Kong. And now Fujian Province, and more specifically the
Xiamen Municipality, has gained as economic relations between
Beijing and Taipei have begun to thaw. As of 1997, Hong Kong
still made up over 50% of foreign direct investment into the Xiamen special economic zone, with Taiwan at 20%, dwarfing the
contribution from U.S. investment at around 6%. By the mid-
1990s, Xiamen SEZ was also growing at 20+% annual rates. In
1995, its GDP was thirteen times the size it had been in 1980.
Such has been the success of the SEZ policy in Xiamen that foreign ventures and enterprises are now the largest manufacturing
force there, replacing the SOE sector in this role. Such foreign
enterprises make up almost half of the Xiamen SEZ's exports.

Undoubtedly, the stunning economic success of Xiamen and
Fujian Province as a whole has had a generally beneficial effect
on the standard of living and consequently reduced the desire
for social unrest or otherwise express protest or dissatisfaction.
Still there is work to be done. An anecdote provides a clue to the
challenges ahead. An investment banker friend of mine told me
a story about how a local manufacturer, in what was for him a
complete loss of face, came to the bank and asked it to intercede,
as the company's ships were being hijacked off the Fujian coast
and the local police seemed disinterested. The bank called up a
few people in Beijing, and Beijing said it would do what it could.
A few months later, after a lengthy investigation by the Public
Security Bureau and the People's Liberation Army, a group of
local transport police who had themselves been responsible for
the hijacking of the said ships were lined up by the dockside and
shot there and then. In retrospect, one can see this as a pragmatic approach to a problem given the challenges involved. But
the very fact that such action had to be taken perhaps shows the
degree of the problem that both Beijing and the local officials are
having to handle.

Hainan Island, just off from Guangdong, while itself being an incredible success story in the 1980s and 1990s, has a reputation as being a freewheeling place. Officially made a separate province from Guangdong in 1988 and also a separate SEZ, Hainan Island has never looked back. Rich in strategic resources such as iron ore, timber, and rubber, Hainan's industry was extractive—rather than manufacturing-based. SEZ status has eventually recreated the island as a service and manufacturing center and distribution point. Situated on the same latitude as Hawaii, Hainan benefits from a pleasant climate and has become one of the key tourist destinations for China's new elites, from both party and business backgrounds. In 1992, some 2.5 million tourists visited Hainan Island.[7] Hainan Island has, however, become somewhat infamous in some aspects. In 1984 after an auto-importing scam was uncovered, the provincial government was dismissed. Equally, as the tourist industry has boomed, so has prostitution. The fact that many of these people are mainlanders and not Hainanese is merely something else for the locals to gripe about. Intercommunity tensions do exist between mainlanders and those who deem themselves local Hainanese, as in born in Hainan and speaking Hainanese Mandarin, despite the rapid economic success the island has achieved. Such tensions at the local level are mirrored at the provincial government level and also between the Hainan provincial government and Beijing. Hainan has always had a fiercely independent streak, though one should emphasize that this is focused nowadays on a desire for greater autonomy with regard to regional economic development rather than any pretensions at political independence or separatism.

The examples of Guangdong, Fujian (Xiamen), and Hainan show how the reform process has been led and has prospered, albeit under trying and difficult circumstances. It is useful to compare these with the interior and the northeast of China where conditions are not so prosperous, where the economic pain resulting from the reform process has been considerably greater, and where the instinct for protest is quicker. One example from the interior is Sichuan Province, birthplace of the late Paramount leader Deng Xiaoping. Sichuan is the largest province in China in terms of number of people. It has a population of 120 million and a workforce of 65 million (more than the entire population of Britain or France). It has traditionally had one of the largest provincial economies in terms of GDP size—RMB280 billion compared with RMB35 billion for Hainan Island. The main driving force behind this economic size is agriculture. As a result, Sichuan boomed in the early phase of the reform process, in the 1980s, but has since lagged somewhat. The fact that Sichuan has the largest population of any province, however, has historically made it also one of the poorest provinces in terms of relative GDP per capita. In addition, Sichuan has been disadvantaged by the fact that 46% of employment is rurally based. The shift in the national government's economic development strategy from reforming agriculture to boosting industry, and more specifically boosting industry on the coast (Guangdong, Fujian, and Shangdong Provinces most notably), has not helped economic prospects in Sichuan. In addition, the restructuring of the SOEs is a further burden to the province since what industry there is in the province is largely heavy industry, which will be hit by unemployment.

The other main type of industry in Sichuan is the defense industry. News in late July that the government under Jiang Zemin has ordered the PLA to get out of commercial activities will not be taken well in Sichuan. There are some positives, though even these have caveats. The massive Three Gorges Dam on the Yangtze River, the largest dam in the world, will benefit much of eastern and central China in terms of electricity production, though its actual benefits to Sichuan itself will be limited. In addition, by the time it is completed in 2008, it will have been responsible for the elimination of 15 counties and cities in Sichuan, with the result that the province will have to resettle almost a million people. The national government has sought to address local government concerns about being disadvantaged by saying that it will help with the development of heavy industry in the Panzhihua southwestern area of Sichuan. However, the emphasis remains on the local government sorting out its own problems—despite the fact that many of those problems are created by shifts in national economic development strategy.

Finally, there is the example of Liaoning Province, in the northeast. Liaoning has a third of the population of Sichuan, at around 40 million people. However, its industrial/agriculture mix in terms of employment is more balanced in favor of industry, at around 30% to 20%. Liaoning is one of three northeastern industrial provinces that represented the industrial heartland of China in pre-reform days. Thus its industrial base was developed along the lines of providing for a centralized command economy. About 75% of industry was heavy industry—steel, chemicals, etc. Initially, the provincial government sought to revitalize the state sector as the core of the Liaoning economy. However, Liaoning's traditional role as part of the centralized industrial base has hindered this process, in that equipment is out of date, products are inferior, and the mind-set within the elite themselves is not so readily able to change.

The challenges in Liaoning are best represented by the contrast of the coastal city of Dalian and Liaoning's capital city, Shenyang. The latter has a population of just less than 6 million. The casualties of the economic reforms and restructuring process are easily visible on the streets of Shenyang, as laid-off workers and the *"xia gang"* offer their no longer valued services at street corners. Shenyang tried to alleviate the situation of massive job losses at its main SOEs by creating the Tiexi industrial district. But unemployment still remains a serious social problem, so much so that protest outside city hall, to demand either jobs or back pay, are very frequent. Shenyang is the equivalent of the northeast of England or Pittsburgh after the steel industry all but closed down. It is an industrial city whose main industrial products are no longer highly valued when cheaper and better products are available elsewhere. In order to restore itself, further rationalization of the SOEs is needed. However, this will bring with it more unemployment and the resulting social unrest. The Liaoning provincial government should in the case of Shenyang seek to boost TVE and private production through subsidies and tax breaks in order to create jobs, thus reducing the burden of what remains an inflated SOE sector. All is not doom and gloom, however, in Liaoning. The example of the coastal city of Dalian demonstrates that success can be achieved. Made an economic and technical development zone (ETDZ) in 1984, Dalian has wisely mirrored its southern counterparts, seeking to attract FDI through attractive terms. Japanese manufacturers (Japan is only 4 hours away by plane) have not been slow to take up the invitation. Job creation has resulted, with both sides—the local workforce and the foreign company—benefiting.

Beijing has used a combination of strategies to try and deal with the growing problems associated with the restructuring process: the rise of unemployment, bouts of social unrest, the widening income disparities between the cities and the countryside, and so on. Fundamentally, they come down to an age-old duo—the carrot and the stick. National and local public security officials have made clear that demonstrations, petitions, and other instances of public unrest will be dealt with firmly and the leaders of such protests targeted for imprisonment. However, government, both local and national, realizes that the protests and demonstrations represent real grievances of ordinary people and have to be addressed if such social discontent is not to become explosive. This has involved both slowing down the reform process in some areas by redirecting state banks to lend to loss-making SOEs and at the same time encouraging more dynamic sectors of the economy to take up the slack by employing those who have been lost from the SOEs. It is a careful—and dangerous—balancing act, and it is far from assured of success. On the one hand, at the national level, Beijing is committed to the reform process: yet the restructuring of the SOEs, which is an essential part of those reforms, has caused and is causing substantial economic pain and as a result, social discontent. This is a classic catch 22 situation where there is no immediate answer. In the meantime, Beijing, in a more traditional manner, has sought to boost its preparedness to fight challenges to its authority. In 1995, it was announced that the size of the People's Armed Police (PAP) would double to 2 million officers. While this also represents a useful counterbalance against the PLA, there is little question that the growth of the PAP (numbering only about 500,000 before the Tiananmen Square events) is reflective of the social mood in the country (despite the economic progress to date) as evidenced by the rising number of incidents of unrest.

In terms of dealing with the provinces, Beijing's tactic of rotating top provincial officials has had some success in reducing local power monopolies, though any hope of eliminating these has long since gone; a return to more draconian methods of stamping out local power bases apparently is not an option any more. However, with top provincial bosses being rotated or retired, this leaves considerable power in the hands of the middle- and high-level bureaucrats who serve under these bosses—and who are not so frequently rotated. The results have been predictable: Some local bureaucrats act in dictatorial ways, and others are easily bribed. It remains a key question as to how to balance the need to decentralize the economy in order to improve its efficiency while at the same time attempting to stop or limit local corruption, independence, or heavy-handedness. It is a question that remains unanswered. Beijing, though, is far from being alone in this. Most Western countries have yet to provide a successful answer. The carrot-and-the-stick approach is generally in line with the overall economic strategy of "feeling for stones underfoot while crossing the river," of gradualism and caution. Yet there is a view that states that this approach can no longer be afforded, that time is not on China's side. Officially, China has a budget deficit of around 1% of GDP. Unofficially, including the SOEs and the deficits of these, which are financed by the government or the People's Bank of China, it is roughly 6% of GDP and rising. This is an unsustainable burden; thus logically the restructuring of the SOEs must be accelerated, not slowed down. But to do that risks alienating more of the population as more and more unemployed clog the streets of cities, and, in turn, as there are more incidents of local unrest. The time has yet to come when crime and unemployment merge fully in a political context, when the unemployed and the disadvantaged use political, revolutionary rhetoric to justify their crimes against the haves. That day is not far off, however. The only alternative is to make everyone better off, and Beijing is doing its level best to achieve just that. But the task is so monumental as to be indefinable.

So what is China today? What kind of country, what kind of society? The country's official name itself denotes that it is a people's republic—for the people, by the people, of the people. And huge swaths of people in Chinese society have certainly benefited enormously from the reforms. In fact, the benefits have been so great that one hears in Asia and in the U.S. hitherto unheard of reports that ethnic Chinese, the overseas Chinese of whom we have heard so much because of their financial potential, are actually starting to move back to China. But a large and growing minority in China feel left out, downtrodden, disadvantaged. China, a country with some 900 million rural people, continues to adopt an economic development strategy whereby the countryside, directly or indirectly, deliberately or not, continues to fall behind the cities. China is split across many plains—between the city and the countryside, between the provinces and Beijing, between the haves and the have-nots, but above all, between the coast and the interior. This is the essential differentiation that has to be dealt with if local and national governments are to ensure that social stability is for the most part maintained.

To many people in China, the name of the PRC has lost any meaning; certainly it has lost its original meaning. The focus is no longer on ideology, but on prospering economically, on bettering oneself. The enthusiasm of the past for democracy has waned, as this represents a destabilizing element to that aim of economic prosperity. The Party and the government have tied their mast to the aim of achieving this economic prosperity for the people. It is a worthwhile and glorious, if extremely dangerous, endeavor. They better not fail. The consequences of failure are unthinkable, both socially and politically.

To others, the name of the PRC still has profound resonance, representing a framework of social equality and justice, a defense against naked capitalist exploitation, the friend of the poor, of the peasants. The fact that modern China is seeing the reemergence of widespread corruption, despite Beijing's attempts to crack down on the corrupt, the fact that income disparities are once again appearing and widening dramatically, the fact that a growing number of people feel a profound sense of injustice over their present conditions, necessitates that Beijing's response be accelerated. For if Beijing, in the form of the current government under Jiang Zemin and Zhu Rongji, does not provide an answer, others will. Nature abhors a vacuum. Jiang and before him Deng Xiaoping have done much to dismantle the effectiveness of any opposition to their plans and aims from the leftist side of the government and Party. Indeed, there are few who would still claim to be leftists of whatever hue. Most of the old ones have died off or effectively been marginalized by Deng in the early 1990s, while the youth have little interest at the moment in the Party given the infinite possibilities of economic betterment. That said, the threat is not gone entirely. Indeed, in a country that "stood up," as Mao put it, in 1949 due to a Communist Revolution led by the peasants against the capitalist excesses of the cities, this would seem unlikely. The threat of leftist opposition to the government remains. In part, the unraveling of the Communist ideology itself has a part to play in all this. While members of the Party no longer see themselves bound by the same strictures and morals as the generation before them, the people themselves no longer feel bound to the community, to a community ethic or moral. Particularly in coastal cities, they increasingly protest as individuals, albeit within groups. Social protest has thus taken on an implicitly if not explicitly political slant. The ethos of the community over the individual is breaking down, as shown by the rising divorce statistics if nothing else! There will come a day when there will be a backlash against this, as surely as a pendulum swings back on itself.

4

The Threat to Reform —
Enemies on the Left?

A BACKLASH MAY BE nearer than many expect, given the degree of economic slowdown that China is witnessing and the amount of economic pain that the people are feeling. Such pain could be used to stir up problems for reformers, pain that could be manipulated, exploiting the growing cultural and income disparities in the supposed People's Republic. It is a great irony that in the PRC, the largest remaining Communist country in the world (if only in name), the left—the Communists—have largely been forgotten as a political force. Is this justified? A cursory glance at Chinese history would seem to suggest that it is not. Who in the 1930s successfully predicted the downfall of Chiang Kai-shek? Or the downfall of the Ming and Qing dynasties? The seeds of revolution cannot be seen. It is only when a seed has become a tree, when the threat is all-apparent, that the danger is realized—inevitably too late.

This is not to overdramatize the situation. It is merely to suggest that to completely ignore the left, as many commentators and China watchers now do, would seem a touch hasty, relative to what history teaches us. Granted, the left has been greatly marginalized. Most of the leaders are now spent forces or have died of old age. Yet surely Mao's forces were spent in 1935, before the Long March revitalized the spirit and popularity of the

Communists. Could we see another political long march in the 1990s and into the next century? I would be the first one to say that it seems unlikely in light of the forces that are combining to drive the reform process forward, and yet a more detailed answer is surely needed than mere guesswork. To dismiss the left out of hand is not a satisfactory response given China's history, and particularly given its revolutionary tradition since the "liberation" in 1949. The answer to what the left does from here, whether it still represents a potent political threat, most notably with regard to the reform process, is surely to be found in an examination of the battle between the various factions since the reform process began. While many in the West still to this day (somewhat incredibly) see the Party as a relatively homogeneous—if obsolescent—organization, this is far from the case. Indeed, the increasing divisions in the country as a whole, which we examined in the previous chapter, are fully represented in the Party. The Party has always been deeply divided along factional lines—much like any political party. Even in the early days of Mao, there were those who wanted to take a more lenient line with regard to class struggle and collectivization—and were purged for their pains in "antirightist" campaigns. The Cultural Revolution itself, that decade of criminal lunacy which ruined so many lives in China, was a manifestation of factional divide, of Mao striking back against growing opposition within the Party itself to his policies.

After Deng Xiaoping's rehabilitation (for the third time) and rise to power, he was finally able to get on track his long-desired economic reform process (the ideas behind the reform are the reason for which he was purged on two occasions). The 1978 Congress was, as noted before, a pivotal point in China's history. It was the point where the core of China's "national work," its ideological soul, was henceforth viewed as economic construction, where persistent and unending class struggle was initially relegated to secondary importance, only to be completely scrapped later on. It is fair to say that leftists were in general not best pleased by this development. However, more specifically they had varying reactions. The traditional propagandists, those who above all sought all ideological purity, viewed this as tanta-mount to treason, to a betrayal of the revolution, of the libera-tion of China from the dark forces of the Guomingdang. Others, on the other hand, those who put greater emphasis on central economic planning rather than ideological purity, went along with Deng's economic revolution. The left itself was thus split. It was on weak ground in any case given the vicious suppression by leftist forces in 1976 of demonstrators in Tiananmen Square who were mourning the death of Zhou Enlai and the subse-quent arrest and imprisonment of the "Gang of Four." Deng's speeches, emphasizing that China must rebuild, that the doc-trine of Mao would always serve as the centerpiece of ideologi-cal thought but that "poverty is not socialism," were persuasive. Deng was an exceptionally persuasive person, and someone al-most uniquely gifted in playing off factions against each other for the furthering of his cause and view.

Initially, Deng emphasized "thought liberalization," stressing that if the economy was to be rebuilt, if the lives of the people were to be improved, much greater flexibility was needed with regard to strategies toward achieving that end. In the 1980s, the decade epitomized by Deng's remark that "to get rich is glori-ous," his philosophy became reflected in his famous remark that "whether a cat is black or white, it is a good cat if it catches mice." Whether people were labeled communist or capitalist, they were good "cats" if they helped increase productivity, if they helped boost the economic reform process Deng himself had set in motion. The leftist central planners, led by Chen Yun, a for-mer finance minister under Mao, became increasingly troubled with this line, partly because of its increasingly lax ideological grounding, but more importantly because it increasingly repre-sented a direct attack on central state planning, on the leftists' own power base. It was Chen Yun who in response to Deng's white cat/black cat philosophy created the "birdcage" philoso-phy: The economy is a bird. Let it fly, but only within the steel confines of the cage that is the state, lest the economy fly away.

To the leftist propagandists, led by Deng Liqun, who indeed became propaganda director of the Party, this was tantamount to

war, a war by ideological revisionists against the purity and sanc-
tity of Mao thought. As a result, the 1980s saw a series of skir-
mishes, battles, and factional movement. On the one side were
the reformists around Deng, who wanted to accelerate the reform process but did not yet have a sufficient power base to be
able to do so. On the other were the leftists, some of whom
wanted to slow down the reforms, others of whom wanted not
only to stop it entirely but to reverse it. The Chen Yun faction
sought to support economic reform as long as it did not impinge
on central economic planning and dominance, whereas the
Deng Liqun faction and those of his ideological viewpoint
waged a very vocal and public attack on the entire reform
process. Deng Liqun went so far as to rail against Deng Xiaoping himself for allowing bourgeois liberalism to develop and
then not doing enough to stamp it out. Not surprisingly, given
his job as propaganda chief, Deng Liqun attempted to revive
class struggle as the key focus of "national work." He was just
too late. His time had been passed on to others who were more
eager to taste the fruits of modernization and the same liberalization he attacked.

It was a close run thing though, close enough for Deng Xiaoping to have to ally himself with the leftists against some of his
own protégés and supporters. Deng was a master at creating and
maintaining balance between the various factions in the Party,
but the price of maintaining that balance for some was high. After the student demonstrations of 1986 and 1987, Hu Yaobang,
picked as the successor to Deng, was sacked, as Deng was forced
to give in to the demands of the likes of Chen Yun and Deng
Liqun, who demanded that Hu be banished from the Party hierarchy. The loss of Hu was a great loss to China. Generally regarded as an exceptionally honest individual, Hu Yaobang
gained a great respect and following among the people—the
Tiananmen student demonstrations of 1989 initially began in
commemoration of his death. And the leftists were to make further gains when Zhao Ziyang, the replacement for Hu as designated successor to Deng and party general secretary, was himself
sacked after the events of 1989. Zhao's attempts to appease the

students and workers were seen as consorting with ideological traitors.

The left itself did not avoid taking casualties, however. At the 13th Party Congress in 1987, Deng Liqun was stripped of all his major Party titles. The Campaign against Spiritual Pollution of 1983 and the Campaign against Bourgeois Liberalization of 1987 had achieved minor victories for the left, but the cost had been heavy. A major effect was to alienate the undecided, who now (quietly) went over to the ranks of the reformists. In terms of ideology, the bloody events of June 4, 1989 (*"liusi"*—literally, the fourth of the sixth month) and their aftermath were the last chance for the left to snatch power. They failed, but again not by much. From 1989 to 1992, the Maoist revival was very evident. The *People's Daily* exhorted the workers and peasants to turn in class traitors and to be ever vigilant against any revival of bourgeois liberalization. The Deng Liqun and Chen Yun factions were unsparing in their drive to rid the Party of the supporters of Zhao Ziyang and Hu Yaobang, of the moderate reformers and relative liberals. Yet by aligning himself with this Maoist revival, Deng Xiaoping was able to stop the complete annihilation of the reformist faction. This was done not only out of a need to maintain a group of supporters for the ideas he himself wanted to push forward, but for pragmatic reasons. If the reformist faction was eliminated, this would unbalance the Party, potentially threatening a return to the type of chaos that had characterized the 1960s and early 1970s and that Deng would do anything to avoid. The reformist faction thus split in two: The "bourgeois liberals" who were seen as supporting Zhao and Hu were purged; more mainstream Party members who favored strong Party control with economic reform were saved.

The years 1991–1992 saw the last fleeting attempts by the left to gain the higher ground, given the impetus of the failed Soviet coup against Gorbachev in August 1991. However, the leftists had missed their chance. The momentum was lost. Reformists within the Party continued to be purged, and Deng Liqun's supporters continued to try to harass and bring down the reform process. Deng Liqun put forward the idea that with communism failing in the Soviet Union and anarchy assured, China now represented the last great bastion of Marxism-Leninism and this must be defended at all costs. The idea of "peaceful evolution," whereby a peaceful transfer from a socialist, centralized state to a market economy, socialist or not, had to be fought at all costs. By the second half of 1991, it almost seemed at one point as if they would succeed. The left was about to underestimate Deng Xiaoping for the last time. Ever the pragmatist, Deng continued to focus on the economy as being the core of the reform process, de-emphasizing the need or relevance of ideological rhetoric or thought.

In early 1992, Deng again took everyone by surprise, embarking on a modern-day version of the Long March. Seemingly unable to get his views across sufficiently in Beijing where the leftists still were in the ascendant, or at least sufficiently powerful to stifle the reform process, he embarked on a *"nanxun,"* literally a tour of the south. Everywhere he went, he urged Party cadres to accelerate the reform process, to strive to achieve ever-greater growth and productivity targets. The people of Guangdong, where the *"nanxun"* was focused, took him at his word. Guangdong has been a place of merchants and traders since the time of the emperors (an emperor banished all traders to the south, and there they stayed), and it had actively responded to the reforms of the 1980s. It was the *"nanxun,"* however, that caused Guangdong to explode. Other provinces saw this and wanted the same. The creation of the SEZs (Shenzhen, Xiamen, Zhuhai, Shangdong, Hainan) and Deng's *"nanxun,"* which effectively gave them the green light to reform the economy at will, forsaking centralist Party controls, was effectively the death knell of the leftists. Whether they controlled Beijing or not, the country was responding to the ideas, to the vision of Deng Xiaoping. It was not long before Beijing too fell into line—much as it had done at the liberation in 1949. The 14th Party Congress of October 1992 witnessed the removal of a number of key leftist leaders and supporters, effectively dismembering the body of the leftist opposition. In their place, Deng elevated a number of key technocrats, notably Jiang Zemin and Zhu Rongji. Whereas Hu

Yaobang and Zhao Ziyang had failed to achieve the requisite balance between political repression and economic liberalization, allowing bourgeois liberalization to take hold, the rising group of technocrats possessed the necessary degree of redness so that they could be trusted to maintain both factional and national equilibrium. Just as he had stopped the complete elimination of the more liberal reformists, Deng did not allow the elimination of the leftists. As ever, factional balance, the need to maintain factional harmony as opposed to chaos, was paramount. The country could yet live to regret that decision. Whatever the case, from 1992 on, the left was undoubtedly in retreat. Encouraged by the *"nanxun,"* reformists such as Qiao Shi and Tian Jiyun really let rip into the ideas and actions of the leftists. Deng himself said that any cadre who opposed the idea of economic reform on ideological grounds "should go to sleep." The message was clear. The reform process was unstoppable. Peaceful evolution had in effect won the day. The leftists were increasingly isolated, forced into irrelevance and obsolescence, not only by Deng's superior political and tactical skills, but by the increasing achievements of the economy. Nothing succeeds like results, and the economy by that time was achieving extremely impressive results. By late 1993, it was clear that Deng had beaten the last major challenge of the leftists. Chen Yun and Deng Liqun simply could not compete against the material gains that the reform process under Deng had achieved.

While the outright leftists had been defeated—albeit temporarily, perhaps—there were a significant number of ardent Communists who, feeling which way the wind was blowing, had taken a more pragmatic approach in not opposing Deng. Indeed, the defeat of the likes of Chen Yun and Deng Liqun still left the Party with a number of major competing factions. First and foremost was the "Shanghai faction." This was led by Jiang Zemin and Zhu Rongji, the former mayor and vice mayor of Shanghai, along with their supporters and acolytes.

In addition, there was the so-called "Soviet" faction, led by Premier Li Peng. These were, as the name suggests, usually people who were Soviet-educated and indoctrinated and were consequently likely to take a harder line ideologically. Li Peng himself has always been viewed as a hard-liner; yet many who forecast that he would be the fall guy, the scapegoat, for the Tiananmen Square massacre were mistaken. Indeed, to suggest this was to fail to understand the nature of the Chinese leadership system, a system that dates not only from the Liberation and 1949, but back through the 1911 revolution to the time of the emperors, the sons of heaven. The emperor ruled according to the "*tianming*," the mandate of heaven. Heaven was seen as bestowing the emperor with his reign on the condition that he rule wisely, fairly, and correctly. Should he make a mistake or be unjust, heaven would make its displeasure known by creating disturbances, whether through natural disasters or social revolts. Ultimately, if the emperor did not take heed, the mandate, the "*tianming*," would be withdrawn and the dynasty would fall. Deng Xiaoping could not have fired Li Peng because to do so would have meant that he was not infallible, that he had made a mistake, indeed that the Tiananmen Square massacre itself was a mistake, an injustice. Such an admission could not be allowed, for it would risk his own downfall. Previously, Deng avoided blame for the sacking of Zhao Ziyang and Hu Yaobang by blaming it on the leftists, who indeed were only too eager to take responsibility. This time, the only people who could have opposed the hard-liners were the liberal reformers, and they were in disarray, retreat. There would be no escaping blame this time.

There were also those within the Party who emphasized the rule of law in the reform process, of impartiality and civil society. These were led by the likes of Qiao Shi—the chairman of the National People's Congress and a member of the Politburo Standing Committee until Jiang Zemin relieved him of these positions at the 15th Party Congress in September 1997—and Tian Jiyun. Finally, there were the remnants of the more liberal reformers who had previously served, overtly or not, under Zhao Ziyang and Hu Yaobang. Ultimately, however, with Party ideology—and thus discipline—in retreat and the emphasis still on getting rich, such factional warfare degenerated into one common denominator, the desire for power. Mao is easily accused by historians of developing a cult of personality. Yet Deng Xiaoping was no less guilty, at the least of doing nothing to oppose this development and even the diffusion of "Deng thought," thus replacing "Mao thought." Deng's strategy had initially been to groom and consolidate a leadership structure that would preserve the Party's dominant role yet at the same time pursue market reforms energetically. That aim degenerated into one of mere self-preservation, of trying to make people rich not because there was a change of ideology but because it was the only way to hold onto power, to avoid chaos. Finally, it degenerated further into the stage of cult of personality. To an extent, this last is understandable. The Party was so divided that of necessity it needed a supreme or paramount leader to keep it together.

Deng thought was used further as the justification for the ascendancy to supreme power of the Shanghai faction, under Jiang Zemin. Throwing his support to Jiang, Zhu Rongji proclaimed, with the approval of the great man himself, that they would carry on the thoughts and traditions that had made the reform process under Deng so successful. These were pragmatists above all, people who embodied the necessary balance between seeking to maintain the Party's dominant role and simultaneously liberalizing the economy with ever-greater vigor and daring. These were and are modernizing technocrats, relatively liberal toward the economy but leftist in ideology (for pragmatic reasons), not given to Westernization but to taking the best of the West and making it essentially Chinese. The faction fighting continued, but no longer on strictly ideological lines. Much in the way of competing political parties in a Western context where ideology is all but irrelevant, the Shanghai faction sought to relieve the Soviet faction of its key positions, one by one. Li Peng himself has remained influential and prominent, but his supporters have been cut down, notably Liu Zhongli, the former finance minister, and Li Gruixin, the former governor of the People's Bank of China. In their place came men who were allies of the winners. As an example, Dai Xianglong, the current governor of the PBOC, has strong links to Zhu, who himself at one time was PBOC governor.

It is interesting to note that even to this day Jiang Zemin, who during the events of June 1989 seemed relatively neutral or at least reluctant to crush social unrest in his city of Shanghai, continues the Deng thought line that June 4, 1989, represented an attempt at counterrevolution or counterrebellion. This is merely the most modern extension of the principle of *"tianming,"* whereby the ruler—or even the protégé of the old ruler, newly crowned—must be seen as just, wise, and above all infallible. It is unlikely that this will change any time soon, that the events of 1989 will be admitted for what they were, a tragic and brutal mistake. Those within China who oppose this view say that chaos would have ensued had the crackdown not happened. Yet even to take the view that some restoration of order had to be achieved, this does not necessitate accepting that 2,000 people had to die. The very reason for the disturbances happening in the first place was surely a sign from heaven that the dynasty's *"tianming"* was starting to fail. Let us trust that China's leaders, whom U.S. President Clinton on his visit to China in June 1998 called the right leaders at the right time for China, have the wisdom and justice to learn the lesson. If they don't, heaven could withdraw its mandate. How could this come about? It seems unlikely that the left could engineer such an event given how systemically their organization has been destroyed, but it is not impossible. The Party now takes a back seat, at least in the economy, and the government now portrays itself as an administrator—much like the mandarins of old. Yet with the government taking over the preeminent position, it also takes over the *raison d'être* of the current administration, of the current dynasty, to make people better off. If the economy turns down, there is therefore a danger that the government—i.e., the Shanghai faction—and not the Party will be blamed, if blame there is. This may seem inconsequential. Indeed, in this modern time, the Party itself appears completely irrelevant to everyday life. Perhaps this is true for those who seek the good life in the cities, but not for the peasants, who see an ever-widening gap between themselves and the *nouveaux riches* in those same cities. Many want not to tear down the wealth of others but to get wealth for themselves. Yet this can only be achieved if corruption does not get in the way, frustrating that very ability to succeed, if the economy as a whole does not turn down. In the latter case, the wealth of the cities is forgotten (yes, life is unfair) and only the pain of the rural areas remembered. This is obviously a gross exaggeration. There are rural areas that, thanks to the TVE drive and selective modernization of the rural SOEs, have substantially improved the livelihoods of their communities—not relative to their past, but relative to their counterparts in the cities. Still, they are in the minority.

The only recent outbreaks of Mao fervor, whether in the cities or the countryside, have been for the purpose of collecting Mao memorabilia. Yet should the economy continue to deteriorate, should growth continue to slow, the *raison d'être* of the government, indeed the government itself, will start to come into question. With no effective opposition, the only alternative to the reformers—whether Shanghai, rule of law, or liberal—is a more hard-line view. This will not necessarily be taken up by the old leftists. For a start, very few remain. Indeed, many of their children have become some of the most zealous "red capitalists" that China has seen. It could, however, be taken up by the Soviet faction and those within other factions who again feel the changing of the wind and tack to the left to catch it. In other words, the threat from the left is more likely to be a pragmatic shift within government and Party circles rather than the return of ardent Maoists. That said, do not discount the latter entirely. Much is riding on the government succeeding in fulfilling its promise, in making the lives of the ordinary people better off. In the past, failure could be justified through revolutionary and ideological rhetoric—the need to work even harder for the glory of the triumph of socialism, and so on—but this is no longer the case. Indeed, the government, if not the Party itself, has nothing to fall back on in the event of failure. The government's new role as administrator is based on the simple principle of self-preservation. While some still believe that the principles of Marxism-Leninism hold true and that the reform process is merely a way to bring socialism up to date and into line with the necessities and demands of modern life, most ordinary people view it somewhat differently. They see that the Open Door policy represents a fundamental shift, in both theory and practice. People are still extremely careful about what views they express and in what company, to be sure. However, it is the change in mind-set that is important. There is no going back, either on the economic reform process or on the modernization of political thought whereby the marketplace has been allowed to take an increasingly important role in the lives of the people.

Whatever the political intentions of the reform process, there is an increasingly large paradox between a rapidly expanding market economy as a proportion of the total and an obsolescent Communist bureaucratic and administrative system. The assumption of some is that this can go on almost indefinitely because of the economic benefits that the combination has brought to the people. While this position seems untenable, it is even more so if one considers that the economic slowdown will mean that such benefits will be reduced or even eliminated. What one has in China is effectively a social contract, as mentioned earlier. It is contingent on the premise that economic progress and liberalization replace the need for their political counterparts. The example of Indonesia shows that this cannot go on forever. All one needs is one good economic downturn and the people will be demanding change, political change. To a certain extent, this tenuous situation is exacerbated by the very progress economic reform has achieved, more specifically in creating a large and growing middle class. History teaches that it is usually the frustrated middle classes that lead revolutions, the working classes that follow. What has been said in this chapter up to now points to the idea that the reform process does face potential opposition from the left, but that opposition is more likely to come from within the government itself rather than from the more overtly Maoist groups, which have largely been rendered useless. Such a move within the government would likely be in reaction to a perceived threat, the most probable one being a renewed threat to the *"tianming"* of the government itself, or more specifically Jiang Zemin. Where would this move come from? The most likely source is those who have become disillusioned with the economic reform process, who have lost out in some way, who have been left behind or fallen afoul of the nefarious side effects of the reforms, most notably corruption. This could include disillusioned peasants who have yet to see the next stage of agricultural reforms and who feel betrayed that they, above all, have been left behind. There would also be renewed attempts by students to push for an acceleration of the reform process.

To summarize, the most likely threat will come from those who see the reforms as not moving fast enough, rather than those who want to stop or reverse them. Now and in the future, the government faces the tough balancing act of attempting to keep the reform process on track, while at the same time seeking to alleviate the suffering of those who have become casualties as a result. The government must try to push the reform process forward sufficiently to avoid political frustration building up in the place of inadequate economic progress, while maintaining a dominant role for itself in that future. It is an unenviable task, and success is far from assured.

In the past, when social unrest or economic dangers (inflation) have surfaced, the government's response has been to slow the pace of reform. While this may seem only prudent at the time, it is not necessarily a prudent long-term strategy. As we shall see in Chapter 8, when we look at the economic fundamentals that make up modern China, the country does not necessarily have time on its side. Even though the banking system is technically bankrupt, the SOEs are running huge losses and will thus have to be propped up, which will mean that the banking system becomes even more indebted. Pollution levels are appalling, and cities are becoming overcrowded. Depending on whether you have benefited individually from the reform process, you might ask where is the "progress" in all of this? Meanwhile, economic growth continues to slow, and China has many of the fundamental weaknesses that plagued the rest of Asia and that caused the Asian crisis of 1997. The risks, political and economic, both of pushing forward the economic reform process and of holding it back to limit the pain it is causing, continue to grow.

Externally, the renminbi's lack of convertibility on the capital account shelters the currency to a large extent from the worst effects of the Asian crisis. However, it does not do so completely. Export growth is slowing down as a direct result of the crisis because most Chinese exports go to Asia. Equally, foreign direct investment into Asia as a whole has slowed dramatically, and, given that China was the major beneficiary of FDI in Asia, that also has a direct impact on China. This in turn hurts the ability of China both to finance the reform process and to alleviate suffering and create new jobs. The real threat to reforms is thus more economic than political, though it is a constant theme of this book that the two concepts cannot be completely separated. Indeed they are inextricably interlinked. If China is being affected by the Asian crisis and if we accept that the real threat to reforms is economic, what does this mean for the currency? Convertible or not, there is no doubt that the renminbi's steady performance relative to its Asian counterparts, which have devalued massively in the wake of the crisis, is having a domestic economic cost. Some domestic exporters are actually complaining that they cannot compete and are having to lay off workers as a result of fiercer export competition now from the ASEAN for their main export markets in the U.S. and Europe. They are demanding that the renminbi should be devalued. Would this be the answer, or would this cause further chaos in Asian and world markets? Is the renminbi overvalued, and if so, what does that mean for the domestic economy? Does renminbi overvaluation in fact have any relevance for the domestic economy? It is to these issues that we turn to next.

5

An Overvalued Currency—
A Renminbi Devaluation?

As THE ASIAN currencies fell, one by one, pressure, both real and perceived, grew on the remaining currencies to follow the devaluation trend. Currently, Hong Kong and China stand alone in resisting the currency market meltdowns of 1997 and 1998, but how long can this last? Clearly, China is the key. A China devaluation, given the immense size of its economy and role in the region, would have immediate and substantial repercussions, not only in the region but in global financial markets. Such a move would precipitate a further series of competitive devaluations by the ASEAN and North Asian currencies and would represent a further significant deflationary impulse to the global economic order.

Yet can such a move happen? Will the renminbi (RMB) be devalued, or can it be successfully defended? Clearly, the answers to these questions lie in a detailed analysis of the prevailing financial and economic trends in China. However, ahead of that, a brief history lesson regarding Chinese foreign exchange policy is in order. In part, to see whether or not the authorities are going to devalue the RMB in the future, we have to see what they have done in the past. Clearly, they have devalued their currency on several occasions in the past. What caused such a move, and are today's circumstances similar or not? The history of foreign exchange policy in China has been like anything else, a matter of proceeding with extreme caution while simultaneously seeking not to lose the momentum of necessary reform. Indeed, "feeling for stones underfoot while crossing the river" has epitomized the way in which the authorities have sought to open up foreign exchange in China in the past two decades. Following the initial reforms set in place in 1978, the foreign exchange certificate (FEC) was issued to represent a partially convertible currency for foreign use.[1] Subsequently, it was used more specifically to ration consumer commodities, particularly imports, and thus was a useful weapon in seeking to avoid unnecessary drain and leakage of China's foreign exchange reserves—which at that time, let us not forget, were minimal. At the time, China's growing need for raw materials and technology imports, together with the awakening of the domestic consumer market, eventually resulted in the FEC becoming an institutionalized part of the regulatory mechanism until it was abolished in 1993. The evolution of the renminbi toward eventual full convertibility has been a parallel of the history of the opening up of China's economy to the outside world. Past nonconvertibility should be understood in the context of China's past policies of self-reliance and strict isolation.

As in many socialist countries, prior to the reform of the trading system that liberalized the process of exports and imports, the value of the renminbi was kept artificially high. Indeed, the USD-RMB exchange rate was fixed at 1. Beginning in 1981, however, there were effectively two exchange rates, the official rate and the "internal settlement rate" that was executed between the People's Bank of China and China's foreign trading companies.[2] The introduction of the internal settlement rate was in effect an admission by the Chinese authorities that the official RMB rate was overvalued against the dollar. Increasing foreign pressure due to the allegation that the internal settlement rate was in effect a protectionist measure (as it made Chinese trading companies more competitive at the expense of foreign trading partners which had to trade through the official rate) and a burgeoning black market eventually obliged the authorities to devalue the official rate toward the internal settlement rate. In 1985, this was fully achieved, and thus there was no longer a need for the internal settlement rate, which was abolished.

The 1980s, as we have already seen, was a time when the Chinese consumer first woke up, when consumer spending exploded, resulting in a dramatic swing in the trade balance in favor of imports. The resulting drain on China's foreign exchange reserves had a predictable effect on the currency. In 1986, the renminbi was devalued by a further 15.8% in an attempt to boost the export side and increase the cost of imports. The results were impressive. China's trade deficit fell from almost USD12 billion in 1986 to just under USD4 billion the following year. Further measures were introduced by the State Council in 1986 to address foreign exchange repatriation concerns among foreign investment companies. In addition, the State Administration of Exchange Control (SAEC) was put in charge of a limited number of foreign exchange adjustment centers (known as "swap centers") where foreign trade investors could trade foreign exchange and renminbi at rates that floated between designated parameters. In practice, these swap center rates fluctuated between the official rate and the black market spot rate, depending on prevailing local sentiment as to the health of the economy. The swap center rate, somewhat predictably, began to move closer to the black market rate, whereupon the SAEC sought to use funds to stabilize the exchange rate if and when necessary. In 1988, the official rate was USD-RMB 3.7, while the black market rate was around 8. By mid-1989, the swap center rate was just below 7.[3] This, needless to say, put increasing pressure on the official rate, which on December 15, 1989, was finally devalued again by a further 21.2%, bringing the official rate up to USD-RMB 4.72. Yet, as seen by the black market rate, which going into 1990 was still above 9, even this adjustment of the nominal exchange rate was insufficient in reflecting the real value of the currency. As a further measure to boost exports, state investment was specifically promoted for export industries, and the official rate was again devalued, this time to 5.73. By 1993, there were over 100 swap centers, reflecting the exponential rise in trading activity. Yet both the official and the swap center rates remained out of line relative to the black market rate, a clear historical symptom of real exchange rate overvaluation. Indeed, the very existence of a black market rate suggests overvaluation of the nominal exchange rate. Of the 100 or so swap centers, 18 became open markets where computers matched bids and offers, the first effective market-driven exchange rate trading system in China.

China was not done with the idea of devaluation, however. On January 1, 1994, the authorities again effectively devalued their currency, removing the official rate peg and floating it. The renminbi's value thus became fully reflected by the rate traded in the swap centers, though of course black market trading remained. This amounted to a de facto devaluation of 35% of the official rate. The introduction in 1994 of the China Foreign Exchange Trading System, based in Shanghai, was the next stage in the development of foreign exchange in China, effectively and gradually replacing the swap centers. China thus has quite a history of gradual devaluation of the value of its currency in order to make it more realistic (relative to the "real effective" value of the exchange rate) and to boost exports. As it has liberalized its trade and foreign exchange markets, China has gradually moved the value of its nominal exchange rate closer, first to the swap market and then the black market rate, in order to make its exports more competitive and, at least early on, to tame import demand. Yet, at every step, the black market rate has remained substantially above (in dollar terms) the official/swap/OTC exchange rate, suggesting that further devaluation or at least gradual depreciation is needed. Currently, the People's Bank of China allows the USD-RMB to trade within a daily volatility band of 0.3%, centering on the 8.28% level. Do current economic fundamentals suggest the need for further devaluation? And whether they do or not, would this of necessity lead to such a move on the part of the authorities?

In the past, devaluation has been part of a gradual move to liberalize trade and more specifically to boost exports. While economic fundamentals and symptoms thereof— most notably in the form of the black market rate—were in all three cases

(1986, 1989, and 1994) suggesting the need for a devaluation, the authorities resisted such a move until they were ready. Indeed, when they did happen, the devaluations were seen as being state policy, rather than something forced on the authorities. The case now is somewhat different. China has truly come of age in terms of foreign exchange reserves, trade surpluses, domestic economic influence on the global economy, and diplomatic importance. It is trying to get into the WTO, allowing it further trade privileges—but also necessitating certain responsibilities and domestic market-opening measures. Granted, China has been attempting this for some years now. Its efforts have been frustrated by U.S. and European demands that it first open up its domestic economy more to Western finance and trade. However, China has a much longer time frame in mind (in general) than that usually adopted in the West. It waited 156 years to get Hong Kong back. It can afford to wait a few years to get WTO status. Indeed, some economists within China itself argue that China does not actually need WTO trading status, that it already has most of the benefits without the increased costs that would result from entering the WTO. To be sure, this is not the official government view, which sees WTO status as being a diplomatic necessity, whatever the trade merits. The bottom line is that, whenever it actually takes place, China is still officially seeking entry to the WTO.

In addition, amid the onslaught of the Asian financial and economic crisis, China has, as said previously, stood out as a bastion of stability. While the yen continued to weaken from 127 to the dollar in April 1998 to close to 150, the Chinese authorities played an exceptionally skillful game with the financial markets. On the one hand, officials and newspapers of obscure source and unknown importance would question the official policy of maintaining the value of the renminbi, while on the other, the PBOC and the State Council would deny such talk, saying that whatever other countries were doing, China would maintain its policy of no devaluation of the renminbi. The message was clear, sometimes expressed explicitly, sometimes implicitly. China was undergoing great pain to hold the value of its currency steady in order to shoulder its international responsibilities and in particular to seek to avoid further economic and financial market distress in Asia. It was up to the U.S. and Japan to equally take up their responsibility to stop the yen continuing to devalue against the dollar. Throughout May and June 1998, while markets ignored the incessant whining of Japanese government officials that excessive yen weakness needed to be avoided and such weakness would be dealt with "decisively" and so forth, they paid close attention to any utterance from Beijing—or from any other part of China—regarding the value of the renminbi. Indeed, the joint intervention by the Federal Reserve Bank of New York and the Bank of Japan was initially seen by markets as a direct response by the U.S. Treasury to the pleas and complaints of China. This was denied by both the U.S. and Japan. But the very fact that the markets initially believed the story shows just how much the diplomatic and economic power pendulum has swung in favor of China—and away from Japan. China's leaders are well aware of the diplomatic benefits of maintaining the value of the renminbi, and as I write this, I continue to believe that they will not forsake these by allowing the renminbi to devalue, at least not this year, 1999. To do so would lose everything they have gained in terms of diplomatic prestige, particularly on a regional scale where China has succeeded in portraying itself as the spokesman for Asia, at least in terms of seeking to maintain some degree of regional stability. Others in Asia may of course not see it that way. However, China has at no time in the recent past had such diplomatic leverage over its Asian counterparts as right now—and largely as the result of maintaining the value of a currency it did not intend to devalue any time soon in any case.

Yet do economic fundamentals justify this stand? Should China keep the renminbi steady by artificial means or devalue it? Will it actually be forced to devalue? As noted earlier, in the past, currency devaluations by the Chinese authorities have been part of an overall strategy of improving export competitiveness. The markets to a certain extent forced these since in 1986, 1989, and 1994 China had minimal foreign exchange reserves with which to defend the value of the renminbi, even in an exceptionally controlled market, and was running large trade deficits at the time in all three cases. Yet, despite that, the authorities probably wanted a devaluation. Thus the devaluations were in all likelihood a matter of the market merely forcing the timing of the move, rather than a forced policy reversal by the government. This, on the face of it, is not the case today. China, as of the end of 1998, had foreign exchange reserves totaling USD145 billion. In 1998, it ran a trade surplus of USD43.6 billion, up from 40 billion in 1997. In addition, while Asian exports in general were getting killed in 1997 and 1998 in the wake of first the rise in the USD-JPY and then the Asian crisis as export finance dried up, China's exports boomed. Thus China gained valuable export market share in third markets such as the U.S. and Europe at the expense of its Asian competitors. The direction of trade data suggests that it was continuing to gain share through the first half of 1998. All this should in theory completely rule out the need for a devaluation of the renminbi. Yet talk of the need for a devaluation has persisted. Why is this so? It would appear clear cut, at least on the face of it, that there is no need for a devaluation. Further analysis of the trade and inflation data at least puts this into question. Ahead of that, however, the actions of the government itself have provided a hint of the seriousness of the situation. For a start, by the end of July, China's government had increased tax rebates on certain export sectors such as coal, textiles, and shipping three times.

Along with such measures to try and improve corporate competitiveness, Chinese authorities have to an extent backtracked on the reform process by demanding that state banks start relending to the SOEs that specifically focus on exports. In addition, the PBOC has cut interest rates three times so far in 1998, in March, July, and October, reducing the domestic costs for exporter operations. Finally, in an attempt to combat the black market for foreign exchange, the government announced a series of measures to tighten foreign exchange controls in light of rising concerns over the amount of hard currency being funneled out of the country. Under the new rules, the PBOC threatened to ban from foreign exchange settlement business any financial institution, domestic or foreign, which was repeatedly linked to irregularities in the foreign exchange market. The regulations, which took effect August 1, 1998, aim to standardize foreign exchange controls. Under them, any financial institution that is found to have conducted USD5 million worth of foreign exchange settlement involving irregularities—i.e., the foreign exchange transactions were not conducted through the Shanghai official OTC market or through regional centers—will be banned from the foreign exchange settlement business. Financial institutions will also be banned if they are found to have been involved in a single year in a total of USD100 million of foreign exchange settlements without checking the client documentation from the foreign exchange control authorities.

All this activity on the part of the authorities begs the question of why a government that officially and theoretically is fully in control of its exchange rate needs to do all this. The answer is of course that it is not fully in control. The situation is not desperate yet, but it is serious. It is serious enough for China's government to seek to do all it can to boost exports at a time when, on the face of it, China's trade surplus remains quite healthy. Why is this so? Let's have another look at that trade surplus. In 1998, China's full-year trade surplus was estimated at USD43.6 billion. To repeat, this was up from 40.3 billion in 1997, a healthy trade balance by any account. Yet even with the trade surplus at USD43.6 billion and foreign direct investment at USD45 billion for the same period, foreign exchange reserves as of the end of 1998 were USD145 billion, up only 5.1 billion on the end of 1997. How is that possible? FDI plus the trade surplus should have theoretically combined to significantly boost foreign exchange reserves, not necessarily by USD88. 6 billion since there are offsetting factors, but by a large proportion of that since the capital account is effectively closed. In 1997, trade accounted for 56% of the increase in foreign exchange reserves.

There are two possible explanations for this. The first concerns the rule put in place by the PBOC in 1997 to allow certain Chinese trading companies to keep up to 15% of their export receivables in foreign exchange (usually dollars) rather than have to translate them immediately back into renminbi. At the time, the PBOC did this to try to improve export competitiveness. The renminbi was too strong against the dollar, and the PBOC wanted to reduce this effect. The State Information Center, a think tank within the influential State Development Planning Commission, indeed attributed the flat foreign exchange reserves to exporters hoarding dollars, as allowed up to a point by the PBOC, rather than translating them back into the domestic currency. However, this alone cannot be fully responsible. It is not arithmetically possible. Exports in 1998 were around USD182 billion. If every exporter in China held on to 15% of its dollar receivables, this would account for only USD27.3 billion, and this would in any case be contravening the law since only certain exporters are allowed to take advantage of this regulation. Perhaps the exporters are holding onto more dollars than the PBOC ruling allows them to. That links us to the second possible explanation for this enigma—that of capital outflow.

To be sure, there are various forms of capital outflow, some of which bend the rules and some of which of course break them entirely. China's current account balance has long had an income deficit—hardly surprising given the huge rise in FDI over the last 5 years. FDI of USD40–45 billion a year inevitably creates a significant drain on the income account in the form of repatriated profit, dividends, and interest. It is unlikely, however, that the income account is responsible for foreign exchange reserve underperformance, as this would necessitate a substantial rise in the income deficit this year—despite the well-known slowdown, which one assumes would negatively affect "barbarian" (Western) companies as well as their Chinese counterparts. On the capital side, FDI is obviously a major positive in boosting the capital account. However, the rate of FDI growth has slowed substantially. Indeed it turned negative in May 1998. That said, we are still talking about a net inflow into China of over USD17 billion (subtracting Chinese outward FDI flow which usually amounts to USD2–3 billion annually). Given the lack of convertibility of the renminbi, the other parts of the capital account such as portfolio

investment are insignificant relative to FDI, though 1997's portfolio investment inflow of USD7.7 billion was still a record. Portfolio outflows in 1997 were USD1 billion. Notably, within the
1997 accounts was a USD34 billion increase in the outflow of
"other assets." The horrifying performance of China's A- and B-
share stock markets in the first half of 1998 could provide one
clue. Yet again this is not the complete answer.

Suppose 1997's record portfolio investment into China of
USD7.7 billion was completely reversed in the first half of 1998,
leading to an equal portfolio outflow. Given the miserable performance of the Shanghai and Shenzhen markets in 1998, this
would be fully justified. However, a casual glance at the trade
surplus would be sufficient to demonstrate that this alone is not
enough to explain static foreign exchange reserves. Given the inefficiencies of Chinese official data, one is required to rely to a
degree on anecdotal evidence (which in any case has its place)
for an attempt at a more complete answer to this perplexing
problem. On the one hand, one hears—and the black market for
the USD-RMB exchange rate suggests—that there is capital
leakage through illegal foreign exchange transactions out of
China. The very fact that the authorities have cracked down on
such activities in Guangdong and Xiamen, and that the PBOC
governor himself, Dai Xianglong, spoke in terms of "crushing"
the black market for foreign exchange, appears to confirm this
(at the very least, it confirms a certain degree of desperation).
And indeed one hears of up to 40% of annual FDI
being leaked back out of the country. Given that this would
amount to USD18 billion using 1998 as a benchmark, this
would seem exaggerated. There is no question, however, that
such leakage is occurring. In addition, again anecdotally, some
FDI is not actually an investment but a loan (booked as investment for tax purposes) and thus is also subject to reversal.

The strength of China's trade and foreign exchange fundamentals is put even more in doubt on further examination of that
trade surplus. Before 1997, Hong Kong was a Crown Colony, a
part of the British Commonwealth centered around the United

Kingdom of Great Britain and Northern Ireland. In terms of Chinese trade statistics, it was thus ignored—by all but the U.S. Commerce Department, which puts Hong Kong and China trade data together when considering U.S. imports from both. On July 1, 1997, however, Hong Kong reverted to Chinese sovereignty (a memorable night for any who were there). Thus, whatever the excuse before, there is a strong case to be argued that when looking at the Chinese trade balance, one should include Hong Kong. While China had a trade surplus of USD40.3 billion in 1997, Hong Kong recorded a visible trade deficit of USD20.6 billion. The net figure cannot simply be derived from subtracting the two to get a net trade surplus of USD19.7 billion, because both trade statistics include intra-Chinese trade—exports and imports to and from Hong Kong. Since manufacturing is barely 10% of the Hong Kong economy, with most of it being moved over the border to Guangdong where wages remain a fraction of what they are in Hong Kong, intra-China trade is not an insignificant amount. Those who wish to find out just how much it is could start off with the U.S. Commerce Department and IMF direction of trade data and work back. For our purpose here, the figure itself is not the issue. The real issue is that China's trade surplus, if one includes Hong Kong—which seems fundamentally necessary given that it is *one country*, two systems—is not nearly as large as it is made out to be. Indeed, Paul Krugman in a typically brilliant article (entitled "The East Is in the Red") debunking the myth of China's supposed trade threat to the U.S. has said as much.[4] Just as if you detached New York from the U.S. (not physically but in terms of economic trade data!) or London from the U.K., you would see a profound effect on the "national" (without New York or London) trade data of the U.S. or the UK. There would be a drastic reduction in "national" trade deficits. So it has been the case with China and Hong Kong. By putting the two together, China's trade surplus, while still very healthy, is decidedly less a threat or even a fundamental economic strength.

Indeed, one could argue that given the huge FDI flows into China over the past 10 years, how is it possible that China runs a trade surplus at all? For a start, it again comes back to how you define China. China's three largest FDI benefactors are Hong Kong, Taiwan, and Japan, with Hong Kong by far the largest contributor. If you take out Hong Kong, FDI into China equally does not look nearly so strong—doubly so if you include Taiwan in the concept of *"dazhougua,"* or Greater China. Yet, still, China would be running a sizable trade surplus despite significant capital inflow. This runs contrary to the experience of much of emerging Asia and seemingly also to the central tenets of economics. The answer lies more in the concept of new capital outflow. This takes the form of illicit capital leakage, along with Chinese corporate investment abroad, some of which is scrutinized by the authorities, much of which is not. The People's Liberation Army, which was given the green light in the 1980s to take part in commercial activity in line with the economic reform process, partly for self-financing reasons, has been a major exporter of capital as well as goods. Running around 15,000 companies, both inside and outside China, the PLA is estimated to have annual goods exports of USD7 billion a year, half of which is civilian. In keeping with the authorities' attempts to tighten foreign exchange controls this year, it was thus no accident that President Jiang Zemin ordered that the PLA cease all commercial activities forthwith. While this announcement was stunning by its boldness, clearly no one expects the PLA to do so, either overnight or in total. That said, given that the PLA is thought to be a major player in illicit capital outflow and thus in illegal foreign exchange activity, it demonstrates both the authorities' concern and determination to tackle the leakage. This is fine in theory. Whether it happens in practice is quite another thing.

So where are we going with all this? We have seen that China is experiencing significant capital leakage, through one form or another, legally or illegally. In addition, China's trade surplus is not the mountain it appears to be. What does that mean for the currency? Does this mean that the renminbi should be devalued? Not of necessity. China's exports, while slowing, are still growing. They are not negative. They are not a burden rather than a boost to the trade balance. Equally, given that domestic demand is slowing, this will necessitate slowing or negative import growth, an actual positive for the trade balance. Yet in order to see whether the situation is likely to get better or worse, and thus whether the pressures for devaluation will increase or not, we have to examine the fundamental situation for both the economy and the value of the currency. Economic performance in the first half of 1998 was of course disappointing. In addition to export growth of 7.6% in the first half (compared with 21% for full-year 1997 and 26.2% for the first half of 1997), first-half GDP growth was a "mere" 7%, with growth slowing from 7.2% in the first quarter to 6.8% in the second quarter. Full year 1998 GDP growth was 7.8%. Compare this with a rate of 8.8% for full-year 1997.

Looking ahead, the risk clearly remains that the economic slowdown that we looked at in Chapter 2 will indeed continue. Four out of five key economic indicators (exports, industrial production, retail prices, and FDI) in China are in a dismal state by recent standards. In particular, the retail price index fell by around 2.8% Y/Y in 1998. China is thus experiencing deflation. In addition, contracted FDI actually fell 1.3% in the first half of 1998, and it seems likely that given the Asian crisis and massive overcapacity in China at present, it will continue to decline. The only support to the economy is fixed-asset investment, which rose an impressive 14.1% in 1998. Yet this cannot alone be expected to make up the slack of slowing exports, industrial production, FDI, and deflation as measured by the RPI data. Deteriorating economic fundamentals remain the key argument of those who seek or expect a renminbi devaluation.

Yet is the renminbi overvalued? Even if it is, should the renminbi be devalued? To answer the first part of that, you have to look at traditional economic measures of valuing exchange rates such as purchasing power parity and real effective exchange rates. On both measures, the renminbi would appear to be overvalued. Much depends of course on where and when you set your base year, but looking at relative inflation differentials between the U.S. and China from 1990 together with the performance of the nominal USD-RMB exchange rate, it would appear that the renminbi is as much as 30% overvalued given the extent to which Chinese inflation has outstripped that of the U.S. during that period. Since 1994, prices in the U.S. have grown just over 10%, whereas those in China have surged 25%. While many talk of China's unit labor cost advantage in light of its huge excess of labor supply, the years 1990–1997 saw a dramatic rise in unit labor costs in China, not only on a nominal basis but in relation to other emerging markets. This was particularly the case in Guangdong, where most Hong Kong "exports" are made. Indeed, during this period, relative to productivity gains, unit labor costs ballooned in China. This is hardly surprising given the general improvement in the standard of living. Yet it is something which many economists miss; the assumption is that China has had and always will have a substantial labor cost advantage over its competitors. While I would argue that this is still the case with most Asian emerging market competitors—the exceptions being Indonesia and the Philippines— that margin of advantage has been substantially reduced as a result of the combination of rising domestic wages and the Asian currency devaluations.

On a REER basis, there is also substantial room for concern. As of the end of July 1998, the renminbi's REER had appreciated 18.2% since the 1994 devaluation. Assuming that Asian currencies still have further downside (against the renminbi as well as the dollar) since Asia's fundamental situation is likely to continue to worsen in the near term, while the nominal value of the renminbi will be kept stable, it is likely that the gains in export competitiveness due to the 1994 devaluation of the renminbi will be more than wiped out and that the REER overvaluation will continue to increase. One further indicator of currency overvaluation is the very fact that China is experiencing accelerating deflation. While this is partly due to massive domestic overcapacity, it is also the result of imported deflation due to currency overvaluation. The same thing occurred in Germany from 1995 to 1997 given past overvaluation of the nominal value of the deutsche mark. In that specific case, the Bundesbank, one of the most hawkish central banks in the world, allowed a de facto devaluation of its currency in order not only to restore export competitiveness, but to allow a modest amount of imported inflation in order to stabilize prices. It achieved this, and now Germany is recovering, while the value of the deutsche mark finally stabilized after a period of depreciation.

Should the same happen in the case of the renminbi? PPP and REER overvaluations suggest, as do the RPI data, that the renminbi should be devalued in order to restore domestic and external economic competitiveness. Yet will China's leaders take this route? Just how much economic pain are China's leaders prepared to take in order to avoid a devaluation? Much depends on how the USD-JPY exchange rate and other Asian currencies perform. If the USD-JPY continues to rise, thus forcing the USD-Asian exchange rates higher, while the PBOC maintains a steady USD-RMB rate, not only will China's exporters continue to lose competitiveness, but the renminbi's REER will continue to appreciate. As noted above, deflation, wherever it occurs, is the result of not only domestic overcapacity but also nominal exchange rate overvaluation. As a currency's REER appreciates, this necessitates that a proportional decline in domestic prices occur if the nominal exchange rate has to be kept stable. This in turn suggests that if China is to keep its promise to hold its currency stable, retail prices must continue to decline at an accelerating rate, which itself will pose both economic and social questions for the government. Falling retail prices will of necessity mean that economic growth will continue to slow. China's government may try to artificially inflate growth through investment—in fact, this is exactly what it is trying to do—but this cannot be maintained indefinitely. After all, where is the money going to come from? China already has a budget deficit problem.

A look at the RPI data, together with the REER and PPP valuations for the renminbi, would suggest that the currency should indeed be devalued. Still, China's government clearly has the resources, in the form of its huge foreign exchange reserve war chest, to avoid this if it wants to and if it is prepared to take the resulting economic pain. China's government has pledged that the renminbi will not be devalued in 1999, and I strongly believe that this will be the case. However, 2000 is another matter entirely. Trade now accounts for 20% of GDP. With exports at around 13 percentage points of that, in value-added terms, a decline in export growth from 21% in 1997 to around 0.5% in 1998 costs around 22.5% of GDP. Rudi Dornbusch, in an article in the *Financial Times*,[5] put the figures at 20% export growth to a theoretical zero and the cost to GDP of 2%, but the point is the same. China's export sector is being hurt and will continue to be hurt in the near term—hence the argument to improve export competitiveness by devaluing the currency. This idea rests on the idea that Asian currency devaluations have resulted in Chinese exporters' losing market share in third markets to their Asian counterparts. But the evidence of this is mixed at best. While anecdotally there has been a steady stream of complaints from Chinese exporters—from shipbuilders and steel manufacturers in the north to service and retail industries in the south—suggesting that they are indeed finding the post-Asian devaluation environment increasingly difficult to compete in, the data do not (yet) support that view. In fact, the data suggest the opposite, that Chinese exporters continue to gain market share on their Asian counterparts. China trade as a percentage of total U.S. and Japanese imports continues to rise, not fall.

While the jury is still out on the question of whether or not Chinese exporters are losing competitiveness relative to their Asian competitors in third markets (inevitably, the verdict will come back as guilty, though the jury will take some time for deliberation, the legal version of the J-curve), there is no doubt whatsoever that Chinese exports have been hurt by the Asian crisis. Some 60% of Chinese exports go to Asia, and of that around 25% go to Japan. There is clearly little that China can do about this situation in the near term apart from seek to make its exports more competitive, which it is indeed attempting. China's exports have historically been very sensitive to microeconomic management by the authorities, and there appears no reason why this should change in the near term. Indeed, exports rose by 1.6% Y/Y in June 1998 and 3.5% Y/Y in July after the government ordered that tax rebates again be increased for certain types of exporters. With China's capital account officially closed, the authorities continuing to close loopholes and tighten capital and foreign exchange restrictions, and the PBOC still with its USD145 billion in foreign exchange reserves, China is fully capable of holding the line in terms of the value of its currency in the near term.

As I said, however, 1999 is another matter. China wants to keep the diplomatic benefits that it has gained as a result of maintaining the renminbi stable and could not devalue in 1998 while Asian currencies remained weak. Should Asian currencies stabilize and start to strengthen in 1999, China's leaders will be sorely tempted to allow their own currency to devalue. To be sure, the move, if it comes, will be couched in terms of diplomatic niceties—we held the line for so long, took all the pain, and now we are letting it go once Asia has been saved—but it will be a devaluation nonetheless. China's leadership, given the memory of the chaos of the Cultural Revolution, abhors the idea of instability, whether financial or social. In the short term it will seek to shore up both the export sector and the domestic economy through a combination of measures. On the export side, if push really came to shove, it could simply reverse the ruling to allow exporters to keep dollar receivables. In addition, it could relax further domestic regulations for foreign joint ventures and cut import tariffs—boosting imports should help the export side given the high import content of exports. On the domestic side, accelerating RPI deflation means that monetary policy remains overly tight. Nominal interest rates have to be cut further, and there is every likelihood that this will happen. The fiscal side will also be loosened, with several hundred billion renminbi earmarked for infrastructure projects. Economic feed-through on the domestic side will take time. It is likely to be mid-1999 before we see any major benefit from these projects. Thus growth will continue to slow, and devaluation talk will persist.

Meanwhile, anecdotal evidence within China that the domestic population is jittery regarding the possibility of a currency devaluation (i.e., the government has done it before, why not do it again?) abounds. For a start, there is the black market itself. By

August 1998, the spot black market rate for the USD–RMB was trading above 9, implying a renminbi devaluation relative to the official OTC rate of around 10%. While the authorities continue to crack down on black market activities, (arresting company officials, bureaucrats, and individuals, indeed anyone who is or suspected to be involved), getting black market foreign exchange is relatively easy. The average tourist (or economist!) taking a casual walk along any of the main thoroughfares in Shanghai—or any other major city in China—will be incessantly pestered by black market foreign exchange traders, armed with mobile phones and pocket calculators, who leap out of alleyways and from behind shop-front awnings in search of new prey and business. Chinese officials correctly point out that official foreign exchange trading through the Shanghai foreign exchange center (averaging around USD150–200 million a day) dwarfs black market trading by a substantial multiple (officials put black market trading at around USD200,000 a day, which in all likelihood is a major underestimation). But black market trading is important not only or even mainly for its size but for its very existence. A black market is after all surely a symptom of economic failure of some sort, of local skepticism with financial and economic policy and with present valuation of the currency and domestic assets, be they property, stocks, or anything else that has a value to it. While the Russian black market is probably larger than the official economy by a substantial margin, the death knell of near-term economic performance was sounded by the very existence of such a vibrant black market, not by its size per se. A further point to make about black markets is—and here we differentiate clearly between random economic crime and an organized and deep market where bids and offers are filled for assets, currency, or anything else of value—that they have historically had a reasonably close link with currency devaluations. For instance, think of the rise of the self-proclaimed Societa Honorata (the Sicilian equivalent—and parent—of the Cosa Nostra in the U.S., aka the Mafia) in recent decades and then have another look at the performance of the Italian lira. Note the crackdown on the Mafia in Sicily and then have another look at a graph of the lira. Equally, note that Mexico was a major money laundering center for the Colombian and Bolivian cartels and then remember the unhappy state of the Mexican peso and financial markets in January 1995. Think too of Bangkok also as a haven of corruption and money laundering for the drug lords of Burma just over the border and remember July 2, 1997.

None of this is of necessity or of itself cause and effect. There were plenty of other variables, some of which may indeed have been more important. The one linking factor is that economic excesses in terms of massive asset bubbles and easy money in the official economy are usually paralleled by similar increases in black market trading. This is particularly the case in emerging markets where regulation and supervision are frequently more lax—and officials are easier to bribe. While China's government has made repeated attempts to crack down on corruption (financial fraud is in theory a capital offense though this punishment has occasionally been commuted to life imprisonment), it is not unfair to say that corruption remains endemic within China's economy. This is not particularly surprising. It is a simple state of evolution. Check out the U.S. economy in the 1920s and 1930s and you will find exactly the same thing. You can easily find the Al Capones of the present lolling in the clubs and bars of Shanghai and Shenzhen—though you do not necessarily want to. And wasn't there some sort of asset crash in 1929 in the U.S.? More seriously, it is best not to run away with this idea. There is, however, a link, and it should not be forgotten. Crime in general and black market trading specifically are both a parallel and a symptom of fundamental economic performance.

Chinese companies are also watching the situation rather warily. Well aware of what happened to unhedged foreign exchange exposures in the likes of Indonesia, Korea, and Thailand in the wake of the Asian currency crisis and the consequences thereof, they are seeking ways of hedging that risk. The most obvious way, in a tightly controlled market where an "unnecessary" foreign exchange market is banned, is to take advantage of the regulation allowing 15% of dollar receivables to be kept in foreign exchange rather than translated. It is not just a question of receivables either. While China's external debt is modest by regional standards (outstanding short-term international bank lending was 24% of domestic foreign exchange reserves as of the end of December 1997, compared with 249% for Indonesia and 145% for Thailand), the fact that companies are seeking ways of hedging that risk, legally or otherwise, is merely a further factor pressuring the renminbi. Should the renminbi be devalued, it would in all probability be a significant rather than a minor move, with the result that required dollar debt payments would increase proportionally. In the past, Chinese companies, whether operating solely on the mainland or in Hong Kong in the form of "red chips," traditionally used equity for funding and expansion purposes given the buoyant stock markets. This avenue would appear closed, unless they accept substantially reduced equity valuations for stock offerings. State lending and debt issues, whether straight debt or convertibles, are the only two remaining funding options in a world where free cash flow continues to be squeezed by the deteriorating domestic economy and falling retail prices—which means falling margins. Of China's external debt of around USD130 billion as of the end of 1997, it is estimated that USD35 billion was issued by the state, USD42 billion by financial institutions, and just 13 billion by domestic enterprises. The State Administration of Foreign Exchange (SAFE) keeps an exceptionally tight rein on foreign debt issuance; yet note that the figure for the external debt does not include red chips or H-shares (the original classification of Chinese companies, listed in Hong Kong), which operate and trade out of Hong Kong but which concern mainland assets. It also does not include FDI, which is in fact a loan, requiring foreign exchange translation when the loan comes due. Say, for example, Chinese corporate external debt was USD50 billion, including all these factors. This would still not represent a major problem since it would be a tiny fraction of GDP. It does add to the pressure of the currency, however.

A final thought—should China's export growth continue to deteriorate as most financial experts expect, with Asian exporters gaining competitiveness in 1999, pressure will continue to grow on the currency whether or not the government's efforts to stabilize the domestic economy are successful. After all, if the efforts are successful, this will necessitate a deterioration in the trade balance with a reduction in the trade surplus; if they are not, this will mean that the economy continues to head south, implying persistent and accelerating deflationary pressures. The renminbi could well be devalued in 1999 or 2000, or through the PBOC either widening the daily volatility band in a series of steps or devaluing it in one move.

The spreading Asian crisis and the possibility of a Chinese devaluation from mid-1999 mean that currency reform in China remains years away. China's capital account will remain closed, as to open it, particularly in the wake of a currency devaluation, would mean a meltdown of China's banking system (which is bankrupt several times over in any case) fully on a par with the situations in Thailand and Indonesia. Indeed, the Asian crisis demonstrates vividly the dangers of fully opening the capital account without an adequate institutional framework to deal with the resulting capital inflows (and outflows!). China will continue with its gradual approach to liberalization, in terms of both foreign exchange and monetary policy. In addition, China cannot yet afford a fully market-driven interest rate market, as it needs to keep the SOEs afloat before they are restructured. While the government has attempted reforms in the banking system, the fact remains that the banking system is technically bankrupt and only stays afloat precisely because the capital account is closed and depositors have little alternative to renminbi deposit accounts (the only major alternative being the stock market). In addition, the SOEs still make up the vast majority of state bank loans. The result of these two factors is that bank asset deterioration will continue, and at an accelerating rate. Developing a deep and liquid government and corporate securities market would be one way around this, by financing the banking and corporate system. However, once again such markets remain in their infancy. In the meantime, the economy will continue to deteriorate, China's exporters will continue to lose their competitiveness, and pressure will continue to grow on the renminbi to devalue despite every effort made by the government to solve these multiple and combined problems. Needless to say, the massive flooding caused by the Yangtze River makes the authorities' task of stabilizing the situation even harder.

If the renminbi does go, what does this mean for the rest of the world? Undoubtedly, given China's increasing political and economic importance in the global economy, it would send significant shock waves around the market. More specifically, what would it mean for Hong Kong, so recently returned to the fold after 150 years as a vassal state of the imperialists? Already, Hong Kong is experiencing substantial recessionary pressures as a result of the Asian crisis and the general de-leveraging process that the region is undergoing. Could a Chinese devaluation sound the death knell for the newly named Hong Kong Special Administrative Region, or could it save it from economic catastrophe? In any case, what lies ahead for the territory, which only a couple of years ago was being touted as the replacement for Tokyo as the main Asian financial center, when pundits were confidently predicting that the value of the Hang Seng stock index would surpass that of the Nikkei 225?

6

Holding the Peg—
China and the HKSAR

So RECENTLY RETURNED to the Motherland, the Hong
Kong Special Administrative Region (HKSAR) has had an exceptionally tough time of it with the economy falling into recession, property prices collapsing, and the current account deficit
ballooning. In the initial stages of the Asian crisis, Hong Kong
was thought to be a safe haven, along with China. However, this
idea was foolish and was swiftly disproved with the crash of the
Hang Seng stock market index in late October 1997 and the
subsequent bear market which drove the benchmark index from
a high of 16,820.31 on August 7, 1997, to sub-7,000 levels. Since
then, the HSI has rallied back through 10,500, in line with the
fall in the dollar and the rebound in the U.S. stock market. But
the fundamental outlook remains decidedly shaky.

Frustrated and deeply angered by the territory's misfortune
and the economic pain that is being experienced, some local
Hong Kong commentators suggested Britain was to blame. The
downturn in Hong Kong's economic fortunes, they said, had
been caused by a British conspiracy to embarrass China. Understandable though this overly emotional view is, it is, needless to
say, rubbish. For one thing, it is doubtful, to say the least, that the
various British services required to carry out such a fiendish conspiracy would actually be up to the job of doing it! For another,

Hong Kong had plenty of problems of its own. Unpleasant though the message is, Hong Kong's current downturn is entirely due to its own economic and financial fundamental weaknesses, and to the need to adjust competitiveness in the wake of the Asian currency devaluations against the Hong Kong dollar. Hong Kong deservedly has a reputation as an efficient and laissez faire economy, and its business and financial sectors as extremely astute, flexible, and fast on their feet. Hong Kong's entrepreneurs will need all their historical ability to adapt in order to survive and prosper this time round. For while Hong Kong does not have many of the problems of Thailand, Korea, or Indonesia, its currency board system that pegs the Hong Kong dollar to the U.S. dollar at a rate of 7.80 necessitates in the current regional environment that asset prices are regionally overvalued (they were in any case under any valuation) and have to adjust downward. How did this situation come about? It was not that long ago that Hong Kong's economy was booming—seemingly without fundamental weaknesses that would otherwise concern investors—and that Hong Kong was being trumpeted as Asia's preeminent financial center outside of Japan. Indeed, there were many who thought that with the continuing economic ascent of China, Hong Kong would surpass Tokyo in regional and global economic and financial importance. As ever, to see the future, we have to, to a certain extent, look back at the past.

Just about everyone now claims—hindsight being 20/20—that the Hong Kong dollar is and always was overvalued and the Hong Kong economy crucially flawed or at the least in need of further substantial downward adjustment in order to make up for a loss of competitiveness. Is this so, and if so, how did it happen? The Hong Kong dollar, as noted above, is pegged to the U.S. dollar under a currency board system. This was not always the case. The currency board system was adopted on October 17, 1983. Prior to this, the Hong Kong dollar (HKD) was pegged to sterling. Then, in the wake of the breakup of the Bretton Woods monetary system in 1972, it broke the link with sterling and was repegged to the U.S. dollar. The dollar entered a significant decline, however, so in November 1974 Hong Kong broke what was a de facto currency board system with the dollar and for the next 9 years allowed the Hong Kong dollar to float freely. But in 1983, fundamental weaknesses—both political and economic—caught up with the Hong Kong dollar. Mounting fears that differences between China and the U.K. could not be worked out and that China might actually invade Hong Kong caused a sharp fall in the value of the Hong Kong dollar, with the USD-HKD rising from around 6 to 9.55 in late September 1983. Hong Kong is largely import-dependent in what it consumes and also in what it reexports. The rise in the value of the USD-HKD exchange rate meant automatically that Hong Kong imported inflationary pressures due to the rising cost of imports, which were due to the decline of the value of the Hong Kong dollar relative to the U.S. dollar, a direct transmission mechanism. Indeed, the headline CPI inflation rate rose from 3.9% in 1976 to a high of 15% during the 1979–1983 period.

The government responded to this by reimposing a currency board system with the USD-HKD peg limit at 7.8. Under the currency board system, every Hong Kong dollar issued and every Hong Kong dollar balance in the system had to be matched with an equivalent value of U.S. dollars under the 7.8:1 peg. Theoretically, a currency board system is self-regulating. If an increasing number of Hong Kong dollars are sold for U.S. dollars—or any other currency for that matter—the balance or supply of Hong Kong dollars is effectively reduced, forcing up the demand side, (i.e., the level of nominal interest rates) until such a time and such a level whereby supply meets demand once more and equilibrium is restored. Under currency board systems, there is in theory no need for a central bank. Indeed, with a currency board system there is no reason to have an independent monetary policy since monetary policy through the level of nominal interest rates is directed by market demand and supply of Hong Kong dollars. From the very start, however, Hong Kong's currency board system was not completely orthodox. In 1978, the government deposited at the Exchange Fund its entire holdings of foreign currency reserves. The Exchange Fund was given the possibility of discretionary policy, which had not been the case between 1972 and 1974 and which should not be the case in an orthodox currency board system. Then in 1990, the Exchange Fund began to issue its own securities, or Exchange Fund bills. While no doubt a convenient instrument of monetary control for the Exchange Fund, the very existence of these securities would appear to fly in the face of currency board system theory. Finally, in 1993, the government created the Hong Kong Monetary Authority (the HKMA), combining the Exchange Fund and the Banking Commission, which, as its name suggests, supervised banks and other financial institutions. The HKMA is not an orthodox currency board. A truly orthodox currency board would hold foreign exchange reserves requisite to the monetary base and would do nothing else. The HKMA, on the other hand, holds and manages government funds, issues securities as described above, and exercises central bank-like operations in the money and foreign exchange markets. In addition, it regulates financial institutions and even disciplines and threatens banks deemed to be speculating against the Hong Kong dollar. We shall return later to this issue in more detail. Suffice it to say for now, however, that the HKMA's unorthodox status relative to currency board system theory has been one of the fundamental concerns of Hong Kong and in addition has attracted the presence of speculators who deem this a systemic weakness.

Whatever the theory, there is no question that the currency board system worked in terms of dampening inflationary pressures, as indeed any revaluation of the currency (in Hong Kong's case, from 9.55 to 7.8 to the dollar) should. The following year, 1984, was a momentous one for Hong Kong, with the signing of the Joint (Sino-British) Declaration of 1984 to return Hong Kong to Chinese sovereignty by 1997, the year in which the lease from China ran out on the New Territories part of the Hong Kong mainland. Hong Kong island itself had been ceded indefinitely when the original Sino-British treaty had first been drawn. However, China had always demanded the return of Hong Kong island as well as the New Territories. Deng Xiaoping, who as paramount leader ultimately conducted the negotiations with British Prime Minister Margaret Thatcher, was asked by a diplomat what China would have done if Britain had not yielded. He is said to have responded that China would have simply "walked in." Return of Hong Kong to the motherland was never an issue for China's leaders. It was always an imperative that the full sovereignty of the mainland, which had been humiliated and damaged as a result of imperialist incursion, had to be restored over the lands taken from it. This was the case with Hong Kong—the claim on which no Chinese leader could have given up—and remains the case today with Taiwan.

The local Hong Kong reaction to this was unambiguously negative. The ensuing panic, though, eventually died down, and long-term thinkers began to see vast, indeed limitless, benefits resulting from this, especially in light of China's growing economic reforms just over the border. In particular, the making of Shenzhen—literally just over the border if you take the train to Lowu—as a special economic zone heralded the dawn of what was to become one of the most, if not the most, successful economic joint ventures in economic history. Guangdong had abundant and cheap labor. Its factory costs were a fraction of those of Hong Kong, and it had been given the green light from Beijing to open up, not just in the sense of internal development and deregulation, but with specific regard to Hong Kong. In under a decade, both Hong Kong and Guangdong were completely transformed. Most Hong Kong manufacturing had moved across the border, leaving over 85% of the Hong Kong economy to the service sector, while Guangdong was growing at over 20%, year in, year out. With Guangdong setting world records for economic transformation and growth, Hong Kong became the sole service center for this dramatic boom. The whole Pearl River Delta exploded as Beijing cut down the barriers to growth. During this transformation, employment in the Hong Kong manufacturing sector fell from around 50% to 15%, while the GDP share of trade and financial services rose from 40% to 55% and its share in private employment from 30% to 65%. Total exports of goods and services rose from around 70% of GDP in the early 1980s to 195% of GDP by the mid-1990s, with the export of services and also reexports from Guangdong taking on an increasingly important role.[1]

As the saying went, Hong Kong was the shop window and Guangdong the factory floor. The combination was irresistible and attracted substantial and growing foreign capital inflow, in terms of both direct and portfolio investment into the area—just as Deng Xiaoping had hoped. By 1994, the integration of Guangdong and Hong Kong, despite British attempts to limit this relationship, was largely complete. Shenzhen was transformed from a collection of poor and backward villages and rice fields into a Hong Kong-like concrete garden of skyscrapers and factories. Foreign consumer goods were abundant, from designer clothes to flashy sports cars (stolen from Hong Kong or bought locally), and the average standard of living in the province had risen exponentially relative not only to 1984 levels but to the rest of Asia. Three-quarters of investment in Guangdong came from Hong Kong, and over half of Guangdong's workforce of 6 million was employed by Hong Kong companies. In return, Guangdong produced 90% of Hong Kong's reexports.

There was serious money to be made. The joint venture produced a geyser of money, showering the area like a new oil strike. In a decade, Hong Kong was transformed from a maker of cheap consumer goods into the preeminent financial services and reexport center in Asia, not including Japan. By 1992, real GDP was expanding at a rate of 6.3%. The Hong Kong dollar M3 money supply growth was 13.7% in 1992 and a stunning 25.2% the following year. The years 1993–1995 saw a further, externally based boost to Hong Kong. The fall in the value of the dollar against major international currencies, precipitated by the apparent official U.S. depreciation policy to reestablish export competitiveness—or at the very least benign neglect—put downward pressure not only on the USD-HKD exchange rate but also on domestic Hong Kong interest rates. Indeed, interest rates turned negative in real terms relative to the level of inflation. In 1996, the benchmark interest rate in Hong Kong was an average 5.55%, while the headline CPI rate was 6%. With negative real interest rates, you were effectively being paid to borrow money. The property market, which in 1994–1995 had actually been in a slump, with residential and commercial property prices falling by around 25% in 1995 from their peak in April 1994, saw this as a golden opportunity, not to be missed. That and the impending handover in 1997, with economic integration with Guangdong and increasing Chinese demand for property further boosting the market, caused a bottoming out in prices in late 1995 and a stratospheric rise in prices in 1996 and the first half of 1997. The combination of lower mortgage rates and the Hong Kong government-run system, whereby supply of property was strictly limited and only allowed through land auctions, proved an irresistible combination. In March 1997, the government announced that it would substantially increase the supply of land for housing development over the next 5 years in order to reduce the housing shortage (and take advantage of astronomical prices), in part seeking to stabilize the property market. However, prices for both residential and commercial property, continued skyward after only the briefest of pauses. Anecdotally, a friend of mine, a local Hong Kong Chinese, offered HKD11.5 million for a house in a chic part of Hong Kong in January 1997. He missed it and it went for 12 million. In June of that year, it was sold again for HKD20 million!

Needless to say, skyrocketing property prices raised concerns about a bubble. However, economic fundamentals appeared to be roughly in line with this move, at least in terms of supply and demand. Only 7,000 private apartments were completed in the first half of 1997, compared with 17,000 in 1996 and an average of 30,000 units per year in the period 1991–1995.[2] At the same time, the population expanded by 3% a year in the 1996–1997 period, compared with 1.5% annually in 1991–1995, while the residential property prices rose an average of 32% since April 1994 compared with a 55% rise in nominal payroll per person and a 28% rise in construction costs.[3] Supply remained strictly limited by the government, while the demand side continued to rise with the approach of the handover and the resumption of Chinese sovereignty in Hong Kong.

It was a marvelous time to be in Hong Kong. While the Handover itself was an incredible focus and centerpiece, attracting several thousand TV cameras, photographers, and journalists from all over the world, the general buzz of the place was something to behold, something that is difficult to describe adequately. Hong Kong in 1996 and the first half of 1997 was a boomtown. History of course teaches that for every boom there is a bust, every bubble, a crash, but most people ignored that. (One of the few exceptions was Dr. Marc Faber of Marc Faber Ltd., who long before the crash predicted the future demise of Hong Kong as a regional financial center.) And anyway, people were having too good a time to care. Money was everywhere, money to burn, money to throw away, and without it being a concern. At the start of the handover year, Hong Kong had more Rolls-Royces per square per capita than anywhere else in the world. The bars of Lan Kwai Fong and Wanchai, the restaurants of Repulse Bay and Causeway Bay, were on fire with demand. If you didn't book well in advance, you simply didn't get in. If anyone had collated data on the number of bottles of champagne and cognac (a local favorite) drunk in 1996 and 1997, they would surely have found that the consumption of Hong Kong matched if not overtook that of France despite the fact that it had barely an eighth of the population. In 1997, Hong Kong's GDP per capita reached USD24,500—higher than that in Britain or Australia. Hong Kong boasted the world's largest and most expensive public works project in the form of the building of the new Chep Lap Kok Airport (sadly, to replace the old chaotic but lovable Kai Tak Airport in Kowloon) out on Lantau Island. The new and impressive—and incredibly expensive—Hong Kong Conference and Exhibition Center was purposely built for the site of the Handover, its shadow looming out into Victoria Harbour. Donald Tsang, assuaging some local fears, while publicly proclaiming his confidence in the handover process and in the fundamentals of Hong Kong's economy, said that the territory would start life as a special administrative region of China "in sound economic shape, with every prospect that we will remain the most attractive business location in the region."

In hindsight, it was a crash waiting to happen, but there were those who argued that economic fundamentals justified this ex-

pansion whatever the anecdotal signs of conspicuous and excessive consumption. After all, the supply-demand dynamics of the
Hong Kong property market surely demanded that prices rise. In
addition, real interest rates were negative, so where else could
property prices go but up? With property being one of the three
key engines of economic prosperity and growth—the other two
being tourism and financial services, both of which were also
booming—there seemed little to be worried about. Markets are
occasionally due for corrections and perhaps in Hong Kong's
case this might be necessary, but there appeared no fundamental backing for the suggestion by the one or two lone voices who
argued that a major fundamental reversal was imminent, so the
view went. Yet this view ignored both external and domestic
flaws. On the external side, the decline in the USD-JPY and the
resulting decline in the USD-HKD and Hong Kong domestic
interest rates had played a major part in the property market
boom of 1996–1997. Yet the USD-JPY began a major recovery
phase from late 1995, in the wake of the April 1995 commu-
niqué from the G7, seeking an "orderly reversal" of previous dollar weakness, backed with active intervention by the Federal
Reserve Bank of New York and the Bank of Japan. From a low of
79.85 in April 1995, the USD-JPY exchange rate recovered first
to the 100 level and then to above 120 in 1996. That recovery accelerated in 1997 and 1998, with the dollar rallying from 127 in
April 1998 (after the Bank of Japan spent over USD20 billion in
foreign exchange reserves trying to force it lower) to over 147 by
mid-August of that year. In addition, the dollar had of course
risen dramatically against the Asian currencies during the initial
and secondary stages of the Asian currency crisis, while the
USD-HKD exchange rate had remained relatively steady. The
Thai baht was depegged and effectively devalued on July 2, 1997,
and the Asian currencies had fallen one by one. Yet the value of
the Hong Kong dollar had been maintained. On the domestic
side, while the headline CPI rate had declined from 6.0% to
around 5.7% in 1997, nominal interest rates had risen. Indeed
they had risen through the CPI rate and were now above it at 6%
and above. The days of negative real interest rates had gone.

In the heady glow of the Handover and the boom time that characterized Hong Kong, most people ignored this, though to be sure an increasing and vocal minority were starting to voice concerns. Parallels were raised between Hong Kong and Tokyo in 1989. By the time of the Handover on Tuesday, July 1, 1997, Hong Kong had become the most expensive place to live in the world as measured by residential property prices. Hong Kong retailers also had to pay the most expensive retail shopping space rates in the world, even surpassing those of the long infamous Ginza District in Tokyo. Hong Kong had at one time been a major bargain center in terms of retail shopping. By mid-1997, this was certainly no longer the case. Indeed, such had been the turnaround in shopping dynamics that I remember vividly a European designer store in the Landmark Building in Central Hong Kong forcing customers to queue outside its door and only be admitted one at a time (when another customer left). Not only was this an insulting and repugnant system, but it was a clear demonstration of excess consumption. When demand reaches such levels—when shoppers clearly have lost their self-respect, not to say their sanity—you (should) know it will not be long before the economy is in trouble. At the corporate level, debt levels were nothing compared with the likes of much of the ASEAN, not including Singapore. However, overall debt/GDP was 150%, ominously in line with that in Thailand and Korea. Figures were not available for how much of that was hedged against the dollar, but the likelihood was—and is—that such hedging would make up a tiny fraction of the total, given the temptation to avoid hedging costs due to the relative stability of the Hong Kong dollar peg and currency board system. In terms of the big picture, however, Hong Kong had clearly lost competitiveness on a regional scale, not only because of the Asian currency devaluations but because of domestic overvaluation of assets.

In addition, productivity was lagging sorely behind, and there were certain fundamental elements of the economy and society which were alarmingly falling behind. The shortcomings of the HKSAR's education system was reflected by underperformance in terms of the high-level skill proficiency needed to run a world financial and service center. In particular, secondary schools place greater emphasis on large classes and learning by rote than on creativity and innovation. The average ability of Hong Kong Chinese to speak English, long an invaluable asset in terms of encouraging and servicing inward investment, had also fallen dramatically. Hong Kong's focus on China, given the handover, had meant that an increasing emphasis was being placed on learning Putonghua, or Mandarin Chinese, and a clearly diminishing emphasis on English. While this is entirely understandable, it is an unquestionable fact that English is the global language of business and that a world financial and service center must of necessity have a high degree of English to survive. Note that this is not the case in Tokyo to the same extent because Japan obviously has a major domestic manufacturing base to service and thus does not have to rely so much on inward investment. This happened just at a time when rivals in Asia, notably Singapore, were increasingly offering advantages for foreign firms that Hong Kong had long held a preeminence in. For a start, the level of spoken English in Singapore is eminently superior to that of Hong Kong. Singapore also sought to give tax breaks to foreign multinationals, similar to Hong Kong's corporate tax rate. In addition, the improvement in Taiwan-China relations after the flare-up between the two in 1996 and the start of direct shipments between the two diminished Hong Kong's role as the middleman in this relationship. To be sure, Hong Kong still had some advantages, some positives, such as its emphasis on the rule of law, honest administrators and a desire to root out any corruption, minimal government, and an openness to new ideas. However, there is no question that its overall advantage and lead in the region had been reduced if not all but eliminated.

Concerns about Hong Kong asset valuations and overall competitiveness came to a head in October 1997, when the Hang Seng, which had peaked in August, finally broke lower, coming crashing down to earth. The initial trigger was the effective devaluation of the Taiwan dollar on October 17, when the Central Bank of China (Taiwan's central bank) let the exchange rate go, after stubbornly defending it for several months despite the devaluations of the ASEAN currencies. The following week, from October 20 to 24, was a torrid time for the Hang Seng. On Thursday of that week, October 23, it lost a record 1,669 points in early trading before managing to close off its lowest levels of the day, as speculators, having defeated CBC, which after all had the world's fourth largest foreign exchange reserves, turned their attention on Hong Kong. The HKMA desk intervened repeatedly in the spot and forward foreign exchange markets to defend the USD-HKD exchange rate at the 7.7500 level. In addition it left the money market to its own devices, providing no extra liquidity to offset the shortage. The ensuing panic to obtain Hong Kong dollar funds resulting from the sell-off in the Hong Kong dollar—as indeed a currency board should work—saw the overnight rate spike to a high of 300% at one point. The USD-HKD collapsed to a low of 7.48, before rebounding. As a result, the smaller speculators saw their positions crushed by the double whammy of capital and interest rate losses, and even the larger ones went home to lick their wounds.

The HKMA desk, which, rightly or wrongly, has a reputation for having a somewhat vindictive streak, had tasted blood, and won what seemed at the time a major victory against the speculators, indeed the only victory by any Asian authority against the forces of the market. Yet it was interesting to note that the *South China Morning Post* issued a stinging critique of the HKMA's actions, suggesting that such methods of attempting to defend the Hong Kong dollar currency peg had recklessly endangered the stability and health of the entire Hong Kong financial system. The HKMA, as we shall see later in greater detail, tends to take things somewhat personally for even a quasi-central bank; and HKMA Chief Executive Joseph Yam responded promptly, denying such accusations and saying that the HKMA had not played an active part in market activity, rather that the currency board system had been simply allowed to work as it should. As I said, a surprisingly personal, if not defensive, tone from the head of a quasi-central bank. In the meantime, both the foreign exchange and money markets eventually quieted down going into November and into the first quarter of 1998, which saw most Asian currencies actually rebound against the dollar as current account balances started to recover (due to collapsing imports). Then there were further attacks against the Hong Kong dollar peg in May, July, and August. Interest rates spiked on each occasion and remained at historically high levels, only to cautiously and gradually pull back.

These repeated attacks against the peg seemed on the face of it nonsensical. The HKMA has the world's third largest foreign exchange reserves around (USD90 billion, including the contributions from the Exchange Fund and the Land Fund), plus it has Beijing's overt and public pledge to help defend the peg. Beijing has a further USD145 billion in foreign exchange reserves. In addition, and perhaps most importantly, the very nature of a currency board should be self-balancing. A currency board necessitates that the manager of the currency board—i.e., the HKMA—does not sterilize the currency inflows or outflows, but simply allows supply and demand to dictate and right the system. Yet speculators continued to show up in one form or another, ready to attack or at least test the resolve of the authorities to hold the peg. Why was this so? To a certain extent, of course, the downturn in the economy attracted the interest of the speculators. Looking at their successes in the past of attacking a currency in the midst of an economic slowdown, thus forcing the authorities concerned to raise interest rates to intolerably high levels which in the end cannot be sustained, they saw the same prospects for success in Hong Kong. Yet under an orthodox currency board system this should be impossible. The truth was of course, as noted earlier, that the Hong Kong dollar peg is far from being an orthodox currency board system. In theory, an orthodox currency board system requires adequate reserves in the currency that the domestic currency is linked to (in this case the U.S. dollar), the monetary authority's commitment of unlimited and unsterilized conversion at a single and predetermined exchange rate (7.80 to the U.S. dollar), nonintervention in the market with no real or perceived bands or trip levels, and finally monetary policy that is de facto a mirror image of the monetary policy of the linked currency (i.e., that of the Federal Reserve). The result should be to convince market participants that any widening of the interest rate differential between the two currencies, if it ever occurs, is a temporary distortion and should and will be eliminated almost immediately by opportunistic arbitrage.

That was the theory. Hong Kong's reality was nothing like this. For a start, the HKMA acted like a central bank, intervening in both the foreign exchange and money markets. The HKMA denied this, with HKMA Chief Executive Yam saying that the HKMA only accepted Hong Kong dollars passively as a currency board should. I have met countless dealers in Hong Kong who say this was simply not the case; the HKMA did indeed intervene actively and more specifically at a rate of 7.7500. Central banks that intervene in the foreign exchange market typically "sterilize" that intervention through money market operations by adding back currency supply to the system. Thus they avoid the resulting tightening of liquidity which would otherwise result from buying the domestic currency (and thus reducing supply in the system). As it clearly and unequivocally stated in its mandate, the currency board system under the management of the HKMA did not enjoy such flexibility. The very nature of a currency board system implies that it cannot sterilize foreign exchange or money market intervention, at whatever exchange rate, and that consequently it does not have the right or the ability to offset tightening in the money market. Thus, the more vigorous the intervention, the more severe the tightening.

To currency speculators, this was a no-brainer. It was not so much that they thought the peg would go; it was that HKMA foreign exchange intervention was an easy way to guarantee them profits. How did this work? Previously, in October, they borrowed huge amounts of Hong Kong dollars and sold them short against the U.S. dollar, "forcing" the HKMA to intervene. The HKMA allowed interest rates to spike to triple digits and the speculators went home with a bloody nose. Then, they changed their tactics. Hong Kong's stock and interest rate markets trade inversely to each other. This is the case in most countries. However, it is particularly the case under a currency board system where supply and demand rule unfettered. What the speculators now did was to go short the Hang Seng futures contract and then force interest rates up by selling Hong Kong dollars in the market and also selling the interest rates through futures and swap contracts. Any loss on the interest rate side due to borrowed Hong Kong dollars to fund the short Hong Kong dollar position would be easily made up for by the collapse in the stock market cash and futures indexes due to those same higher interest rates. HKMA intervention in fact exacerbated the tightening in the money market! This was easy money, and a lot of speculators made bucket loads doing it, at the expense of not only the HKMA's reserves, but also the level of the Hang Seng and the health of the economy. In addition, the HKMA's order to its agent banks to buy any Hong Kong dollar in the system when the exchange rate was 7.7500 compounded the situation (and the error), for this allowed a theoretical perfect arbitrage opportunity for the "note-issuing banks" themselves. Three banks, Hong Kong Bank, Standard Chartered, and Bank of China, are allowed to issue Hong Kong dollar notes. Under the Exchange Fund guidelines, note-issuing banks could exchange dollars for Hong Kong dollars with the HKMA at 7.8000. Yet with the HKMA's standing order to intervene at 7.7500, they can exchange Hong Kong dollars back for dollars (whatever their intervention on behalf of the HKMA) at 7.7500. The fact that the arbitrage window existed at all was a further negative for the Hong Kong dollar. Such apparent imperfections in the Hong Kong currency board system as have been outlined allowed speculators to manipulate liquidity in such a way as to have a disproportionately large impact on the Hong Kong market. The measures put in place by the HKMA in August 1998 increased the transparency and liquidity of the currency board system, eliminating for now the window of opportunity for the speculators.

What of the fundamentals? Currencies, just like asset markets, experience temporary domestic and exogenous shocks. However, in the end they revert to long-term economic fundamentals. In the case of Hong Kong, do these suggest that the

Hong Kong dollar is ripe for renewed speculative or fundamental attack, that it is fundamentally overvalued? Or is, as potentially suggested above, something else at work here? The answer is actually a bit of both, but let's have a look at the detail, as shown in Table 5.

Needless to say, Table 5 is a morass of data, but what does it all mean? The bottom line is that the Hong Kong dollar was undoubtedly overvalued at the end of 1997 and remains so as of the end of 1998, albeit less so. How do we know this? A number

Table 5
Hong Kong's Economic Fundamentals

	1996	1997	1998 (my forecast)	1999 (my forecast)
Real GDP growth (%)	4.9	5.3	−4.0	1.0
Budget balance (% of GDP)	2.1	5.8	−2.5	Flat
Visible trade balance (USD bln)	−17.8	−20.6	−10.0	−5.0
Goods and services balance (USD bln)	−2.6	−6.6	−2.0	−1.0
Goods and services balance (% of GDP)	−1.7	−3.8	−1.5	−1.0
Current account balance (% of GDP)	−3.1	−1.7	−2.5	−1.5
Consumer price inflation (%)	6.7	5.7	1.5	−0.5
Nominal wages (%)*	6.3	6.0	2.0	Flat
Real wages (%)*	−0.4	0.3	0.5	0.5
Labor productivity (%)†	1.3	2.3	3.0	4.5
Unit labor costs†	4.9	3.8	2.0	1.5
HKD REER valuation‡	134.5 (Dec. 96)	149.7 (Dec. 97)	141 (Dec. 98)	135 (Dec. 99)
HKD Trade-weighted valuation‡	119.3 (Dec. 96)	129.1 (Dec. 97)	126 (Dec. 98)	122 (Dec. 99)

Sources: Standard & Poor's MMS, Hong Kong official data.

* Based on averages of semiannual (March and September) data.

† Based on employment data up to the first half of 1997.

‡ Both the real effective exchange rate and the trade-weighted Hong Kong dollar (i.e., the nominal effective exchange rate) are based at 1990 = 100.

of indicators show this, but let's start with the trade data. Hong Kong had a stunning visible trade deficit of USD20.6 billion in 1997. This was mitigated somewhat by a substantial surplus on the services' side. However, it still led to a goods and services deficit of USD6.6 billion that year, equivalent to 3.8% of GDP. While the current account deficit was more than otherwise expected, it remained clearly in negative territory and thus a drag on the economy as a whole. This is not wholly unexpected because Hong Kong traditionally runs a trade deficit since most of its manufacturing base is in China. But in order to retain competitiveness Hong Kong has to offset its trade imbalance through higher rates of productivity and low rates of wages and unit labor costs. In this, it clearly failed. Labor productivity fell from an annual rate of 6.9% in 1992 to 1.3% in 1996, while unit labor costs rose in that same period from 2.9% to 4.9%. The CPI rate, meanwhile, was growing at 6.7% in 1996, while that in the U.S., to which the Hong Kong dollar peg is linked, was around 2.5%. This brings us to the Hong Kong dollar's real effective exchange rate, or the trade-weighted exchange rate valuation adjusted for inflation. A rising REER is a clear sign of a loss of relative competitiveness. From 1994 to 1997, the Hong Kong dollar's REER boomed. In nominal terms as well, Hong Kong has lost competitiveness, with the value of the nominal effective exchange rate, or the trade-weighted exchange rate, also rising sharply through the end of 1997. During the period 1984–1997 (1984 was the first full year that the currency board system was in place), Hong Kong's CPI rose a cumulative 146.7% against around 53.5% in the U.S. Logically, looking at real exchange rate valuations, the nominal Hong Kong dollar should lose around 93%. Yet the USD-HKD exchange rate has remained relatively steady. Indeed in that period the Hong Kong dollar actually appreciated over 1%. There is no question whatsoever, according to these data, that Hong Kong lost relative competitiveness and thus the Hong Kong dollar became overvalued.

That's the bad news. The good news is the market is already correcting that overvaluation, not only in terms of the decline in the Hang Seng and property prices, the most obvious correction, but with regard to the peaking in the REER and trade-weighted values in December 1997 and the pullback from there. As imports collapse because of the decline in domestic demand due to high interest rates, the overall trade balance deficit should improve. In addition, with retail prices falling, threatening deflation by the end of 1998, consumer price overvaluation will in the end right itself. Hong Kong may not have been cheap in 1997, but it will soon be! Yet asset prices cannot by themselves take the full burden. The Hang Seng fell from 16,820 to 6,544.79, with property prices back to mid-1996 levels; yet the HKD REER as of the end of June was 145.1, well shy of the 134.5 recorded as of December 1996. This suggests that there is significant pain still to come.

While the nature of a currency board system necessitates that assets rather than the currency take the adjustment needed to regain relative equilibrium, productivity and cost-cutting gains can also help. Along with efforts to retrain the workforce by raising the level of technical and general education, competition must be increased within the service sector. This may seem nonsensical since the assumption is that Hong Kong is completely laissez faire. This is not completely the case. Transport facilities, for instance, are effectively run by a cartel, with small companies marginalized. The government controls the housing market, while a small group of *"Hong"* (trading groups) effectively control commercial property. What effect does this have? As in any such case, it acts as an inflator of prices and thus is damaging to overall competitiveness. In addition, Hong Kong manufacturing and service industries need to go further up the value-added chain by seeking not only cheap labor and cost bases but also innovative and creative processes that will add to total factor productivity— the residual of growth when all inputs such as investment are taken out. Total private and public R&D expenditure amounts to just 0.2% of GDP, as against 1.2% in Singapore and 2% in Taiwan. The establishment of the Industrial & Technology Center Corp., which is nurturing thirty technology start-up companies, was positive news, but, to repeat, more needs to be done overall to bring Hong Kong further up the ladder in terms of value-added. Just being a good trader and service center is not enough. Hong Kong now faces easily the strongest competition, in terms of both quality and pricing, that it has had since the currency board system was first put in place in October 1983.

Even more fundamentally, the government needs to sort out the housing problem. Only around half the population of 6.5 million own property. The government sought to alleviate this problem by announcing in October 1997 that a further 85,000 apartments a year would be built and be available for purchase. The subsequent collapse in asset prices caused a rethink on this, with land auctions canceled for 1998 and the initial plans for new apartment buildings scaled back. While this is perhaps understandable, does it actually make sense? The answer is no. For a start, anyone looking to buy a flat of the start of 1999 would know that the 1999 supply is likely to be greater than that of 1998, and therefore there is no point buying now since prices are likely to go lower, whatever is happening at the time to property valuations. The 40% fall in property prices in 1998 merely exacerbated this view. To pretend otherwise is to adopt the ostrich approach to economics. In addition, with Hong Kong's population growth rate accelerating, the problem of inadequate housing can only get worse. High property valuations have had profound effects on companies, more specifically on worker turnover, since many young Hong Kong people regularly switch jobs specifically in order to try and make the 30% down payment needed to buy an apartment. This high employee turnover rate adds to the lack of Hong Kong corporate competitiveness. The government needs to increase supply. It might as well do it now, because waiting until later will not have the desired effect of stopping or slowing the collapse in property prices. It will simply reduce market liquidity—while prices continue to slide.

While the asset adjustment process continues, in whatever form, the authorities can also play their part. Already, the government has announced a fiscal package. It includes measures to improve corporate competitiveness such as the scrapping of the tax on corporate deposits in Hong Kong dollars, which will result in a budget deficit of HKD21.4 billion, or 1.5% of GDP for fiscal 1998–99. It is almost certain that despite the basic law which necessitates that the government not run large deficits, except in special circumstances, and the government's pledge that no further measures are planned, another package will take place before the end of the 1998–1999 fiscal year on April 1, 1999. Hong Kong can well afford this given the significant surpluses that it built up from 1992 to 1997. In addition, there was a need for the HKMA to change its tactics; indeed its present tactics are part of the problem rather than being the solution. As mentioned previously, the HKMA was not acting in the way an orthodox currency board system should. Its active intervention was exacerbating the tightness in the money market. This may seem a contradiction, since without the HKMA intervention interest rates would undoubtedly have moved higher. However, I would argue that they would also have reverted to equilibrium far more quickly. The initial effect on the economy might have been even more dramatic and severe than the current downturn, but it would be over and would start to reverse much sooner. While certainly not deliberately, the HKMA's actions were, to my mind, exacerbating and prolonging the pain. The result is that nominal (and real) interest rates stayed at high levels rather than spiking higher and then falling back. To Hong Kong business, this was a disaster. Unusually high and volatile interest rates hurt companies across the board, the healthy and the less so alike. The fact that the overnight rate hit 300% on a single day does not matter in the great scheme of things. The fact that it remained at or near double digits for several months certainly does. Indeed, with interest rates straying so high, the perceived sentiment was that there remained no hope in sight. Thus, the massive contraction in asset prices—added to, to be sure, by speculative activity—was perceived as a reflection of the fading attractiveness of Hong Kong, rather than as an opportunity for bargain hunting. With no bottom in sight, why would you buy here? So the thinking went—the same argument as in the property market.

The very fact that the HKMA continued to intervene at 7.7500—something completely contrary to the spirit of an orthodox currency board system—attracted speculators, in both the currency and stock markets. It suggested to the speculators that the HKMA and the government did not actually believe in the currency board system, that maybe the 7.80 peg would not hold. It suggested weakness, not strength. While the HKMA's foreign exchange reserves of USD90 billion compared with the M2 money supply of cash and deposits of around USD210 billion, it clearly has enough reserves in theory against the monetary base to defend against speculative attack. Joseph Yam is entirely correct when he says that the people of Hong Kong ultimately are the only ones who can defeat the Hong Kong dollar peg (he added, of course, that they showed no signs of doing so). The weaknesses of the Hong Kong currency board system in 1998, together with the HKMA's tactics of moneymarket and foreign exchange intervention, did, however, exacerate the HKD's overvaluation, thus adding to and extending the correction in Hong Kong's economy and its asset markets. To be fair, however, the HKMA has done much to address the situation through the measures announced in the autumn of 1998. The expansion of systemic liquidity and credit availability through the scrapping of the discount window, thus forcing banks to keep intrabank liquidity in the system rather than lending it to the KHMA, caused a domestic change in interest rates, forcing them sharply lower. Equally, the convertibility undertaking at 7.7500 to supply all market needs for dollars, together with a commitment to change the convertibility undertaking by 1 pip a day from 7.7500 as of April 1 toward the 7.80 peg level, should eliminate further the uncertainty in the market and lack of creditibility surrounding the currency boards system. The HKMA should add to such improvements by separating foreign exchange reserves aimed at specifically backing the monetary base, preferably under a new body with separate management and control! Alternatively the reserves needed to back the monetary base could be kept at the HKMA while other assets were separated, thus making the HKMA into an orthodox currency board. With such measures, the uncertainty over just what is the role of the HKMA is removed and with it the opportunity of anyone for arbitrage.

Theoretically, there has been a further alternative for system refinement that the authorities of Hong Kong have occasionally mulled and that drew attention and comment from August 1998 on: the idea of "dollarizing" the Hong Kong economy, or effectively replacing the domestic currency with the U.S. dollar. The very idea might seem ridiculous given that Hong Kong has only recently been returned to China. Yet it actually does not contravene the letter of the Basic Law, which demands that (some) Hong Kong dollars continue to flow through the system but does not in fact specify that the current exchange rate system be maintained. In the wake of the Mexican peso crisis of December 1994–March 1995, Argentina, feeling the blast of currency market contagion, threatened to dismantle its currency board and dollarize the economy. The speculators, seeing that the threat was real, quickly departed the scene of battle. If Hong Kong threatened dollarization, it would have to do so convincingly. Still, this measure could theoretically be effective given that anticipation of narrowing of interest rate differentials (to those of the dollar curve) would be irresistible and would crush speculative attempts to go the other way. Because a currency board holds reserves equal to or more than 100% of the monetary base, it has the option to dollarize the economy at any time. Hong Kong dollars in this scenario would be exchanged at a fixed 7.80 to the U.S. dollar. This would not be a devaluation. The currency in the system would simply be exchanged. In practice, however, Beijing would probably take a dim view of such an idea since it would be politically unacceptable.

Two final ideas to chew on. First, it is notable that prior to the measures announced at the end of August 1998, the note-issuing banks were the only ones with access to the Exchange Fund. If every bank and financial institution had had similar access, there would have been far greater opportunity for arbitrage between whatever the spot rate was at the time and the peg value of 7.80 (as long as the HKMA gave up its line in the sand of 7.7500). This surely would allow for self-reinforcement of the 7.80 peg, albeit with minor distortions and divergence (which would swiftly be corrected). Last, but not least, there is the idea of unifying the

Hong Kong dollar and the renminbi—and thus the HKMA and the PBOC. This also would be politically unacceptable since it flies in the face of the "one country, two systems" approach, which is the hallmark of bilateral Hong Kong–China relations. In sum, in theory at least, the best way to stabilize the financial system as a whole and interest rates more specifically would be to increase domestic competitiveness and at the same time make the currency board system much more orthodox in order to eliminate the uncertainty off which the speculators are feeding. As long as the authorities remain prepared to take the pain, the rest would right itself and Hong Kong would regain its equilibrium.

So much for the theory. August 1998 brought with it a different type of intervention by the HKMA. On Friday, August 14, the HKMA intervened for the first time in the stock market, buying both individual shares and the August Hang Seng futures contract in an attempt to burn the speculators who had been shorting both the HSI futures and cash stocks while at the same time receiving increased floating-rate interest payments through interest rate swap transactions. The HKMA came in again on Monday, August 17, and all that week, supposedly spending up to HKD6.5 billion in reserves in the process. Was such action, while at the same time maintaining that line in the sand at 7.7500, justified? Exceptional circumstances sometimes merit exceptional responses. Yet the HKMA's intervention initially drew a hail of criticism, domestically and internationally. The objective after all was surely to bring interest rates down and to stabilize asset prices, yet that can happen only when people perceive value. Such a concept and a calculation of value surely becomes distorted when the HKMA itself is buying the Hang Seng index. Those looking to bargain-hunt in the market would wait until the HKMA finally stepped out of the way and the market fell again until such a point where fundamental valuations suggested prices were a screaming buy. As of August 1998, with the Hang Seng at around 7,000, this was not the case and certainly not with the HKMA, deliberately or not, actively propping up valuations.

Just as in the case of the workings of the currency board system, confusion is allowed to persist. Why did the HKMA intervene in the stock market? Suspicion remained that it was for the purpose of propping up prices rather than to specifically hurt the speculators. Certainly the authorities did *not* initially make it crystal clear that such an operation was *definitely not* to support valuations, but was aimed as a surgical strike at speculative and manipulative positions, and that the market would be allowed to find its fair value, wherever and however low that was. The HKMA's words and actions seemed to many to suggest the complete opposite. While the HKMA, justifiably, is known as an extremely skillful and prudent financial authority, it also has a certain reputation in Hong Kong as being vindictive to those it deems its enemies. It is not unique in this. The history of central banking is littered with cases of central banks seeking revenge on banks and other financial institutions for daring to attack their currencies—but that is exactly the point. The HKMA is not and should not be a central bank. It is supposed to be the manager, the administrator of a currency board, a system that is completely neutral and unemotional, translating and covering the full value of the monetary base if necessary at the peg level of 7.80. Needless to say, this was not seen as the case in practice, with the perception prevalent that the HKMA desk was purposefully seeking to hurt sellers of the Hong Kong dollar and the stock market (so much for a free market!). To a certain extent, it did not matter whether or not this was reality. If it was not, the authorities had clearly failed to clarify and rectify what was a false impression. That autumn of 1998 I met with representatives of the Honk Kong authorities in London and attended a luncheon for Financial Secretary Donald Tsang. At the time, it was clear that the Hong Kong authorities considered they had got the message across that they had not intervened in the stock market for the purpose of propping up valuations, but instead to eliminate market manipulation. I made the point, however, that it was not yet that the market's understanding that the HKMA would tolerate further, asset market weakness, for whatever reason, be it manipulation or price correction. The Honk Kong authorities assured me that the pledge not to prop up valuations per se specifically meant a toleration of further market weakness if needed. This assurance helped assure international investors that transparency had returned to the market.

Economic projects remain gloomy near term. Yet does this mean Hong Kong should devalue or otherwise abandon its peg? The answer is a resounding *no*! As severe as the economic pain undoubtedly and presently is, it is nothing compared with the resulting meltdown and chaos that would be seen if Hong Kong depegged or devalued its currency.

In free-floating or even pegged exchange rates, a devaluation of a currency is not necessarily a bad thing. It can restore export competitiveness, though of course there are negative side effects such as the potential for imported inflation. If Hong Kong devalued, there could only be one reason for doing so—the hope that interest rates would fall and set prices would subsequently stabilize. Yet this would most likely not be the case. While Hong Kong's corporate base has a relatively modest gearing (debt-to- equity) ratio at around 30%, much of that is unhedged. A devaluation of the Hong Kong dollar which would automatically result from a depegging would cause a panicked flight by these companies out of Hong Kong and into U.S. dollars—just as happened in Thailand— exacerbating the upward move in the USD-HKD exchange rate. Investors, whether in fixed assets or the Hong Kong asset markets, would also panic, and the subsequent capital flight out of the territory would cause a severe contraction of the monetary base, which would in turn send interest rates skyward rather than lower.

There would be a further reason for higher, rather than lower, interest rates—imported inflation. Because Hong Kong traditionally runs a trade deficit, a devaluation would mean sharply higher import costs that would feed straight through to inflation at the retail level. The precedent for this was September 1983 when on "Black Saturday," September 24, 1983, the Hong Kong dollar hit a low of 9.60, resulting in the present currency board system being imposed.

This brings me to a final and crucial point. Hong Kong is not a free-floating or even a pegged exchange rate regime. It is a currency board system, with the requisite distribution of U.S. dollars and Hong Kong dollars within both foreign exchange reserves and the monetary base that that necessitates, according to the 7.80 currency board peg. A devaluation of the Hong Kong dollar by, say, 30% would wipe out at least that proportion of the territory's financial capital base given the distribution of Hong Kong and U.S. dollars in banks under the currency board system. Hong Kong's banking system is uncharacteristically healthy by Asian standards in terms of overall solvency and capital adequacy ratios, which remain well above the Bank of International Settlements (BIS) imposed limit of 8%—in fact, most in Hong Kong are more than double that. A Hong Kong depegging and devaluation would critically injure what is otherwise a supremely healthy banking system by regional standards. The result would be even higher interest rates as greatly increased credit risk was taken account of, as has been the case in Korea, Thailand, and Indonesia this past year. A devaluation is unthinkable. It would mean the end of Hong Kong as a world financial center, a fall from which it would never come back.

The alternative of course is more of the same—more economic pain. However, the pain has to be born if Hong Kong is to reemerge from this present downturn. Hong Kong is one of the few places in Asia to be able to undergo such a wrenching economic experience without incurring a major social backlash (to date). While this is likely to be tested in the next year or so, Hong Kong benefits from being as pure a free-market system as there is in Asia. Its entrepreneurs have traditionally had to be nimble and fast on their feet. They will have to be to survive and prosper this time around. Various ways of improving Hong Kong's competitiveness and thus accelerating the adjustment process have been suggested above. For all the gloom, however, Hong Kong still has certain major fundamental strengths that should see it through. The authorities have significant foreign exchange reserves, the government historically has a strong fiscal position and no debt (though this may change if the government seeks further fiscal expansion), and the workforce has an entrepreneurial spirit. Where Hong Kong falls down, relative to, say, Taiwan, is that it needs to improve productivity and go further up the value-added chain by investing in higher value-added and creative manufacturing and service processes, with the requisite retraining of the workforce. What does China make of all this? China is no doubt aggrieved to find its progeny so recently returned to the fold under attack and in the midst of deep recession. Yet, besides token public announcements of support for the Hong Kong dollar peg, there appears little China can do in the immediate term to alleviate Hong Kong's pain.

If China devalues its currency in 1999 or at least allows it to depreciate modestly, would this mean automatically a Hong Kong dollar devaluation? The theoretical answer is no, since China devalued in 1986, 1989, and 1994 and this had absolutely no lasting effect on the peg. That said, it would of course cause an immediate and renewed speculative attack against the Hong Kong dollar, though China would no doubt seek to help the HKMA to rebuff this. Mutual noninterference in each other's societies—a central part of the concept of the "one country, two systems" approach—is one thing, but not helping each other is quite another. If China did devalue, this would have a mixed fundamental impact for Hong Kong. On the one hand, it would hurt Hong Kong exports to China; on the other, it would make Chinese exports to Hong Kong, which are reexported elsewhere and are counted as Hong Kong exports, more competitive. It would be deflationary to Hong Kong, and yet it would initially cause a spike in interest rates as the system sought to defend the peg. Ultimately, more competitive reexports from Hong Kong would be a major benefit. For China, Hong Kong stands not only as testament to the return of sovereign Chinese territory from imperialist hands, but in a more relevant context as an export processing and regional financial center, and finally as an airlock to the outside world—which Shanghai is not and will not be for some time.

Chinese companies will continue to look to tap international investor interest through the Hong Kong asset markets (albeit, perhaps not at present asset valuations!) rather than Shanghai, which will continue to be the *domestic* financial center. In addition, Hong Kong stands as a model of what "one country, two systems" could be like for a reunified Taiwan. Granted, Taiwan for the most part continues to reject this idea, but who is to say that given the increasing interdependence of the economies of China and Taiwan this will remain the case? Much will of course depend not only on the economic but on the political and social development in China itself. In the near term it would appear that political development remains glacial at best, though there are positive signs that Beijing is planning for the long term and seeking to further justify its administration through a Singapore type of administrative model receptive to popular demand and opinion.

In terms of China's economy, the slowdown is likely to continue for the foreseeable future, given that to slow the reform process—and thus to keep loss-making SOEs afloat—will mean continued stagnation in the financial system, while to continue it or speed it up will mean more economic pain through job losses and corporate and bank restructuring in the immediate term. China stands on the brink indeed, of either being reborn or plunging down an abyss. Both have major global implications that are addressed in the next chapter.

7

China in the World—
Global Tremors

WHY ARE DEVELOPMENTS in China and even Hong Kong so fundamentally crucial to the health of the global economy and more specifically to that of the U.S. and Europe? To some this may seem obvious. But for those who are not directly focused on Western-Chinese bilateral trade and capital flows in their daily lives (the vast majority), even the suggestion of such a link between the health of the Western and Chinese economies is shocking and alarming news. Yet such a suggestion is no more and no less than present-day reality. China's economy and overall international importance have both risen exponentially since the start of the reform process and now have a profound effect on the global economy as a whole. Equally, in the diplomatic field, China's star is also rising. Recent Sino-U.S. summits have taken on the air of past Soviet-U.S. meetings, the suggestion being that these are the two dominant nations in the world. In the case of China, this is highly debatable. However, the very fact that the suggestion is even entertained is testimony to the increase in Chinese influence on a global scale.

This is no less the case in terms of its role in the global economy. Only 10 years ago, the idea that China might ever overtake the U.S. in terms of total economic output would rightly have been laughed at. This is no longer the case. Indeed, books and other commentaries have sprung up, suggesting that China will become the world's preeminent and largest economy. It is a central theme within this work that this suggestion is dangerously reminiscent of the suggestions only a couple of years ago that the global economic locus was shifting from the West to the East and that the heady growth of the Asian tigers would continue forever. Needless to say, these ideas did not prove to be the case. In fact, the Asian crisis proved the persistent Asian dependency on the West rather than the reverse. And the days of Asian tiger growth seem so very long ago, amid the disastrous contraction that the region is undergoing. The risk is, I would suggest, that the same will be the case with China. China is presently being proclaimed as the new superpower, not simply in military terms, which it undoubtedly is, or even in the political sphere, which is increasingly evident, but in terms of economic might. Indeed, the explicit suggestion is that China will soon be the preeminent economic superpower, surpassing the U.S. To suggest such a thing is of necessity to expect that China's economic slowdown will stabilize and reverse in dramatic fashion and that China will again in record time sort out its massive financial system and SOE problems. Not that this is impossible, but it seems unlikely.

My view is that China's economic peak, at least in the near term, has already been seen, not simply in terms of GDP growth (which peaked in 1992 at just over 14%) but in terms of the economy's overall strength and ability to adapt and recreate itself. To some, this may appear near heresy. Indeed, many who pinned their hopes and beliefs on Asian supremacy now cling to the idea that at least in China's case it will prove true. The East has always held a particularly strong fascination for many in the West; some would say a compulsive one—like a mirage in the desert, or a focus of mysticism and ideological and religious purity that are attractive to those in the West who are disillusioned and disgusted by the cynical, impersonal secularism which now predominates in their own societies. Economists are of course not impervious to this. It was one of many factors that drew me there, myself. There remains so much in Asia that has not yet been tamed, that is raw, uncharted (or at least poorly charted!).

There is so much potential. To many in the West living in mature industrial societies, this is heady stuff, the chance for adventure in Asia seemingly infinite and certainly far greater than where they come from. The tens of thousands of bankers and backpackers who, I would humbly suggest, go to Asia for reasons that are closer than they both would like to think are surely testimony to this phenomenon. Yet one should not exaggerate. Many and great as the advantages and qualities of Asia are, the severity of everyday living conditions for a large proportion of ordinary Asians remains a reflection of the region's development status. Some may take offense at this. I do not offer explanations about why the West generally is at a more advanced economic stage of development than is Asia—how many Asian (ex-Japan, which for this I count as the West) countries are lending the West money? Rather, I simply state what is an unquestionable fact—a fact which reflects the present day situation. No doubt that situation will change, and I will be among the first to cheer. But let us not get ahead of ourselves and use imagination to extrapolate present-day gains into future potential. Emerging countries are so called for a reason, not least for their great potential, to be sure.

Consequently, the suggestion that China is or will be any time soon "number 1" in economic terms, surpassing the U.S., looks overdone. In 1991, the official estimate for GNP per capita was USD370. However, this was measured in domestic prices. The IMF subsequently revised this higher to take account of international price comparisons, using purchasing power parity, and came up with a figure of USD1,450. Larry Summers, then of the World Bank, now the current deputy secretary to the U.S. Treasury, forecast that China's total economic output would surpass that of the U.S. by no later than 2010. Since making this forecast, he and others have somewhat retreated from such aggressive predictions, with even the most bullish China watchers expecting China to take until at least 2020 to catch up with the U.S. In my view, even this is overoptimistic. In terms of total GNP, there is a case to make that China could match the U.S.; however, this will be a result, not simply of economic improvement, but of the sheer size of the Chinese population. China, let us not forget, has around five times the population of the U.S. Measured in GNP per capita terms, however, a very different picture emerges. You don't have to go to New York or Beijing, Chicago, or Shanghai. Take a trip around the Midwest in the U.S., and then take a plane to Xinjiang or Xian or Wuhan and that different picture will be eminently clear. The likes of Beijing, Shanghai, and Shenzhen have grown by leaps and bounds in the last 5 years alone, but they are not in the same league as New York, Chicago, or San Francisco. China's leaders are rather more sanguine and realistic about all this than some Western forecasters, describing themselves as essentially a typical developing country and admitting that there is no possibility in the short term at least that China can catch up with the economic prosperity of the developed countries. Indeed, the official ninth 5-year plan (1995–2000) talks about the intention of making China economically successful by the first decade of the twenty-first century and into a "middle developed country" by the middle of the century. This would suggest that China would have the same economic might and influence as a relatively strong European country, in GNP per capita terms. Even this target is ambitious enough, but it is useful, as it puts the more aggressive prognostications in the context of the relative and persistent wealth disparity between China and the West.

It seems to me that there are three clear, possible scenarios when it comes to China. The first is that China's economy will continue to slow at an alarming rate, that the banking system's problems will continue to mount, that the currency will be devalued in 1999, and finally that any talk of China overtaking the West any time in the near future will shortly be consigned to the same dustbin as that of the idea of Asian economic supremacy. The second possibility is that China will somehow manage to revive itself from its present slump and that such talk of economic preeminence will only grow, until it becomes reality by one measure or another. Finally, there is the idea that China will continue to muddle through, maintaining a high though slowing level of economic growth while trying to tinker with the banking system and the SOEs, not seeking to advance too aggressively on this for fear of a social backlash, but still trying to maintain an underlying momentum. All three ideas will have profound consequences for the world, not only in economic terms but also potentially in social and political ones as well.

The first idea is potentially the most attractive to me, not least for the simple reason that it is completely contrarian. There is little question that most people saw China as unequivocally in the ascendancy in 1997, and some still stubbornly cling to this view in 1998—much as the survivor of a shipwreck seeks to cling to a life raft. Contrarianism, by itself, is of course insufficient reason to support an idea. Let us look at this view, that China will continue to slow down, that it will not be able to cope with the huge fundamental problems in the economy, and that this will be yet another devastating deflationary blow for world financial markets. It seems unquestionable that China's economic and political rise would not have occurred, or certainly not to anywhere near the same degree, were it not for the persona of the late paramount leader Deng Xiaoping. This is stating the obvious. It was Deng who began the reform process. It was Deng who fought off the attempts by the leftists to handicap or even reverse the bolder, more progressive reforms that sought to roll back the economic predominance of the state. And finally, it was Deng who conducted the "*nanxun*," seeking to accelerate the reform process in the south which had traditionally been a mercantilist region and was thus fertile ground for plowing. Without Deng's leadership, forged without question on the anvil of the Long March, much of this would not have happened. With Deng gone, the argument could be made that factionalism could return, stifling the reform process. I, myself, would not support this particular idea. For one thing, Deng successfully defeated the leftists and managed to bind together several factions of varying allegiance to the reforms into a cohesive and predominant grouping. The head of that is his successor, Jiang Zemin, who has already proved himself an extremely skillful and able leader. Jiang, through his declaration that the PLA must get out of commercial activities, has also disproved the suggestion that his lack of military experience would be his downfall. Someone who feels confident enough to start pushing around the PLA and get away with it clearly does not have a problem with lack of experience. Nevertheless, the unifying force of Deng Xiaoping is gone and that leads to at least the potential for renewed factionalism.

On the economic side, the arguments that anticipate a continued slowdown were put forward in detail in Chapter 2. However, it is useful to summarize them again here and put them in the context of their likely consequences to the global economy. China, for one thing, suffers from massive overcapacity relative to demand in everything from cars to foodstuffs (China has had record harvests for 3 years, forcing food prices lower). This, and the renminbi's REER overvaluation, is causing deflation, which is hurting asset values across the board, in terms of both hard and financial assets. China's SOEs, faced with tighter credit conditions as the PBOC tries to restructure the financial system and make it more efficient, and also faced with slowing domestic demand, are experiencing mounting losses. The PBOC has responded by encouraging the state banks to renew lending to loss-making SOEs. However, this puts further strain on an already bankrupt banking system. Those SOEs that are continuing the restructuring process are putting more and more people out of work, causing economic pain and the growing potential for a major social backlash. If they don't restructure or slow the process down, however, they will represent an increasing burden on the state budget. In more "big-picture" terms, China has a burgeoning population (some economists say it is excessive relative to resources by around 400 million people), rising worker discontent, and diminishing agricultural resources due to environmental pollution and the growth of cities across the country. Growing regional wealth disparities, rampant corruption, and rising political influence at the provincial level are all arguments that support a dire scenario in China. Indeed, in its history, whenever the center has ceded significant power to the provinces, particularly with regard to tax raising and other forms of monetary and political dominance, the result has usually been the country breaking up into warring factions and mini states. From a leftist point of view, almost every ill that China suffered from before the liberation in 1949 is reemerging today. Finally, with China's economy already slowing, the Asian crisis is a body blow to an already staggering economic pugilist.

Supposing this view came true, what would it mean for the world as a whole? The first issue to look at would be that of the continuing decline in Chinese domestic demand. China remains the emerging markets' largest recipient of FDI, second only to the U.S. in the world as a whole. FDI in the first half of 1998 was USD20.6 billion, down 1.5% year-on-year. While still a substantial amount—many countries would love to have this amount of FDI—the trend is clearly turning bearish. Overcapacity in China suggests that new FDI will achieve lower returns going forward, which will affect the growing proportion of FDI aimed at tapping the domestic Chinese market. FDI targeted for other markets with manufacturing plants in China now finds tougher price competition in the ASEAN as a result of the Asian devaluations. A continued slowdown in China would of necessity mean a continued declining trend in FDI. Indeed, we could see a reversal of FDI—i.e., factories being dismantled and moved elsewhere—for the first time since the beginning of the reform process. The bottom line would be greatly diminished profit potential in China for foreign companies, both perceived and real. Foreign companies with exposure to China would thus be rerated by the international markets to take account of this.

If China devalues its currency (remember that it has quite a track record of keeping the value of its currency steady, only to devalue it by 30–40% for a specific economic purpose), this will also have a profound effect on world markets. There is now little question that the Asian currency devaluations have had a significant— an increasing—negative effect on world asset market valuations. These devaluations amounted to a sizable deflationary impulse in world markets and economies. Initially, economists said that since trade with Asia amounted to only a small amount of U.S. GDP (total trade being only around 12% in any case), any impact from Asian devaluations would have minimal effect on growth. Sadly, such a view was decidedly misplaced. As I said at the time, in *Asia Falling,* a friend of a friend bought a brand new Korean car for USD2,000, straight off the factory floor. If enough of those cars reached the U.S., U.S. automakers were in trouble. In this type of case, it is not so much whether people like a specific brand or not, but whether a sufficient amount of people—however small on a relative basis—buy that product (in this case, the Korean car) to change the domestic pricing mechanism, forcing prices lower.

As a result of the devaluations, Asian countries have exported deflation to the U.S. and Europe. The effect of this is substantially greater than the simple trade data might suggest. One can compare it with the process of diffusion in science, where molecules hit each other, spreading the effect of a chemical process throughout a widening area. This exported deflation has two main effects—forcing the trade deficits with Asia to expand substantially and forcing domestic prices lower for a wide variety of product classes. Regarding the trade side, note that as of the end of the year, the U.S. trade deficit with the Asian NICs (newly industrialized countries), such as Singapore, Taiwan, Korea, and Hong Kong, was at its highest level for a decade.

Meanwhile, import prices continue to decline, forcing domestic manufacturers to cut their prices and their cost base as a whole, resulting in price-cutting wars across a whole variety of sectors. While consumers may benefit from this, manufacturers and retailers no doubt see things differently. After all, it is their margins that are being cut. Bearing in mind that the U.S.-China trade deficit is the largest with any single country (before any sort of a devaluation), a devaluation of the renminbi would have extremely serious consequences. As we have seen with the cases of the ASEAN and North Asian currency devaluations, it is not merely a case of the simple percentage of trade that those countries have with the West, but also the proportion of the Western economies that compete with those products that are imported from Asia. Needless to say, the latter is significantly larger than that of direct trade between the two countries.

Not only would a Chinese devaluation cause a further significant deflationary impulse to hit the global economy and financial system, but in the present treacherous and uncertain financial market conditions it would probably also result in a further wave of competitive devaluations among the other Asian currencies. While the outcome of this would be to cut into the price and export benefits China had gained from the initial devaluation, in terms of the global economy it would be devastating. U.S. and European companies would have to compete with this new ultralow Asian pricing mechanism. Otherwise many that did not have a clear technology advantage that might offset adverse price movements would be priced out of the market. Emerging markets around the world would fall, as positions were liquidated in other markets to offset renewed losses in Asia. In addition, the suspicion would grow that Latin American and East European currencies would also have to be devalued, either out of necessity to compete with Asia and now China or simply in the wake of a series of currency devaluations around the globe.

In the event of a China devaluation any time soon, the U.S. trade deficit, already at record levels by the end of 1998 to return to that subject, would balloon to hitherto unheard of levels, even in comparison to the days when the U.S. and Japan practically conducted a trade war with each other (1993–1994). Aside from having a likely significant deflationary effect on the U.S. economy, this would put serious downward pressure on the dollar's exchange rate value. While economists cite the supposed "new economy" of high growth with low inflation as being behind the success of both the U.S. asset markets and the dollar's value, in truth it is more a case of substantial inward capital inflows that more than offset the significant and increasing current account deficit. It is a well-known—and no doubt well-worn—argument that U.S. citizens' savings are insufficient relative to consumption. In order to offset this, capital inflows have to be attracted. The balancing of the U.S. budget and productivity improvements have gone a long way to achieving this, particularly the former. Yet how different is this from the supposed "hot money" argument of old which was supposed to be behind the Asian currency devaluations. Granted, there are significant differences, not least of which is the fact that in a time of global financial market turmoil, the U.S. is now considered a safe haven. However, it remains the case that the dollar is supported by capital rather than trade flows. The former is much easier to reverse than the latter. In short, in the present difficult and unsteady financial conditions, a devaluation of the Chinese renminbi would seriously hurt global economies and as a result global financial asset markets. We are already hearing the political backlash resulting from the Asian devaluations, both in the U.S. and in Asia, in the form of increasing cries for reregulation rather than deregulation and calls for the imposition of trade and capital controls to limit the negative consequences on a domestic level of market disruptions. Just think what would happen if China devalued any time soon, while the Asian crisis was still ongoing. The result would be global market chaos, not simply or even mainly because of the size of China's economy but because of the timing and the fact that global markets are already in a jittery mood following the Asian devaluations.

Of course, China's leaders know all this. As I said in Chapter 5, they have gained so much international prestige by holding the line on the renminbi, they are not likely to let it go any time soon. That said, the risk remains that once the worst effects of the Asian crisis are over, by the middle of 1999 they might seek to devalue in order to loosen their own economic straitjacket and inject just a modest amount of inflation into their economy in order to offset the deflationary impulses that are already prevalent there. In between, this scenario still holds to the view that China's economy continues to slow down, that the trade surplus continues to increase due to declining import growth—which will by itself cause a protectionist backlash on Capitol Hill—and that the strain on the financial system equally continues to grow.

The second scenario is not nearly so bearish. It suggests that the fiscal attempts to boost the economy, through increased fiscal expenditure in particular, will be successful in reviving domestic demand. China's fiscal expansion program should certainly not be underestimated. For a start, the authorities have sought to persuade state banks to start lending again, even to poor-quality credits. In addition, aside from the purely fiscal measures, they have issued RMB270 billion in domestic bonds with which to recapitalize the banking system (inadequate by itself to be sure, but certainly an excellent effort), and finally they are going to issue a further RMB100 billion in bonds to fund infrastructure projects including roads, railways, telecommunications, power stations, and also projects to repair the damage done by the flooding in central China.

If China succeeds in arresting the decline in GDP growth while simultaneously avoiding a banking crisis, first of all it will be a miracle, but also it will be a major positive for the global economy as a whole. On the one hand, it will be a relief to those companies that are nervously looking at their balance sheets and more specifically their cost bases, given the potential prospect of a global recession under the more bearish scenario, with a revival in Chinese domestic demand likely to substantially boost imports. On the other, it will contribute to overall global growth levels. In that environment, those who suggest that China not only is the next superpower but will be the predominant superpower in the twenty-first century will be seen to gain ground in the advancement of their argument. This is not to say that they will be right. Rather, the fundamental backing for their view will be seen to have increased. Whenever this has occurred, as in the late 1980s when Japan was in the ascendant, the result, at least in the U.S., has been considerable domestic concern. Given that the U.S. is of the view that it is not only the military defender of the free world, but also the political, democratic, and economic leader, any challenge to any one (or all) or those self-appointed titles is deemed a threat to the country itself. We have already seen instances of this, in the political and media hysteria in the U.S.—and the outrageously biased reporting in many cases—which has greeted the political and economic treatment of China. And this is in a time, let us not forget, when China is in a period of economic slowdown. What would happen if China were getting back on its feet? One can only shudder to think. Much like any imperial power in the past, the U.S. can only conceive of its global role in terms of dominance. Note that this is not to judge the issue one way or the other; this is merely to state facts. Either the U.S. runs the world, or it goes back into its shell and the world be damned! That is of course a horrendous generalization, but that is pretty much how the U.S. has seemed to treat the world since its very inception.

Indeed, to digress just a touch, there is a strong correlation between the revolutionaries of France, Russia, and the U.S., who all sought to persuade their neighbors of the "obvious" merits of their political arguments and when on occasion their neighbors did not succumb to these arguments, invaded them. While the U.S. is no longer willing to invade Mexico or Canada any time soon, some theoretical semblance of that belief in the inherent correctness of one's cause—and thus the incorrectness of anyone else's—lives on. No one else can be allowed to succeed, for that is tantamount to a threat, not only to the nation but to the nation's belief system. Some readers may view this with varying skepticism or even annoyance at the very suggestion—the nerve of it! But seeking a higher plain of objectivity, let us remember the hysterical reaction in the U.S. to the rise of Japan, and in its more modern form to that of China. The lesson one learns in the East, rightly or wrongly, is that the U.S. is prepared to play the game of capitalism only so long as it wins. When it starts to lose ground, then the rules of the game start to change. For instance, U.S. trade negotiators are happy (or at least they do not do anything about it) to ignore the fact that U.S. manufacturers charge vastly inflated prices abroad for some products, despite the fact that nothing forces them to and they could wipe out the competition if they chose to undercut them, and yet get hugely upset when lower prices appear in the U.S. market, particularly from foreign manufacturers.

Thus, while an economic rebound in China would help global growth, it could also add to the concerns of those within the U.S. and Europe as well (though Europe finds it difficult to mobilize itself for its own causes, let alone against any external threat), who fret about losing global economic predominance. Of course, at the corporate level, such concerns would be relegated by the prospects for tapping ever more into what would be the world's largest consumer market. Already, some U.S. companies sell more of their products in China than they do in the U.S. If China did manage to rebound and heal itself, this process could only accelerate. Unlike in the first scenario, companies with such exposure to the China market would be rerated higher, while those without such exposure would lose out on a relative basis. FDI into China would also rebound. China, after all, has the world's largest workforce. It also has one of the world's cheapest and most productive workforces. Highly skilled by emerging market standards, its workforce would be a major positive for many corporate bottom lines, just so long as the iron rice bowl benefits continued to be reduced.

Finally, there is the third scenario, the one where China continues to muddle through, continuing to see lesser growth on a year-on-year basis but managing to avoid either economic or financial crises, while at the same time seeking to gradually reform and restructure both its SOEs and its financial system. This would indeed be a fine balancing act, though not out of character with the type and the quality of economic progress that China has made since the very start of the reform process. If it succeeded, it would help further in the stabilization process of Asian markets and currencies. While the massive turnaround in current account balances witnessed since the start of the Asian crisis has been a key factor in the rebound in Asian assets and exchange rates, the fact that the renminbi has not devalued and that China's government is seeking to stabilize the domestic economic situation has in turn helped stabilize Asia, albeit at a very depressed level. The "muddle-through" scenario, however, while in line with the "feeling for stones underfoot while crossing the river" approach that has predominated in Chinese reform thinking, could lead to domestic problems, which in turn could have international financial and economic consequences. This will be dealt with in greater detail in the next two chapters. Suffice it to summarize here the concerned arguments.

There is a case to be made which suggests that China can no longer afford the gradualist approach that has characterized the reform process to date, that China is fast running out of time.

This view suggests that as time passes, the reforms of the banking system are insufficient to offset the gradual deterioration in asset quality. This in turn either reduces lending, thus causing the deterioration in the economy to increase, or causes the authorities to print money, which leads to inflation and puts increasing pressure on the currency's exchange rate value. China can only offset this by putting an increasing amount of people out of work within the banking system, which if they are to survive will have to be paid, if only a minimal allowance. This will, either way, hurt the budget. Either China reforms its banking system now and risks serious financial, economic, and social upheaval, or it allows the banking system to continue to deteriorate—the speed of its reforms inadequate relative to the speed of the banking system's deterioration—thus causing the economy to continue to slow and stagnate and storing up a financial and economic crisis of one kind or another. On past performance, China is likely to progress slowly. Yet if this argument is right, that it no longer can afford the luxury of going slowly, investors in China should beware.

Clearly, deciding between these various scenarios is a difficult business. For my part, I look at China and I expect it to seek the third scenario, reforming only so far as it does not threaten the delicate social and economic balance that prevails, yet not fast enough to offset or reduce potential economic and financial threats down the road. China's leaders, as we shall see in the next chapter, are indeed gifted. However, the challenges that they face are so monumental as to be too much for almost anyone to handle. If this third scenario is the path taken, what does it mean for the world? Well, those looking for or fearing a near-term devaluation of the renminbi should be able to breathe a sigh of relief, which should in turn cause similar relief in world asset markets—though the latter are likely to have enough to fret about for some time given the Asian, Russian, and Latin American devaluations. In addition, it is likely to give Asian economies and asset markets further breathing room to try and find a floor. That said, it will probably mean that import demand will not pick up to any significant degree any time soon. Also, consumption, while stabilizing, will remain muted, relative to early 1990s levels. Thus this should depress further both imports and FDI—most of which comes from Asia—into China. Further out, another of the many lessons of the Asian crisis is surely that trying to prop up the economy and the financial system in order to avoid a near-term crisis simply results in a more serious crisis further down the road. Just when Asian economies may think it is safe to go back in the water, they are likely to get bitten by China's financial and economic crisis. Given the size of China, in terms of not only its population, but the importance of its military, domestic economy, and trade balance within the global system, the world cannot afford a China crisis, for it would have devastating results. Indeed, an economic crisis in China, if history is anything to go by, could have widespread social and even political repercussions, threatening the very fabric of the country itself and sending shock waves around the world. Granted, this is somewhat of a doomsday scenario. But anyone who thinks that China is inherently a stable place has not picked up a single history book.

Whatever the case, whichever of the three suggested scenarios actually takes place, one thing is certain—China's growing influence in the world is set only to continue to increase. Indeed, history tells us that the last 200 years, whereby China was dismembered by imperialist adventurers, were but an aberration in an otherwise powerful, even dominant, past. That said, the embarrassment of the last 200 years for China's leaders cannot simply be wiped clean. Wrongs, however long ago, have to be addressed. A lesson of the past is that the sovereignty of the motherland must remain inviolate, that no territory, however small, however seemingly inconsequential, can be ceded and that those taken in the past must—and will—be returned. The return of Hong Kong, just as much as China's economic successes, has done much to restore national pride. It was interesting to note that the celebrations of the handover event were far more joyous north of the border between Hong Kong and the mainland than in Hong Kong itself! This is a positive thing, for the world cannot afford an insecure China, nor an economically weak one. Maintaining national sovereignty is nonnegotiable for China, and that means regaining territories lost, whether in the more obvious case of Taiwan or with regard to sea lanes and small islands in the South China Sea. Indeed, the area that China claims in the South China Sea would not coincidentally protect the whole of China's oil and other commodity imports that pass through those waters.

For such a huge nation, China is in reality an exceptionally insecure state, a reflection of past humiliations. It is with this in mind that Western nations should examine what is perceived by some to be overt Chinese expansionism. When some elements within China call the U.S. "the enemy," they do not necessarily mean this in an overtly aggressive and militaristic fashion. China has no desire whatsoever to invade other Asian countries or start wars (with the obvious exception of Taiwan, if it comes to it). Such comments are surely the reflection of those more defensive-minded individuals responding to what they perceive as an attempt by the U.S. to "contain" China—memories of the U.S. containment policy with regard to the Soviet Union—and possibly even to seek to exploit weaknesses within China. That is the way it is seen by some in Beijing. It starts with the constant suspicion that the U.S. and other Western powers will try to divide the motherland by not letting go of Taiwan, and it goes on to consider the possibility that the U.S. could seek to use other Asian nations for the purpose of damaging Chinese interests and ensuring China stays weak and vulnerable. To the U.S., this may seem bizarre, not to say paranoid, but it should be understood in its historical context.

In general, Beijing does not accept the rules of the past, whereby the U.S., after the collapse of the Soviet Union, is the only superpower left and effectively dominates the world for good or ill. China's history in the last 200 years of being dominated and humiliated by the so-called "Great Powers" indeed dictates that it cannot accept such a geopolitical and strategic framework. There is no reason why it should. China has in the past two decades "stood up" to a far greater degree than even Mao meant when he said those immortal words on the podium of the Tiananmen.

With economic success, even measured in relative and historical rather than very recent terms (which would take account of the recent slowdown), should come increased political and strategic influence. This is already the case in a number of ways, most notably with China being on the UN Security Council. However, such influence is set to continue to grow.

There are those in the U.S., notably two authors of a book that described the coming clash with China, who view this as deeply alarming. The U.S., according to this view, is entirely benign and benevolent, while China is seeking regional and even global domination. Such a view seems decidedly skewed. Faced with the prospect of trying to maintain an exceptionally fine balance of power and influence at home, what country has sought to build an empire abroad? Historically, it is only when a country has been assured at home that it has sought to increase its influence elsewhere—only, in every case, to overextend itself. China, needless to say, feels far from assured at home. While the Party rules with assurance and even severity in Beijing, some of the provinces seek to go their own way. China has one of the longest borders in the world with a historical foe, Russia. There remain independence movements in Tibet and Xinjiang, despite all efforts to crush these—the implicit danger to Beijing being that if it lets one go, a hundred will rise up and demand the same. With the maintenance of national sovereignty being paramount, there is no question of giving up Chinese sovereign territory, whatever the cost—and in the case of Tibet, the cost to local Tibetans has been on a genocidal scale. China is seeking to maintain its own territory, not expand into other people's. It has enough trouble at home without wanting other people's as well! Historically, China has oscillated between expansion and contraction within what it conceives as its historical boundaries. U.S. political hawks see China as seeking to expand and dominate Asia, by force or otherwise. Chinese hawks see the U.S. trying to contain and even strangle China's reemergence on the world scene. This is the blind leading the blind—a world in which the rule of an eye for an eye means that everyone ends up being blind! Nothing is solved by such views and rhetoric. And furthermore great harm is done, for lack of knowledge leads to insecurity, insecurity to fear, and fear to aggression.

In Asia at the very least, there is no reason why China should not achieve a greater and more constructive role. Indeed, in the past couple of years it has done exactly that. China's leaders have to a certain extent used the Asian crisis to their benefit, seeking to portray themselves as a major source of regional stability and global influence with the Western powers. The trick for the Western powers is not to seek to contain China but to ensure that there remains a balance in the region, and that the balance is understood and respected both by the West and by China. Given its rapid economic growth of the past two decades, China seeks not only to lift its position in the international hierarchy, but essentially to achieve a new balance of power. Such an arrangement could be extremely constructive and positive for the world as a whole, not just in economic terms. This is particularly true when one considers the alternative, which is an isolated, insecure, angry China, always focusing on past grievances and thus vulnerable to domestic hotheads who seek to right the wrongs of the past through aggressive action.

A relatively senior Chinese government official said following the 1996 incident with Taiwan, in which the U.S. was seen to intervene with the deployment of an aircraft carrier, that if the U.S. saw China as an ally, then it would get an ally, and if the U.S. saw China as an enemy, that is what it would get. It is important for the U.S. and the West as a whole to understand that China does not seek to dominate. Instead, it seeks better and more respectful arrangements according to Chinese interests and capabilities. Its focus is largely on the development of "comprehensive national power," or "*zonghe guoli.*"[1] Official definitions of this concept refer to the totality of national economic, military, and political power in a given period, reflecting the level of national development within the international system. More specifically, the aims of comprehensive national power can be summarized in the need to protect Chinese sovereign territory and national interests, the need to protect the country's socialist system (however unsocialist it is in practice), the ability of China to defend itself militarily, and finally the capacity to both raise China's international status to a more suitable level (relative to national self-worth) and continue to drive forward the economic restructuring and reform process. It should be immediately obvious that these aims do not focus or even touch on the possibility of territorial expansion. Indeed, the concept of the comprehensive national power dictates that expansion would represent a destabilizing influence that could not be tolerated.

William Overholt, in his excellent and groundbreaking work, *The Rise of China,* called China the next economic superpower. To a certain extent this is already true, if measured in population, military, foreign trade, or total GDP terms. In the recent past, China's economic might was limited to cheap consumer goods, just as was the case in Japan after its initial recovery phase following the devastation of World War II. This is no longer the case, though China is not yet synonymous with manufacturing quality the way Japan has become. No doubt, it will only be a matter of time before this situation also changes, but when we speak of time we are talking decades. China is having an increasing influence on the world's commodity markets. Having been a net oil exporter for one thing, China is now a net importer of oil because domestic demand has outstripped China's current ability to tap existing domestic oil fields. China is also a regular and significant buyer of soft commodities. Its presence in the metals markets also continues to rise. In terms of global wages, there is an argument to be made that, given the widening international trading system, the inclusion of China's workforce is acting as a natural depressant on price pressures—whether in terms of wage "prices" or consumer or asset prices—around the world. This looks to be an attractive idea on balance and indeed has its merits. However, to blame China alone for this would seem to be clearly overdoing it. A major reason we are seeing disinflationary and even deflationary pressures in the global financial and economic system is the fact that on a global scale the world is suffering from significant overcapacity. Simply put, the opening up of economies for the purpose of creating trading systems as a precursor to a global trading system has resulted in significant increases in transnational competition and productivity. Eventually, relative to demand, there is an excess of productivity, which in terms of prices is the nail in the coffin.

This is of course not to say that the 600 million or so Chinese workers are not having an effect. Clearly, they are in terms of intra-Asian competition for third markets such as the U.S. and Europe. In jittery market and economic conditions, the cries of those who in any case hold traditionally protectionist views will no doubt grow more obvious and shrill. These are to be heard all over the world, from Malaysia to Continental Europe and Capitol Hill. In terms of China, the argument in the U.S. will be made (it has already started) that China is in effect stealing jobs from the U.S. and that "something" should be done about it. Of course, to any non-U.S. citizen, this draws one back to the idea predominant in the U.S. that only the U.S. is allowed to win the game of capitalism. In addition, however, it is an erroneous argument since Chinese technology in its present state can in no way compete with that of the U.S. Lower technology and more labor-intensive industries are indeed migrating to cheaper parts of the world—and U.S. shareholders are cheering them for doing this given that the process produces better earnings results (as long as work skills are similar). If China "stole" (a misnomer in any case since the whole point of the exercise is competition) jobs from anyone, it was from its Asian counterparts in the ASEAN and North Asia. Indeed, this was a part cause of the Asian currency crisis.

Beijing has not proved to be the massive market for U.S. exports that was once hoped. This is due to the fact that China is experiencing an economic slowdown. In addition, China remains a developing rather than a developed country. Having just managed to regain a sense of national dignity and prestige following past humiliations due to imperialists, the last thing China will do now is allow Western businesses to dominate China's markets, stifling the ability of Chinese companies to emerge and grow and replacing the exploitation of the past with merely a more modern and technology-advanced version. The West does not see it this way, but then the U.S. at least has not experienced what China went through. Beijing will thus continue to place an emphasis on quid pro quo, for allowing Western companies to expand in China in return for providing technological help to Chinese companies to allow them to grow too.

From the vantage point of Washington—or Detroit or Pittsburgh—this may seem unfair. Yet China does not have to allow Western companies in at all. The alternative would be mutual trade sanctions where the result would be a huge backlash in the U.S. against higher prices and product shortages. China was seen to be the next stage of the "great game," played out along economic rather than political or strategic lines, where the supposed Great Powers battled for influence and power. Needless to say, China has no intention of allowing this to happen since the implied relationship is one of dependence and subservience on China's part, a relationship that is no longer valid or tolerable to Beijing and rightly so. That said, competition for the Chinese consumer market remains the most important challenge for Western multinationals in the twenty-first century—with the caveat that those who enter should tread carefully! Many are the pitfalls and the costs, and indeed of late some have viewed these costs as being too prohibitive. What is certain is that there is no "easy money" to be made in China, at least not for foreigners, and that is exactly the way Beijing wants it. Companies have to bring something to the table with which to trade in order to gain access, and they should be warned that the Chinese have always been master traders. As Singapore Senior Minister Lee Kwan Yew is supposed to have said, "China is not only just another player, but the biggest player in the history of man." The point of this book is that it isn't the biggest player quite yet and will not be for some time, but it is already a substantial player and one that has to increasingly be taken account of.

That said, as mentioned before, one should put this in perspective. China is not even in the same league as those in the West when one considers the so-called "information economy" attributed to the U.S. and which Europe is now seeking to achieve. There is still widespread poverty in Beijing, let alone in the countryside where malnutrition and disease remain important fundamental problems. In addition, China's economy, in contrast to the massive achievements of the past two decades, continues to slow down. In other words, the rate at which China is catching up with the West is itself slowing down. In addition to its many advantages and gains, China continues to have many structural and fundamental weaknesses that have yet to be fully or even partially addressed. It is to these weaknesses and the ability of China's various leaders to address them that we turn to next.

8

Leaders and Fundamentals — Strategies for Coping

DESPITE THE ECONOMIC successes of the past two decades and despite still high levels of growth, there is little question that China's present economic situation is extremely serious. China may be "the biggest player in the history of man," but its fundamental and structural problems are also among the biggest faced by any country. Clearly, before we go into an overview of the main fundamental strengths and weaknesses of the Chinese economy, not merely in terms of the macroeconomic and microeconomic issues but with regard to the "big picture" for China as a whole and what strategies can be used to turn the situation around, it is necessary first to have a look at the emerging group of leaders in China whose responsibility it is to achieve this. These are men (women as yet play a minimal role in the upper echelons of government despite the supposedly egalitarian nature of the PRC) who for the most part have little in common with the previous generation who had war experience. Nevertheless they lived through the insanity of the Cultural Revolution and are determined to ensure that such chaos—some would say evil—never reoccurs. Some, not all by any means, are the progeny of powerful ministers and leaders of the previous generation, benefiting as a result from the influence of their fathers. Others have done it the hard way, simply by being better at their job than most and gaining favor with those in influence. Most are from cities rather than the countryside, in stark contrast to Mao and his acolytes.

First and foremost, of course, there is Jiang Zemin. Aged 72, Jiang holds the three key state titles of power—general secretary of the Chinese Communist Party, chairman of the Central Military Commission, and state president. Whereas Deng Xiaoping sought to distance himself from such titles, which could both limit his power and attract and focus attacks on himself, Jiang has gone the other way, seeking first to eliminate pockets of opposition and then to unify the central levels of power under himself. Going into the 15th Party Congress in 1997, Jiang was clearly Deng's favored successor but had yet to prove himself. The ruthless and skillful way he eliminated his main rival, Qiao Shi, not only removing him from his post as chairman of the National People's Congress, but also from the Politburo Standing Committee, showed, however, that those who had seen Jiang as somewhat of a dull and even blundering statist politician were clearly underestimating him. Jiang went into the Party Congress the favored son, yet with powerful rivals. He emerged as the unquestioned and sole leader. The new, more media-friendly Jiang is verging on the charismatic and is clearly now more at ease with life than when he was first groomed for the post from 1995 on. He is seen now as being pro-market reform and even pro-political reform in some quarters after his stunning comment during the handover proceedings in Hong Kong that the day would come when Hong Kong would have universal suffrage. Yet he is in truth the ultimate pragmatist. In the early 1990s, he was much more of a hard-liner, not coincidentally when the hard-liners still had strong influence, consorting with Li Peng and even Chen Yun. He changed when the leftists were soundly and unequivocally defeated, using an anticorruption drive as his mode of bridging the gap between the left and the "right." He was the third successor named by Deng and the only one to stay the course after Hu Yaobang and Zhao Ziyang fell by the wayside, apparently demonstrating insufficient ability, as seen by Deng, to balance the need to maintain the Party's dominant position with the need to continue to push forward the reform process.

"Balance" is a key word that comes to mind when examining Jiang Zemin. In the West, he would be called the consummate politician. It is no surprise that at Clinton's visit to Beijing in 1998, the U.S. president said of Jiang that he was the right man at the right time for China. This was not simple rhetoric. Jiang and Bill Clinton have more in common than either might like to think. They both know the need to take control of the center in order to command the wings—and in China, Jiang is the center. And they both have shown significant finesse in dealing with various factions, pairing one off with another. The main similarity, however, is that they are both extremely adept at taking good ideas from their opponents and using those ideas against them. In the past Jiang was undoubtedly a hard-liner. Yet now he is reputed to have sought a more moderate line with the students in Shanghai who took to the streets in June 1989 in support of their comrades in Tiananmen. Indeed, he is supposed to have mollified them personally by reading from Lincoln's Gettysburg Address. It is Jiang who is now remembered as trying to take the middle road during those tragic days, rightly or wrongly.

Whatever the truth of the matter, such images do not appear by accident. It was Jiang who is credited with the term "socialist market economy," though it is thought to have been Deng's idea and most probably was. Deng and Jiang no doubt also saw themselves in each other, particularly with regard to their political opportunism and ruthlessness. What Jiang did at the 15th Party Congress, in quietly eliminating his rivals as effective forces, was equally as impressive and clinical as Deng's demolition of the leftists and enforcement of his desired reforms at the 13th and 14th Congresses. Jiang is probably the right man at the right time because China's situation is very much in the balance and thus needs someone who is a master in creating and maintaining such balance. When Jiang first moved from Shanghai to Beijing in 1989, few China watchers, either internally or externally, gave him much chance of lasting the course in terms of achieving a prominent position on a national scale and certainly not as the successor to Deng. The first two men Deng had groomed for the job had after all been discarded, and Jiang was seen as an uninventive, if jovial, statist bureaucrat. He was seen as a lightweight, not someone one could ever mistake Deng for being. Comparisons were made with Hua Guofeng, Mao's chosen heir—albeit briefly—whom Deng effectively deposed. Even those who expected some degree of initial success out of Jiang viewed him as a transitional appointment, with a more serious candidate likely to step out of the shadows in a year or two.

All this surely demonstrates one of Jiang's key strengths, and perhaps the major reason why he was picked in the first place by Deng—stealth. Let others think you are funny, a fool; let others underestimate you and let down their guard. It is a game that Jiang has played brilliantly. Jiang was the first leader of the Party and the first state president not to have had active military experience. This was counted against him at the time, seen as a fatal flaw. His ability to create and deepen relations with the top echelons of the military was confirmed with the confidence that he displayed in announcing in July 1998 that PLA commercial activities would henceforth cease. No one who was not completely assured of total support from the PLA generals would have dared to attack PLA businesses. Following that announcement, the two generals on the Politburo Standing Committee indeed confirmed the need for the PLA to clean up its act, attacking the "black hats" who have apparently sullied the name of the PLA. This is not to say that we have seen the last of this particular issue. A great many vested interests have been and will be damaged by Jiang's order for the PLA and the armed police to close down their businesses (which produce exports of up to USD5 billion a year), and they could well decide to strike back to defend those interests. This is no doubt something upon which Jiang pondered long and hard before making the original decision, and upon which, equally clearly, he has made contingencies against. It is, however, part of a consistent theme for which even Jiang's detractors have acknowledged—his devotion to fighting corruption. This stems from Deng's belief that the greatest threat to the dominance of the Party came not from democratic movements or external threats but from internal corruption—which was indeed behind the defeat of the Guomindang in 1949. Senior leaders of the PLA support the effort to root out corruption, at least those who are not tied to it themselves. Meanwhile, the sentencing at the end of July of the former party secretary and mayor of Beijing, Chen Xitong, to 16 years imprisonment for corruption was greeted with jubilation. No doubt it was a coincidence that Chen had always been a political foe of Jiang. Consolidating his power base and making key alliances, while removing his enemies and the corrupt—the two sometimes overlapping—constitute the hallmark of Jiang's reign to date. The result has been total control.

Jiang rose to his position of complete and unquestioned dominance from his power base in Shanghai. Having gained a degree in electrical engineering, Jiang spent time at the Stalin Automobile Factory in Moscow before returning to Shanghai for further industrial experience. The latter proved an excellent springboard for entry into government. Jiang rose to mayor of Shanghai in 1985 and subsequently party secretary—and member of the Party Politburo. He has subsequently surrounded himself with former colleagues and subordinates from Shanghai, to the extent that his—and therefore the leading—faction is derided (quietly) as the "Shanghai Mafia." Foremost among these is Zhu Rongji. Great as China's problems are, if you had to bet on one person who could or would save the country from either stagnation or disaster, then it would have to be Zhu Rongji, the current prime minister and previous economic "czar," as he was termed in the Western media—which no doubt baffled their Chinese counterparts. Known as "the boss," *"Lao ban"* in Putonghua or *"Lopan"* in Cantonese (the "p" being pronounced as a "b"), Zhu has justifiably gained a reputation as a no-nonsense architect of industrial reform and restructuring. Zhu is someone who gets things done, the person who walks into a room and fires those who need to be fired, the person who makes enemies everywhere, but not so many as to derail the course of the reform process or his own career (for now!). Zhu is very much a "can-do" type of person, someone with whom U.S. industrialists and bankers can associate. He has a reputation for eliminating those people who get in the way, either of him or of reforms, and is roundly hated by provincial bureaucrats as a result. Aged 69, his most impressive achievement to date was in taming inflation through an austerity drive in 1994. His present main task, formidable as it is, is to turn around the SOEs, a challenge that most before him did not even seek to attempt, not necessarily for ideological but for purely practical reasons. His background bears strong similarities to that of Jiang, graduating also in electrical engineering from Qinghua University. In February 1988, he was named deputy party secretary in Shanghai under Jiang and then became mayor in April of that year. He replaced Jiang as Shanghai party secretary in June 1989 as Jiang himself got promoted. In 1991, he was made vice premier and moved to Beijing. Subsequently, he was appointed as head of Deng's financial and economic team the following year, led and carried out major tax reform, currency devaluation, and a fiscal austerity package in 1994, and is seen as having almost single-handedly defeated inflation. In hindsight, one could argue that he actually did too good a job, pushing the headline CPI rate from above 20% to negative on a monthly basis in 1998.

Zhu replaced Li Peng as prime minister in March 1998. In theory, this would have marked a radical departure both in economic policy since Li Peng remains more of a hard-liner and in a purely economic sense where a key policy was to stamp down on inflation. However, with Deng's guidance, the policies that Zhu had advocated had gradually gained in the ascendance in any case. Like Jiang, he is also a pragmatist when needed. It was Zhu who led the drive to cut off wasteful lending from the state banks to the SOEs, and yet it is also believed to have been Zhu who rescinded that order when the apparent results were an explosion in the level of unemployment. Politically, it has always been hard to nail him down, simply because he focused on economics and driving the economy, on practical rather than theoretical matters. Sometimes such an approach proved costly, as in the 1957–1958 anti-rightist movement when he was purged and persecuted. Like the Cultural Revolution itself, this was no doubt a sobering experience, not only from a purely personal and emotional perspective, but from the point of view that reforms were needed, but stability was needed above all. Zhu's style can be encapsulated in the example of his first taking the reigns of economic power in 1993, despite having no major power base in the capital. On doing so, one of his first acts was to fire the head of the central bank and take over day-to-day operations himself in order to ensure that credit growth was forced down. Zhu has been the main force behind the drive to restructure the banking system itself. Still he too has pulled up short when needed—the need being to ensure that the banking system does not go under precisely because of the reforms!

Going forward, his challenges are many and daunting: to stop deflation but to continue the restructuring process, to limit unemployment growth so as to limit any social backlash and yet also to continue the process of making Chinese SOEs more efficient (most of them could hardly be less), to enforce a profit-based lending criterion for the state banks and yet to ensure that the SOEs do not go under en masse for lack of funding. It is an unenviable task, and if something major goes wrong, there is little doubt that Zhu and Zhu alone will get blamed for the fallout. Jiang and Zhu were the heads of the Shanghai faction of the Party before they rose to greater things, and indeed before the faction itself merged and absorbed other factions in Beijing in such a way as to dominate. As influential as they have been and are, they clearly could not have risen to this status without a retinue of supporters and subordinates, many of whom were also part of that Shanghai faction and who did the real work while they took the honors. What became the "mainstream faction" was really a merger of unequals—the Shanghai faction absorbing the pro-Soviet faction under the likes of Li Peng and those technocrats nimble enough in the liberal faction of Hu Yaobang and Zhao Ziyang to change their colors to shades of a more pragmatic and less idealist approach, under the banner of Zhu. The focus of Zhu's technocrats is unquestioned. It is to liberalize the market further. The only questions are how much and how fast, not if. "If" is no longer even in the equation. The last point to note about Zhu is that he shares with Jiang a deep and passionate dislike of corruption. There can be little question that he played a leading role in persuading Jiang of the need to free up unproductive elements of the economy over which the PLA exercised control such as the rail lines, factories, infrastructure projects, port facilities, and property. In this case, the need to make the economy more efficient and the need to stamp out corruption coincided.

It was expected by some that Jiang would feel uneasy, even insecure and defensive, at the rise of Zhu. However, those who suggested this ignored the way the partnership between the two had formed and consolidated in the early years as mayor and party secretary. Jiang, if anything, has displayed a growing ease and trust with his prime minister. The two understand and by all accounts respect each other. Granted, to a large extent, that understanding is based on pragmatism—the pragmatism of a kind that necessitates Zhu take the fall if the economy does not perk up. However, Zhu does not seem the sort who would much care about such trivialities. Unlike Jiang, or Deng before him, it is thought that Zhu has no wish to be the paramount leader. Indeed, several years ago, he muttered that he would be quite happy to pack it all in and go back to the university to lecture. Jiang and Zhu, together, head up the Shanghai faction, dominating with an emphasis on pragmatism and business. They are part of the new, modern, internationally oriented technocracy. This is not to say that they are Western-style democrats, for that is not the case. They do, however, see China's interests in the future—that is to say, the interests of the government they lead—as being synonymous with greater political as well as economic deregulation. Being pragmatists, they realize that an authoritarian state apparatus cannot coexist forever with a freewheeling economy, even a "socialist market economy" at that! If the Party is to continue to dominate going forward, it will have to create political escape valves for the rising political and social aspirations created as a result of economic advancement, particularly among the new economic elite.

A classic example of both a member of the Shanghai faction and also a Zhu supporter is Li Lanqing, China's vice premier, who succeeded Zhu to this post in March 1998 when Zhu himself was promoted to the post of premier. Fluent in English and Russian, Li, who is 65, has a strong background in domestic and international trade issues. Notably, he studied business management at Shanghai's Fudan University. Interestingly, while Zhu has recently adopted a reserved stance toward dealing with the international press, Li and a few other hand-picked men have taken up the task of explaining China's policy to an international audience. Li is well qualified to do this and is at ease, unlike some of his colleagues, in matters of international relations. He was seen a pro-liberal reformer, in the mold of—if not an actual follower of—Hu Yaobang, but has made the shift to the Jiang/Zhu faction seamlessly. Two men directly under him are well worth noting. The first, Wu Bangguo, a vice premier, is well versed in industrial matters—a common theme of many of those who have come to serve under Zhu in some capacity. In particular his experience in managing the reforms of the SOEs makes his knowledge and experience crucial to the Zhu government. No problem is of greater importance to the Chinese economy than the restructuring of the SOEs. Alongside Wu is Wen Jiabao, also a vice premier. Wen, a 55-year-old technocrat, the youngest of the four vice premiers, manages agriculture and finance under Zhu. Next, there is Sheng Guareng, the minister for the State Economic and Trade Commission, Zhu's old department. Sheng also has a strong industrial background, having been the head of the China petrochemical group. His role is largely to extend the government's role in macroeconomic management, while at the same time reducing its influence at a microeconomic level, allowing the economy at that level to function on its own, indeed demanding that it does so and thus effectively taking away the state's presence in everyday life.

A true protégé of Zhu is Lou Jiwei, vice minister in the Ministry of Finance. Previously one of the economists under Zhao Ziyang who helped create and orchestrate the initial reform process in the 1980s, Lou managed to escape being purged as a result of the dismissal of Zhao, and in the post of head of the State Commission on Restructuring the Economy he came to the attention of Zhu. Another Zhu protégé is Li Jiangje, 48 years old, who as a former personal secretary to Zhu is truly a rising star in the new technocracy under Zhu. Previously in the State Office for Restructuring the Economy, he is attending the Party School in Zhongnanhai, usually a precursor for high appointment. Li is apparently well versed in Western financial market theory and does his own economic research on the Internet. Then, of course, there is Dai Xianglong, the current governor of the People's Bank of China. Dai has been in banking all his career, which despite the appalling state of the banking system in China is undoubtedly a good thing. No one is more qualified to know just how appalling it really is than Dai. The former head of the Bank of Communications—a Shanghai-based commercial bank—Dai was tapped by Zhu to replace him as head of PBOC during the 1993–1994 financial reforms that sought to deal with the problem that continues to plague the Chinese banking system, namely "triangular debt." Though Dai appears sometimes ill at ease with the depth of international media attention and curiosity with regard to China's economy, he handles himself with apparent ease at international press conferences. Indeed, it is interesting to note how well the Chinese financial and economic authorities have adapted to the routine of international financial news coverage. They deftly use it to their advantage, as in the case in 1998 when a number of Chinese officials, seemingly independently but of course not so, hinted that China was experiencing great pain as a result of its pledge to hold the renminbi stable and might have to devalue its currency if the U.S. and Japan did not do something about excessive yen weakness. The PBOC, under Dai, would always deny such talk, saying that China would solemnly uphold its pledge, whatever the actions of lesser responsible nations. This act of "good cop, bad cop" was highly effective in sending a message to Washington and Tokyo and was undoubtedly a factor in the June 1998 intervention by the Federal Reserve and the Bank of Japan (BoJ) to sell USD-JPY. Under Dai, the PBOC has gradually become more open, though this has of course to be seen in relative terms. It has certainly adopted a more international profile and regularly communicates with Western central banks regarding market and economic developments. Indeed, such has the profile of the PBOC changed in recent years, that there was widespread speculation in the media that the PBOC might join the Fed and the BoJ in their intervention effort to defend the yen, though all sides denied the possibility. Needless to say, not that long ago, such a concept would have been unthinkable. The PBOC's more international profile, it is probably fair to say, has risen not only as a direct result of the efforts of its governor, but in line with the rise of China's economic presence on a global scale, particularly with regard to its foreign exchange reserves; they are now the second largest in the world at a stunning USD145 billion. Indeed, the PBOC, through its agent banks, is now a major player in the world's markets, seeking to achieve the best available returns in investment products for its reserves.

There has never been a more important time for careful management of China's foreign exchange system. In charge of that is Liu Fuxiang, director general of the State Administration of Foreign Exchange. Liu is China's foreign exchange regulator who replaced Wu Xiaoling in November 1998. Under Liu, SAFE is both preparing the way for full convertibility of the renminbi—which China has committed itself to before 2010—and cracking down on black market currency operations. Fears of a renminbi devaluation in 1998 caused domestic companies to hoard foreign exchange instead of immediately converting it into renminbi and caused individuals—in many cases from within the Party itself —to smuggle currency out of the country (usually in dollars since the renminbi is not convertible abroad). This in turn resulted in SAFE seeking to tighten controls on foreign exchange transactions, including banning four banks in Shenzhen from conducting foreign exchange business because of supposed irregularities in their accounts. The difficulty of SAFE's task should not be underemphasized. If you walk along one of the main thoroughfares in Shenzhen or Guangzhou or even Shanghai, as a foreigner you are besieged by black market currency traders, all armed with mobile phones. In Hong Kong itself, you are supposed to only receive or sell renminbi at specific banks. Yet there are many places in Kowloon which offer extremely competitive rates—the other end of the chain of the money smugglers from China. Two more Zhu people who should be mentioned are Gao Jian, director general of the State Debt Management Department, and Wang Xuebing, president of the Bank of China. A Ph.D. in finance and an author, Gao played a crucial role in the reform process of the renminbi bond market. Wang, a former head of the Bank of China in New York, has extensive dealing room experience, which is no doubt very useful in confronting the practical aspects of financial reform.

So much for the technocrats. Of course, Beijing has more than just them. In the Party itself, there are important changes going on in terms of not only style but personnel. Among those to keep an eye on is Hu Jintao, vice president of the PRC. The youngest member of the Politburo Standing Committee at 56, Hu is head of the Party School in Zhongnanhai. Previously a protégé of Hu Yaobang, like the latter he also rose through the Communist Youth League. Such has been the rise of Hu Jintao in the past 2 years that it appears likely that he could leapfrog Zhu himself to be the chosen successor to Jiang. His position as head of the Party School would satisfy those leftists or near-leftists that remain, while his ability to avoid the purge of Hu Yaobang supporters clearly shows his political skills. Hu Jintao made a number of key speeches in public support of Jiang's move to ban commercial activity in the PLA. If one goes by the rule that little in Chinese political life is by accident, then these speeches were aimed at confirming publicly Hu's devotion to his master. And there is usually only one reason one does that—when one expects to benefit from such confirmation. Li Peng, now chairman of the National Peoples' Congress, taking over Qiao Shi's old job, continues to adopt an ideologically more cautious approach to reforms, though any overt opposition to the Zhu line is never voiced since this would be seen as opposition to Jiang himself. He is seen to be supported by Luo Gan. Luo is a relative hard-liner and as secretary general of the State Council is attempting to maintain the State Council's powers rather than the Zhu/Sheng Guareng line which is to devolve the state from the economy rather than maintaining or increasing its role. Finally, there is Li Ruihuan, a Politburo Standing Committee member who heads the Party consultative group and who is known as a liberal reformer, and there is Wei Jiangxing, 66, the head of the Central Commission for Discipline Inspection, the Party's internal watchdog. At the ideological level, the mainstream faction, the result of the merger of the Shanghai and Soviet factions, along with opportunists—and pragmatists—from the Zhao Ziyang and Hu Yaobang factions, clearly dominates. In terms of the economy, with the leftists having been defeated, the technocrats under Zhu rule unopposed. What differences there are usually deal with the pace of aggressiveness of the reforms. The direction has already been chosen. The men under Zhu are far better equipped than any generation in China's modern history to deal with the economic problems and challenges that China faces. Yet such is the extent of the problems that it remains to be seen whether they will be able to achieve their task.

Before looking at the strategies that these men are adopting—or should adopt—to try and cope and turn the situation around, a detailed analysis of the problems themselves is in order, that is, an examination of China's fundamental weaknesses. These can be divided into short-term problems and medium-term challenges. Needless to say, the main short-term problem concerns the economic slowdown itself. Slowing growth is a direct reflection of weaker domestic demand. This can be easily seen by the consumption data and is a major concern for the government because the government's—and thus the Party's—mandate is nowadays to achieve economic results, to benefit people materially and financially. To fail to do that is to potentially put the leadership of the government and the Party in question. Needless to say, the government will do anything to avoid that. From the supply side, the government's mandate is to provide economic success. On the demand side, the present generation of people who are in their 20s and 30s is much less willing or equipped to deal with economic hardship—or a reversal of economic success—than were its parents or grandparents. By relative standards, they have been used to an expanding consumer goods market, which will be discussed more in depth later, of rising salaries and standards of living, of luxuries. Many of them are "little princes," only children, the result of the one-child policy, on whom their parents have spared no expense.

The dangers of the economic slowdown are, as I noted earlier, not only economic but social and even political. While most of the Western press that focuses on China looks at the rising underclass, the floating population of *"mingong"* who commute from the countryside to the city in search of work, the real danger in a political sense lies with these comfortably off young bourgeois. It is usually the bourgeoisie that lead revolutions. The Communist liberation in 1949 was an exception, but previous revolutionary movements in China, including the 1911 revolution, were led by the bourgeoisie. They are not likely to want to go back to the Communist days. Instead, they will be pushing for greater speed, at the expense of others in society who are more directly becoming victims of the reform process, the unemployed, those who have lost their iron rice bowl benefits. The latter, while many of them seek only to better themselves and indeed to achieve a "Chinese dream," remain susceptible to a resurgence of the leftists, particularly if they perceive that the young wealthy are seeking to pressure the government into advancing policies at their expense. There is already substantial resentment at the way the reforms have cost millions their jobs, at the way the new young elite parade their wealth, at their benefits, at the links between Party officials and business, at the corruption. In any country, worsening economic conditions bring with them an upsurge in crime. Those who deny the link are simply sticking their heads in the sand. This is not to excuse the crime in the first place. Rather, it is to seek an understanding, which is surely half the battle. This is undoubtedly the case today in China, where the crimes of corruption followed in the wake of the boom time, and the crimes of poverty followed the economic downturn. Should the latter ever start to be justified along ideological grounds, the Chinese government will potentially face a major threat to its own survival.

In *Asia Falling*, I sought to explain a key fundamental weakness of the Asian "tiger" economies, namely, that of "external overreliance." In the case of many of these economies, this referred in the main to external debt. In the case of China, what external overreliance that exists is mainly concerned with the growing influence of trade. The latter now makes up over 20% of the entire Chinese economy, up from 2% at the start of the reform process. Throughout the 1990s, exports have been used as a key engine of economic growth. It is no coincidence that exports are slowing at the same time that overall growth is slowing. In addition, within those export data, exports from foreign plants and joint ventures make up around 60% of the total. While this makes sense from the foreign companies' point of view, China's dependence on these companies is a vulnerability. What happens if they leave?

China's cost base is significantly lower than that of the West, but now that Asian countries have devalued their currencies significantly against the renminbi as well as the dollar—in most cases up to 40%—their competitiveness with China has been significantly enhanced. As well as competing on price with other Asian countries, Chinese exporters increasingly face the risk of continued slowdown in the rest of the world. Overdependence on external demand can potentially, as we saw earlier, threaten the entire reform process since slowing external demand means slowing exports. This hurts the ability of China to finance the growing economic and social costs of that reform process. Finally, a key lesson of the Asian crisis is surely that countries that compete on price alone will eventually get undercut—if you live by the sword, you are likely to die by it. Chinese exported goods are known for their volume and for their cheap prices, but they are not necessarily synonymous with quality and they are certainly not known for their technological content. If you go into the average clothing or toy store in the U.S., the likelihood is that the vast majority of products there will have been manufactured in China, either by foreign joint venture companies or outright by Chinese exporters. China's policy of technological expropriation—as in, if you want to manufacture in our country, give us some of your technology—will no doubt change this. In an increasingly open trading environment, bringing value-added to the table of global commerce is the sine qua non of long-term business and economic survival.

Paul Krugman of MIT suggested that the Asian economies were devoid of TFP, total factor productivity. That is, their growth, and thus their export growth, was largely due to investment, to inputs. Take out those inputs and there was little or no creativity, no technological or cerebral advancement. While I would disagree with this prognosis, the idea of TFP is particularly relevant to China. TFP is the residual of growth after all the inputs have been taken out. The true test of whether China's economy possesses TFP to any major extent will come in these next few years when China has to compete with new supercompetitive versions of the Philippines, Thailand, Indonesia, and Korea for third-market economies such as the U.S. and Europe. My bet is that the results will show that Chinese companies on the whole possess minimal TFP and that their export share as a result gets eaten into. Ironically, some of the highest TFP companies are those run by the PLA and concerned with military exports—if one can include stealing or buying other people's military technology as a TFP-type activity!

While one could argue that China's government has not done enough to focus and target export strategy, the same could clearly not be said about the banking industry and the financial system as a whole. The Asian model of growth in the 1970s and 1980s demanded targeted credit policies, and China was no exception. From the very start of the reform process, Chinese state banks were directed to provide adequate funding and liquidity to specific industrial sectors that at the time were deemed to be worthy of growth. The policy of boosting these sectors worked well; indeed one could say too well. Excess capacity was created since demand was not a consideration. For a time, this did not matter because the surplus was exported. However, the inherent and critical weaknesses in this policy became evident when external demand began to slow.

This type of national policy, while appropriate at the earliest stages of economic development, quickly becomes a burden since it sacrifices efficiency and productivity—not to say profit!—on the anvil of production for production's sake. This is not to pick on China. Any such "national economic policy," whether it is in manufacturing or finance, will inevitably lead to both price and quantity distortion. Why? Because the emphasis is on production, not on profit, on supply, not on demand. Markets are far better at determining price than governments and bureaucrats. Price in turn determines future activity, which in turn determines future price.

Targeted credit policies of necessity produce credit overcapacity and thus manufacturing overcapacity. History teaches that no matter how long the delay before the inevitable, overcapacity in any sector eventually leads to falling prices and a reduction in that capacity until such time as demand returns. In terms of credit, credit overcapacity, if sufficiently excessive—and irresponsible—leads to credit crunch. China is certainly seeing the first of these two—falling prices—as witnessed by the retail price index data which confirm the presence of significant deflationary pressures within the economy. As for the second, this has yet to occur, primarily because the government and the PBOC have dictated that the credit taps remain on to avoid the SOEs' facing further difficulties in the immediate term. This is merely delaying the problem. Eventually, the government will have to reduce the burden of the SOEs on the national budget by stopping credit to them or it will run out of money. Of course, it could print money, but this would be inflationary and the result would be either a repeat of the Asian banking crises on a monumental scale or a current account crisis. The government realizes this and thus is attempting a twin-pronged strategy of seeking to provide sufficient credit to ensure the continued running of the SOEs while seeking to make them more efficient so as to reduce the need for credit in the future. Needless to say, given the size of the problem and the external shocks to the Chinese economy, its regulatory defenses notwithstanding, time is not on its side.

The attempt by the government to crack down on corruption and the commercial activities of the PLA is a positive. "Crony capitalism"—demanding the interlinking of business and government at the least and in China's case the PLA—leads to many things, but in a fundamental sense to diminishing returns. Why? Because it distorts the pricing mechanism. Where crony capitalism is dominant, the market is inhibited from pricing goods and services correctly, and this has dangerous consequences for business. In effect, it means that businesses are being propped up, not by the value or price of their produce, but by artificial means. That prop can be easily kicked away, in many cases leading to the demise of the business. In the case of China, the elimination of the armed forces' presence in business (in reality, the reduction since PLA commercial activities will never be completely eliminated) should free up assets for more productive endeavors. At the provincial level, however, there remain excessive, and unproductive, ties between local governments, Party bureaucrats, and business. No doubt for the individuals concerned, these are extremely productive, but for the economy as a whole they represent a considerable burden, not least because they result in insufficient investment in new production and technology.

In addition, such corruption results in worker resentment. Give people hope but no way to advance and you create a problem for yourself. Put in China's historical context, such "brushfires" can develop into uncontrollable, incendiary situations. Taken as a whole, rather than examined purely in the military or provincial context, corruption remains a key fundamental problem within China. Corruption runs from the grass roots straight to the top, or near it, of the Party and the government themselves. In 1996, the authorities discovered over 60,000 individual cases of corruption. Corruption has itself jumped several levels in terms of TFP! It has moved up the scale of technology. It is no longer a simple case of businessmen or Party cadres exploiting the difference between cheap state prices and the black market pricing mechanism. It is now much harder to detect and all-pervasive within the society despite continued attempts by the authorities to deal with it. Corruption is in essence a symptom of fundamental weaknesses within the economy. A black market functions precisely because enough people take the view that the official economy does not function properly. It does not simply appear as if by magic. Black markets usually occur because distribution choke points have arisen, distorting the pricing mechanism to a point whereby sufficient demand for black market prices is created.

A final short-term problem for China, in line with those instances of external over-reliance which we have already looked at, is the idea of low skill-sets. This may seem bizarre to those who traditionally think of China and the Chinese in general as being very focused on education. The elite universities in China set a high standard, and Chinese families are usually extremely focused on economic improvement as a direct result of educational advancement. However, the very fact that thousands of Chinese students study abroad, as a result of being part of the "overseas Chinese" diaspora or having been sent abroad by wealthy or influential parents, suggests a fundamental weakness in the domestic educational system. This should not need to be the case, and yet it clearly is. It is stating the obvious to say that education is the foundation for long-term economic prosperity without which growth will surely flounder. While China has without doubt created the largest educational system in the world, a direct result of its population being the largest, the quality of that education has suffered, I would suggest, given the imperative since the liberation to use education as a tool of political indoctrination rather than as a means of social advancement.

Indeed, the very idea of social advancement was anathema until quite recently in a society that preached socialist egalitarianism. The proportion of national budget expenditure which is devoted to education (around 9%) remains woefully inadequate measured in the context of a nation that is seeking great power if not superpower status, taking its rightful place in the world and seeking to catch up with Europe and the supposed "information economy" of the U.S. Chinese education spending as a percentage of GNP was only 2.4% in 1987 compared with 4.9% in Japan, 6.8% in the U.S.—and 7.5% in the Soviet Union![1] The general world level for education spending as a percentage of national expenditure is around 15%, and yet China remains at 9–10%. In the cases of the industrial ascendancy of both Japan and the U.S., investment and spending on education during those periods was a multiple of growth. For instance, in Japan from 1905 to 1960, education spending rose by a factor of 23, while personal income rose by only 10 times. Between 1960 and 1975, Japanese investment in education increased a further 11-fold! By comparison, investment in education in the U.S. rose 13-fold from 1900 to 1970.[2] In China, investment in education increased 7.3-fold from 1952 to 1978. It goes without saying that China will have to more than eliminate this imbalance if it ever is to catch up. From the liberation through the Cultural Revolution, not only were educational establishments used for political purposes, but their pupils and students were targeted for certain industries, usually the heavy manufacturing industries, leaving more modern light manufacturing and service industries woefully short of trained student material. Improving China's education system, from primary school right through to the postgraduate level, is a prerequisite for qualification to superpower status. In addition, it is not just a question of improving the quality but also the style. Learning by rote is no longer enough. In a global economy where trade and capital market boundaries are lowered, free and creative thinking takes on much greater significance and importance. In China's case, this is a dangerous if necessary component of education. Where will free thought stop, after all?

In addition to these short-term problems, China faces a series of medium-term challenges. First among these is to integrate further into the global economy while trying to make sure that this is not disruptive to the country's economic and social stability. Unlike many of the ASEAN or North Asian economies that now lie in ruins, China has expanded over the past two decades through a careful balance of deregulation in trade, while keeping the capital account firmly closed. There has thus been no speedy withdrawal of "hot money" since there was no hot money to begin with, at least not the foreign variety. Having witnessed the financial typhoon blowing beyond its borders, China might take the lesson that capital market deregulation is wrong per se. This would, I would suggest, be the wrong lesson to take from the situation. Instead, a better lesson would be that while capital is vital for growth, it needs to be better managed and channeled in order to achieve superior returns for both sides. Over the long term, China has pledged to dispense with both trade obstacles (regulations and tariffs) and capital and exchange controls. A fundamental lesson from the Asian crisis is that emerging markets that open themselves up to trade and capital investment from outside require adequate financial infrastructure in order to deal with resulting inflows. In short, they need deep and liquid domestic bond markets in order to provide an efficient funding market with which equities must compete— thus making the domestic equity market more efficient—to channel inward investment appropriately and to tap the domestic savings base.

China is indeed in the process of creating a domestic bond market. Though this is not yet open to foreign investors—since that would mean an opening of the capital account—it has grown substantially in size, with outstandings now making up around 7.3% of national GDP. For the most part, the Ministry of Finance issues Treasury bills or bonds for budget finance purposes, though occasionally as with the RMB270 billion and RMB100 billion issues, it is for a specific funding task. In the former case, it was to recapitalize the banking system, while in the latter, it was to finance infrastructure projects. The Chinese authorities are attempting to encourage further domestic retail and institutional investment in the renminbi bond market, while at the same time seeking to avoid damaging the capital base. It is, as with everything in China these days, a very fine balancing act. From 1998, a limited number of foreign financial institutions with branches in the Pudong district of Shanghai were to be allowed to invest in the domestic renminbi bond market, though these holdings would have to be retained and could not be traded on. For now, however, capital investment in China remains limited for the most part to portfolio investment in the B-share stock market (portfolio investment in China totaled USD7.7 billion in 1997) and foreign direct investment. The A-shares are limited to domestic investors.

FDI from January–August 1998 fell 1.45% year-on-year to USD27.417 billion. This suggests that the resumption of preferential tax treatment for FDI in the form of tax rebates has been more than offset by the adverse impact from the region's slowdown on foreign investment flows. In response, it is likely that Beijing will introduce more preferential terms for FDI in China in the near future. Meanwhile, domestic banks are likely to be directed to make up for the shortfall. A crucial lesson from the Asian crisis, however, is that capital, whether foreign or domestic, has to be used more efficiently. China, despite a more mercantilist mind-set (particularly in the south), is still dangerously close to the Asian model of growth, which, as we have seen in the last 2 years, has, if not failed, then confirmed to the skeptical that it is seriously flawed. Deep domestic asset markets allow capital to be allocated and priced efficiently, helping to support productive asset growth. If Asia as a whole is to escape its present recession, then the idea of targeted credit policies must be jettisoned. Instead, a much more Darwinian approach must be taken. The history of socialist states teaches that you do not help the prosperity of companies by pumping money into them. Indeed, the reverse is true. They actually become worse off because they become dependent on your funding since you have taken away their instinct and need to survive through their own means and capabilities.

What is true for Asia as a whole is true for China. Credit should be apportioned to productive enterprises. One way of ensuring that, rather than depending on the discretion of individual lending officers, is to develop those deep asset markets we talked about earlier. The government argues that some of the SOEs need to be propped up until such time as they are able to stand on their own feet, until they are reasonably profitable. Yet, at least in theory, what incentive do they have to become profitable under such circumstances? After all, to do so means eventually to lose guaranteed government funding. While there is a clear need to avoid a dramatic worsening of the unemployment situation by continuing to help some elements of the SOEs, conditions need to be added to such aid—namely, that there are specific deadlines for government funding to be cut. These companies that in the past have been as unprofitable as their Soviet counterparts that went to the wall have to be forced to become profitable; otherwise they simply will not. In addition, there is in general no better way of inducing profitability than creating competition. Needless to say, the private sector in China remains in its infancy, despite spectacular growth rates in the past couple of years. While China's government is right to be concerned that private companies do not grow at the expense of state companies before the latter are able to support themselves without aid, the government would do well to give a modest helping hand to those same private companies. There is no greater incentive for the SOEs and the TVEs to shape up than the threat (but not the reality) of extinction at the hands of competition. China's approach to economic integration with the global economy will continue to be characterized by the slow and steady approach, dominated by trade, with specific sectors deregulated and opened up on a case-by-case basis. This may be frustrating for those in the West who seek quicker access to China's domestic markets, while at home facing rising competition from Chinese exports. Yet unquestionably it is the right approach for China to take, given the imperative to maintain economic stability at home as a prerequisite for growth.

A further challenge for China is for the Party to become more responsive to the people. While there are actually "opposition" parties in China, they have no effective power base. The Party continues to dominate, forming the foundation of what is now the "socialist market economy." China has never had a democratic tradition. Indeed, its tradition has been in direct contradiction to the Western ideas of limited government, universal suffrage, an executive who is ultimately responsible to an elected legislature, and an independent judiciary. Instead, China's tradition has been focused on centralized power, with a bureaucracy and a judiciary responsible only to the architect of that centralized power, be it the emperor or the general secretary of the Communist Party. Many in the West continue to call for China to "democratize" itself, as if somehow there were a uniform version of Western democracy.

This is patently not true. Democracy in the U.K. differs in substance and style from that in Europe, or in the U.S. for that matter. In China, Deng Xiaoping effectively changed what was a revolutionary political apparatus into an administrative one. The Party and the government's legitimacy come from adequately administering economic progress; yet the leaders of both the government and the Party know that eventually that will not be enough. Again, history teaches that revolutions happen when the economically advantaged are frustrated by political elites. It is in China's nature to have a political elite since this stems directly from Confucian tradition. In addition, in a country with almost 1.3 billion people, 95% of whom are Han Chinese, 5% of whom are not and speak different languages and come from different ethnic—not to say national —identities, the idea of a centralized, political elite that provides stability makes perfect sense. There are many who argue quite cogently that Western-style democracy would cause chaos in China, that it would for a start require a degree of decentralization that would cause the provinces to openly rebel. This point is debatable, but there is no question that going forward the Party itself will need to legitimize itself through more than purely economic means—particularly in a period when the economy has been slowing down for the last 6 years.

The creation of the rural elections in 1987 appears to be an initial step along these lines. The idea is to give the people a voice to the extent that that voice does not endanger the position of the Party itself. There has been talk that President Jiang Zemin has been conducting surveys about how to increase political reforms so as to achieve greater political legitimacy without endangering stability. Several Chinese officials have mentioned Singapore as being an example of what they, the Party, and the government are considering for their nation in the future. It is easy for the West to criticize China on the grounds of not taking up the mantle of democracy and on other matters. But it is a shame that the West does not notice the progress that has been made—progress not in purely a Western sense but with regard to China's requirements and China's traditions. Those in the West who seek greater democracy in China do their cause no favors by harping on about the inadequacies of the present system in China. Let us not forget that China is a nation that for more than a century was humiliated by the Western powers. Now that it is growing, regaining its former state of wealth and influence, there are those in the West who seek to contain it and to criticize it. In such circumstances, it is not surprising if there are elements within China itself, both in the government and outside it, who react defensively to this. China's government, at least since the reforms began, has largely practiced what we know as *"realpolitik"* in the field of international relations. Brought down to its base constituents, this can be summarized as the concepts of domination, balance of power, and chaos. While in the international setting, the idea of a balance of power has been the appropriate one—whether that between the former Soviet Union, the U.S., and China or now between the U.S. and China—domestically, the necessity has been one of domination simply because a balance of power would ultimately end up as chaos. Whatever the merits or lack thereof of the Party itself, there can be little doubt that if China were to change to a Western-style democracy overnight, chaos would ensue. Since chaos must be avoided at all costs—and most people agree on that at least!—while the Party needs to seek a higher level of legitimacy going forward, a gradualist approach to political reform would seem advisable. Given that reform will only happen constructively from the top down—the alternative again being chaos—this will only occur when the Party feels sufficiently secure to permit such a loosening.

The consolidation of Jiang's power base is an important prerequisite for that to happen. In all likelihood, China will not be become a Western-style democracy, of whatever hue; neither will it be completely authoritarian as understood in the West. It will seek its own way and rightly so. That way, however, needs to be devoid of corruption and needs to satisfy the rising civil as well as economic aspirations of the people if it is to be sustainable over the long term. China may (or may not) be following the example of Singapore in terms of administrative government and control. However, another example that it might learn from is that of the U.K. In the nineteenth century, Britain was the only country in Europe not to experience revolution. Why? Because those who would otherwise have led the revolution, as they did elsewhere in Europe, had the most to lose. In continental Europe, by contrast, bottlenecks were created; entrenched political elites stifled the aspirations of the rising middle classes. Granted, this is a huge oversimplification. The bottom line is that political reform has to come in China, and that it has to be gradual and has to conform with the needs of Chinese tradition and the emphasis on stability. In its early stages, it will be a very different animal from Western-style democracy. That said, the West should note the progress that has been achieved in China, rather than continuing to harp about the negatives, which will do little or nothing to change them anyway. China will not become more humanitarian and less authoritarian because the West wants it to. It will only do so if it sees this as being in line with its own national interests. At the very least, a balanced view is needed by the West. The prisoners of the *"laogai"* are not helped by anything less, for to just focus on human rights violations, while ignoring the improvements, will only result in China's government reverting to a more defensive and nationalistic stance. That is not in anyone's interest.

Whether we like it or not, a new balance of power is being created before us, one in which China will play an increasingly important role. To China, this is merely the resumption, after a rude interruption caused by Western imperialism, of its rightful place and status. Such a balance of power, involving the U.S., China, and to a lesser extent Russia, given its present economic difficulties, can be constructive or destructive. The choice is clearly for both the U.S. and China to make. The views of both sides need to be clearly heard and clearly debated. Only through such debate can the extremist tendencies within both countries be effectively negated. In terms of domestic Chinese politics, this is the only realistic way that China's national insecurities can be tamed and its more authoritarian voices quelled, for the benefit of its government, its people, and indeed the world as a whole. China does have a role to play, an increasingly important role. It is when China feels secure within that role, not as a dominating nation—which it does not seek to be—but as a respected and equal partner, that the kind of political reforms that Westerners look for will be most likely to occur. The alternative to this type of respectful relationship (which Presidents Bill Clinton and Jiang Zemin have indeed done much to foster) is for the U.S. to seek to contain China. This would have negative consequences for all concerned, not least for domestic Chinese politics, which would likely regress in the face of such perceived aggression.

A further, less esoteric, and more immediate challenge for China is the sheer immensity of its population. Such is the importance of this issue that some have deemed it not only China's most important challenge but the greatest single threat to national stability. China has, to recall, a population of around 1.2 billion people. Despite the one-child policy, the annual population growth rate is still around 1.1% in the mainland. Aside from the demands that this population is placing and will place on China's resources, which we shall examine later in this chapter, the sheer size of the population is itself a problem. Granted, much of the "problem" is due to the policies since the liberation in 1949. Indeed, from 1949 to 1989, China's population grew by over 570 million. Those few bureaucrats who were brave enough to speak out concerning the dangers of this were purged. While the current population growth rate is substantially down from the 2.5–3% of the 1960s, it will still mean a population of around 1.5 billion in 50 years. Thus, in that period, China's population will have increased by more than the entire population of the U.S. How are these people to be fed? Or clothed? It goes without saying that such an occurrence will shake the global economy to its foundations, for either good or ill. The demands that this increase in population will place on world, let alone Chinese available resources, will be substantial.

Yet it is not simply a case of the size of China's population which is a challenge, but its structure. China has one of the youngest populations of any country in the world. Over a third of the country is under 15 years of age, and two-thirds is under 30.[3] As of a 1992 census, the average age was 27.2.[4] This is not untypical for an emerging market country, indeed this type of demographic development is relatively normal. There are, however, benefits and dangers resulting from this. A young population moving into the workforce can of course be a major economic advantage.

An important concept with regard to this is the idea of "demographic transition." This concerns a crucial period of change that takes place, altering the demographic structure in terms of age dynamics of a country, and thus having a profound effect on the economy of that country. As countries increase their general standard of living, demographic forces combine with improvements in medical and living conditions to result in higher birth rates, lower death rates, and thus accelerating population growth. As the children of these countries become young adults and join the labor force, this gives a major added boost to the industrialization process and thus the economy as a whole. This is indeed what happened in Asia during the 1970s and 1980s. However, as countries reach a certain degree of prosperity, birth rates start to fall back again because of government policies or due to improved living conditions that reduce the necessity, focus on, and even the desirability of having children. Equally, as economies progress, women gain greater equality, freedom, and choice (to have children or not). The result is a major and fundamental shift in the demographic structure. The declining proportion of children means that the "population bulge" is pushed further down the line, which in turn increases industrial production, and also has fiscal consequences given that it leads to higher taxes and higher savings rates. In such periods, budget deficits are likely to fall or even turn into surpluses. Higher savings in turn provide the fuel for higher investment. This is exactly what occurred in the case of the supposed Asian model of economic growth. In truth, it is much less an Asian model of growth than a "growing (and passing) phase" within the demographic cycle. However, what happens when that population bulge, that significant increase in the adult labor force, moves further down the line, becoming middle-aged and then elderly? The proportion of the dependent element within the population increases, which in turn acts as a burden on government coffers, leading to higher taxes even to maintain the budget level, let alone to improve it, reducing the savings rate. The key is how investment performs while this is happening. If the level of investment is maintained while the savings rate declines, then the country is condemning itself to import capital, which in turn means that it becomes dependent on that imported capital.

What has all this to do with China? The answer is because China has, as we saw earlier, one of the youngest populations in the world. There are over 400 million "young people" (aged 1–20) in China, of which around 65 million come from one-child families. While the growth levels of the 1980s and early 1990s show that the demographic transition has already started, to the benefit of the economy, this would suggest that there are several further waves of children due to hit the labor force, which should give a further boost to output (though not necessarily to productivity). However, as the cycle of the demographic transition shows, young populations inevitably become old populations. The elderly within China amount to around 120 million. This is expected to grow to over 400 million, which is likely to place a significantly larger burden on China's budget. A falling birth rate indirectly increases the proportion of senior citizens in the population. In addition, improved health conditions exacerbate this process. Before the reform process, just under 15% of state employees were drawing retirement benefits. While the government is seeking to substantially reduce the general number of state employees so as to reduce the burden to the state that they represent, this effort will be offset by the these types of demographic changes whereby the proportion of the middle aged and elderly increases relative to the labor force and children.

Hu Angang, deputy researcher at the Research Center for Ecology and the Environment, has done substantial work with regard to this subject and on the issue of Chinese demographic development in general. Hu predicts that if the current population growth rate is maintained for the next 50–60 years, the basic requirements such as housing, clothing, and food will be needed for a population that exceeds 1.5 billion people[5]—in line with other forecasts, and indeed conservative according to some. Over the next 30–40 years, work will need to be provided for 300 million more people, with the workforce to increase to 800 million over the next 20–30 years. Over the next 50–60 years, social security will have to be provided for that 300 million that joined the workforce and has now passed through it. In turn, in this time, food and infrastructure will be needed, it is estimated, for a further 700–800 million new urban residents.[6] It goes without saying that these are daunting tasks.

A further aspect of the structure of the population is the mismatch between males and females. According to a 1990 census, the ratio of males to females was just under 1.07. In mature economies, the usual trend is for the ratio to revert toward par. The Chinese ratio favors males over females to a significant degree because of traditions, and strict enforcement of the one-child policy to try and reduce the population growth rate (the need for which should appear obvious given the figures in the previous paragraph) is likely to exacerbate this since it would cause families, particularly in the countryside, to ensure a male child. While the issue over families preferring a male to a female child has not completely died away in the cities, economic advancement and the invasion of foreign concepts and traditions have greatly reduced it. The problem remains to a significant extent in the countryside, which after all makes up the major part of the population. In the poor areas, where the vicious cycle of poverty continues, a large number of children are born due to poverty, and precisely because of that large number this burden keeps them in poverty. Daughters are married off and leave home; thus sons are considered the sole source of support for the elderly. While tradition plays a part, the economic aspect marks the necessity of having a male child. Therefore, with the proportion of elderly increasing, so will the desire to have male children increase in these poor areas so as to provide support, particularly in a time when the state is itself cutting back on state aid for all sorts of economic and demographic sectors. These problems have a way of feeding off themselves. Who knows what might happen to that one son? And if something does, how are the elderly to support themselves? Thus there is an incentive to have more than one son, which in turn increases the overall demographic burden. The disparity between the number of males and females can only be offset by the exporting of "excess" males. In the absence of this, the result has important social implications.

A final point is the distribution of the population. This is exceedingly uneven. Indeed, if you take roughly half the landmass of China, examining the provinces of Xinjiang, Inner Mongolia, Tibet, and Qinghai, the population of that area is only 4% of the total population. Obviously, the remaining 96% lives in the other half of the landmass. Thus, largely to the north and west, there are hugely underpopulated (and in some cases unpopulated) areas, whereas in the south and east, the exact reverse is true. Overpopulation of an area has social and even political implications. On the social side, it leads to inflation since too many people are chasing too few goods. When the reverse happens— that is, when the amount of goods catches up with and surpasses the population demand in that area—deflation occurs. Again, the only way for this to be offset is for excess population to be exported—not necessarily to other countries but certainly to other, less overpopulated areas. Either that or the deflation has to be sufficient so as to meet population price demand; that is the level where people are prepared to buy. Needless to say, this last is extremely painful for the economy. Politically, it has been the historical norm that overpopulated areas are more susceptible to social and political unrest. Aside from feeling crowded and oppressed in a demographic sense, the needs and desires of the population in such areas are difficult to meet since there is excess demand relative to supply. Instability can be the result.

Looking at the population issue overall, there is little question that China's population level is reaching or has already reached saturation level, and the situation will get considerably worse before it gets better. This in turn has crucial implications for resources, both internally and externally, and more specifically for China's energy requirements. In 1994, China imported 3 million tons of crude oil. By 1996, that figure was 22.6 million tons. It is estimated that by the year 2000, it will have to import 50 million tons, or around 30% of its total requirement.

The performance of its own energy production in general has not been impressive, and oil production is certainly no exception. Indeed, as a percentage of total energy production, crude oil peaked at around 24% in the late 1970s and was below the 20% level by 1990. Although the large Daqing oil field has boosted production, the recent floods that reached that area have not helped. And in any case it is thought that production capacity in Daqing itself has peaked. According to the *Statistical Yearbook of China, 1993*, we see that the export volume of oil was 36.3 million tons in 1985 (imports were 0.90 million ton), falling to 29.3 million in 1991 (12.50 million). [7] Meanwhile, in that period, consumption rose from 91.69 million tons to 123.84 million, while production volume rose from 124.9 million tons to 141 million. China became a net oil importer for the first time since the 1960s in 1994. This together with the fact that the production-consumption gap is narrowing will necessitate that China either develop new oil production bases internally, increase imports, or look outside to buy foreign oil fields.

Exporting crude oil is not necessarily a positive thing to do for a developing country, or for that matter exporting any form of energy. The former Soviet Union experienced severe shortages in oil and other forms of energy, not because the production capacity was not there, but because domestic prices were kept artificially low. As a result, there was little incentive to increase production for domestic demand, and the "excess" was exported, resulting in increased foreign earnings, which promptly went into the back pockets of the powers that be in the Party. Aside from this political angle, low domestic pricing of energy which adds to the incentive to export has a further negative consequence. It means that domestic manufacturing production has insufficient energy available and either must import it or, if it is not able to do so, lie idle.

Inefficiency is a further significant problem with regard to China. The country's energy consumption as a percentage of GNP is the highest in the world, eight times higher than that in

Japan and four times the world average.[8] China's total energy consumption is roughly equal to that of Japan, and yet its GNP is a sixth of Japan's. Given inefficiencies, wasted production, low domestic pricing, and so on, basically a distortion of the pricing mechanism and resultant distortions in supply and demand, China needs a multiple of Japan's energy consumption in order to achieve the same increase in GNP. Finally, China's need for oil risks potential conflicts in the South China Sea where there are known to be large though as yet unquantified amounts of oil. The case of the Spratly Islands resulting in tensions between the Philippines and China is an example, though there are equally similar tensions between China and Vietnam over areas that coincidentally or not possess significant quantities of oil.

Coal, however, remains the key energy source in China. Traditionally, coal has been the most important form of energy there, and this is still the case, with coal presently representing three-quarters of the total energy supply. Aside from the need to increase coal production as the overall energy needs of the population increase, there is the issue over transportation. China's coal fields are to a large extent in the northwest and are all to the north of the Yangtze River, but the consumption areas are largely in the south and east. As a result, it is estimated that half of all transportation in China is transportation of coal. Aside from the sheer cost of this, which must be phenomenal, there is also the issue over such transportation clogging up China's transportation arteries. Similar inefficiencies exist in coal as with oil. China has just under 15% of the world's known coal reserves, but per capita recoverable reserves are around 40% of the world average. Outmoded equipment exacerbates other inefficiencies, resulting in waste. A similar phenomenon exists with regard to China's hydroelectric power capacity. A key problem with regard to this is the low price of electricity. Up until recently, in many cities in China it was cheaper to consume electricity than it was to produce it, i.e., the price of electricity to the consumer was cheaper than the cost to the producer. Given such a situation, there was no incentive to increase efficiency or even to increase production. Needless to say, the result is shortages—or an increased dependency on importing energy sources. In terms of absolute numbers, China's natural resources and those able to be produced, such as electricity, are relatively abundant. However, the distorted pricing system that serves to reduce available supply and the comparison of total energy reserves to the population reduce this somewhat. China's total population is so huge that energy reserves per capita seem pitiful. Indeed, China's natural gas and crude oil reserves are only around half the world average. In 1986, China's urban electricity per capita consumption was only around 1.1% of that of the U.S.[9]

There can be little doubt that the issues of pricing and transportation are two key issues with regard to China's energy problem. Deregulation of pricing is crucial if shortages are to be substantially reduced. As with anything, people have to be given an incentive to increase production. If pricing power is artificially undercut by subsidies or enforced domestic pricing, there is no incentive to increase either production or efficiency. Regarding transportation, while it is the case that highways are being built across many provinces, particularly in the south, the national transportation system as a whole remains inadequate relative to demand. Anyone who has traveled "hard seat" on a Chinese train knows not only how unpleasant that experience is but in economic terms how congested trains are. China's railway capacity is inadequate. Also efficiency of railway usage is not just a question of the amount of rail track but the speed of the trains. It goes without saying that more trains can use the same stretch of rail track if they all run at a faster speed; yet China's trains run considerably slower than the more modern versions in the West. The issue of improving China's transportation system is clearly one of the most crucial issues in the development of China's economy, perhaps even *the* most crucial one—just as it was in the initial stages of the U.S.'s industrial revolution. It is beyond doubt that the U.S. highway and railway systems were the largest contributors to the rise of the U.S. economy, indeed to its ascendancy to superpower status. If China is to achieve the same feat, it must put considerably more effort and investment into improving its own transportation network. Yet, even then, we have just been looking at China's present needs, its present energy and transportation requirements, not even considering what will be China's requirements in the year 2025 or 2050, whenever it is that China's population increases from its present 1.2 billion people to 1.5 billion.

Of course, having enough coal or oil is one thing, having enough food quite another. Inadequate food supply would have major social and political implications. Wars have been fought for this kind of thing. As the *State Statistical Yearbook of China* shows, in the 1980s, grain production peaked at 407 million tons in 1984, a level not seen again until 1989. The first 3 years of the 1990 decade, however, saw production average over 440 million tons. This was followed by 1995–1997 being record harvest years. Clearly, improvements are being made; however, problems remain. The official target for grain production for the year 2000 is 500 million tons, while the official target for grain holdings per capita (grain production divided by population) is 400 kilograms.[10] Given the current population growth estimates, it seems unlikely that this target will be met. Finally, there is the issue of available land for cultivation. In 1952, when the population was 574 million, cultivated land totaled 107 million hectares. In 1992, the figures were 1.17 billion and 95 million.[11] Cultivated land per capita has fallen significantly over that period—from 0.1864 hectare to 0.0812—and continues to decline. Thus, labor productivity in terms of food supply production must increase proportionally, not only to offset the decline but also to offset the rate of population expansion, or China will be creating major problems for itself. A joint study by the State Statistical Bureau and the Academy of Sciences showed that the current "population support capacity" of China—the production capacity of available resources relative to population—is around 950 million people. Extrapolating for anticipated production increases, it would rise to 1.16 billion people in the year 2000; yet this would still represent an overpopulation relative to the actual size of the population of around 140 million people. Assuming the population continues to grow at current rates, China's resource productivity capacity will be reaching its absolute limit relative to the population by 2050 at the very latest. Based on the estimates that China could have a population of 1.5 billion by 2025, that would mean that the limit could be reached in only 26 years' time. Once that limit is reached, either China's surplus population will have to be exported or there could be war. Historically, surplus populations have usually led to war, nature's way of reducing the supply side. The other possibility is that in the run up to that point China will have accelerated its import program to an extent that will devastate world financial markets. This brings us to another issue that is of key importance, that of the environment.

Various parties have warned of an impending ecological disaster in China. The merits—or lack thereof—of such an argument can be debated in the data, but actually seeing for yourself the smog on a warm day in Beijing or the fetid moat around the Forbidden City, or the choked and lifeless rivers gives one a better understanding of the situation. It puts it in context. Such things do not happen by accident. To a certain extent, they happen because of the stage of economic evolution which the country is experiencing. Japan went through the same situation in the 1950s and 1960s when it experienced its own economic boom, until finally the people rose up and demanded that the government do something about it. Today, if you go to Tokyo—apart from the human debris in the likes of Shinjuku or Roppongi—it is one of the cleanest cities in the world. The same could not be said for any Chinese city. In Hong Kong, it is the same case. Victoria Harbour, truly one of the most splendid sights at night, is extraordinarily polluted. Air pollution levels have recently reached alarming levels, even for a city where the level of bronchial complaints is already a scandal. The average back alley in Hong Kong will contain impressively sized rats. This is not just a question of education. It concerns incentive. People have to have an incentive to improve. If people have an incentive not to produce pollution, then they will avoid doing so. The incentive does not have to be purely financial, but there has to be some sort of inducement. Life in general comes down to supply and demand. Whatever the case, there is little doubt, either through the data or actually going there, that China faces an increasingly serious environmental problem, or rather a series of problems. China is currently experiencing severe deforestation, reduction of the water base, reduction of available cultivated land, pollution of lakes and rivers, and rising health costs due to air and other forms of pollution. According to a study by the Academy of Environmental Sciences, economic losses due to environmental pollution and ecological destruction total around RMB85 billion, or just under 8% of GNP.

Amazingly enough, there was a time when China, in its overtly propagandist phase, proclaimed victory over the "three wastes"—wastewater, waste gases, and waste materials. Needless to say, this "victory" has proved Pyhrric. The industrial north, where much of China's natural resources are found, also has the worst record for the number of pollution incidents concerning the likes of industrial wastewater, sulfuric gas emission, and coal dust. Toxic emissions have been a key source of environmental pollution in China—as is the case worldwide. The results are plain to see—befouled rivers and lakes, smog, and rising health costs due to pollution of human food and water resources. A further reason is over utilization of existing resources. According to official data, China's arable land has fallen by 35% since the start of the reform process, and desertification—arable or cultivated land turning to desert—has been a major cause of this. How has this happened? The available resources have been decimated by excessive logging, herding, and use of water resources. The industrialization process itself requires huge amounts of water for purely industrial use—in the oil and coal industries, for instance. This makes the water unfit for human consumption and too polluted for maintaining the ecological balance. In the last three decades, it is thought that China has lost around a quarter of its forests. This is of course due to overlogging, but for two reasons. In the first instance, again the industrialization process is to blame. However, a second reason is that rural areas that are short of energy have to resort to such tactics as chopping down wood. This may seem comical, but it takes a heavy toll on forest resources. Furthermore when deforestation occurs next to rivers, the resulting soil erosion leads to sharp increases in silt in the rivers. Deterioration in the strength of river banks and an increase in silt content increase the likelihood of major flooding if heavy rains occur. There are no such things as acts of God—they are all manmade. To put it in context, the Yangtze River discharges the same amount of silt annually into the East China Sea as discharged by the Nile, Mississippi, and Amazon Rivers combined.[12] The pollution and silt discharge of the Yellow River is a more well-known example. Given such context, the results such as desertification, flooding, reduction in available cultivated and arable land, and air and water pollution should not be particularly surprising.

To be fair, China has not stood idly by while all this has been happening. The government has passed laws and created environmental bodies to try and deal with the problem. However, the scope of the problem dwarfs the existing resources being offered to deal with it, and this can only increase as environmental pollution and ecological destruction feed on each other until such point where the economy—not to say popular tolerance!—is severely damaged and the authorities see the problem in a more immediate light.

Meanwhile, millions of tons of untreated industrial waste and sewage are being dumped into Chinese rivers every day, and the available water supply and food resources—fish stocks—continue to decrease. The air, for its part, does not escape this environmental and ecological degradation. While the smog in Beijing or Shanghai is an obvious reminder, more fundamentally China produces every year around 10% of world emissions of sulfur dioxide, 10% of carbon dioxide, and 15% of ash. The result is not only increased global warming but acid rain— which further increases ecological deterioration through damage to water supplies and forests, and so it goes on. In environmental terms, pollution depletes needed and available resources. In economic terms, it reduces productivity and increases expenses—production and medical expenses—thus reducing the available capital that could be used to finance modernization programs to reduce pollution going forward. In China's case, it is a problem for both the cities and the countryside, a potentially life-threatening problem. Disease accompanies pollution. It is no coincidence that the most polluted cities in China or elsewhere also possess high rates of disease.

This brings us to the subject of dealing with the problem, of the strategies that the government has used, is using, or should use to try and deal with its many and varied existing problems and challenges for the future. In the case of the environment, there is a general strategy in dealing with pollution and ecological destruction which might serve to somewhat alleviate the situation. It comes back to the economics of supply and demand, of price. A look at Asia, in general, over the last three decades shows that it has lost around 50% of its forests and fish stocks, in line with the industrialization process and resultant expansion of its economies. This situation is mirrored in China, and urban pollution is likely to continue to increase in the near term in both China and Asia as a whole given that an increasing number of people will migrate from the countryside to the cities. One of the few rules one can generally say about this situation is that the longer a government waits to tackle it in earnest, the more it eventually costs to clean up. This has been the case in the industrialized nations, and there seems no reason why this should not be in the developing ones. Indeed, data from China and other Asian nations confirm this very point.

Something can be done, however. As I noted in *Asia Falling*, much of agricultural pollution is actually linked to trade, or more specifically to trade-oriented government subsidies and protectionism—to supply and demand, to price. By its very nature, government interference in any pricing mechanism leads to pricing distortion, which in turn leads to production distortion. In practical terms, this usually means overproduction and oversupply, though in the case of energy, it has led to the direct opposite. It has led to underproduction since there is little incentive to increase production in an artificially low pricing environment. Trade protectionism leads to overproduction, which in the context of agriculture leads to overfarming of arable and cultivated land. Agricultural policies lead to farmers using more inputs than are necessary or desirable. Thus farmers rely increasingly on chemicals, which in turn leads to chemical runoff, exacerbating the problem of soil erosion. This leads to a reduction in the amount of available land, which leads to overfarming, which leads to soil erosion, and so on—a vicious circle. The way to deal with this is to eliminate the protectionist element, eliminate agricultural subsidies, and allow the market to eliminate the need for overfarming by correcting the pricing mechanism. This would clearly be a painful—and perhaps unacceptable—process, leading to significant job losses. Yet what is the alternative? To continue to let trade protectionism help in the process of destroying the countryside? Eliminating agricultural and natural resource subsidies leads ultimately to environmental gains.

Clearly, this is not all that has to be done. Industrial waste and sewage have to be treated, desalination plants have to be built, and stricter controls have to be enforced to ensure conservation of natural resources. However, incentives also have to be included in order to ensure that there is a reason for the people to follow the rules. At the moment, people in rural areas in China who are without fuel or energy due to shortages have an excellent reason for chopping down the available forests and no reason whatsoever for not doing so. As noted before, that is partly a result of underpricing of domestic fuel capacity, which in turn leads to underproduction and shortages. Note that in both cases, overproduction and underproduction, it is because the pricing mechanism is being distorted. Such distortions usually happen as a direct result of government interference. Lack of education and technology are further traditional reasons for pollution and environmental degradation.

The pattern of Japan and of the other industrialized nations is such that major improvements in environmental protection and resource conservation are usually not achieved until enough of the population has reached a certain comfort level of economic prosperity, sufficient to be able to focus on matters other than economic necessities. This can include luxury consumer items, but it can also deal with social and political issues. Giving people wealth is one thing. Making them "happy" is quite another. Historically, the problem has usually arisen in the transition phase between the two, when aspirations have increased due to rising general standards of living and yet obstacles to advancement remain. Aspirations can be in the context of class, job, social, or political advancement or even to have a higher standard of living by being able to open the window and breathe fresh air! Better for China's government to deal with these issues in a preemptive manner, before the people "ask." The realists who surround Jiang Zemin are well aware of this; yet clearly they have a plethora of problems to deal with and no doubt prioritize. And if China's government has anything in common with those in the West, then it does not place a high priority on environmental protection until popular discontent has reached a level whereby it has no choice.

The difference in China's case is that popular discontent in general has a history of being explosive. Ahead of any popular backlash, some sort of effort has to be made with regard to improving the technological base, to reduce pollution emissions not only directly but also indirectly as a result of reduced inefficiencies. In general, the biggest polluters are the state factories, which means that the environmental protection laws are relatively ineffective since the prosecution of state factories would call into question the state itself. It is to be hoped that deregulation of state factories, with the state's role being reduced or even eliminated, will allow incentive to again play a part in reducing pollution emissions—the incentive of fear of being prosecuted.

Returning to the issue of the economy, the key strategy that China's government has used to date is one of gradualism, a cautious, step-by-step approach to economic reform. As we saw earlier, the government authorities are highly capable of maintaining this approach. But is it still the appropriate approach to go forward with? One could argue that China's many economic problems—slowing growth, rising unemployment, massive excess capacity in practically all forms, a banking system that is technically bankrupt several times over, increasing social and economic schisms between the haves and the have-nots, between the coast and middle China—necessitate a more aggressive approach to solving them. To be sure, China has made extraordinary progress in deregulating its economy. Still, key issues remain to be re-solved. The strategy of "grab the large and free the small," explained at the 15th Party Congress in the context of the SOEs, still leaves China with substantial productive capacity that is not directly open to domestic competition. Freeing the small is an excellent idea, but it would be even better if small businesses were given tax breaks and other sorts of incentives (though this may be jumping the gun!). By doing so, the market will decide who sinks and who swims. This will result in an increase in the productivity of these assets and ultimately in the profitability and employment levels of the companies that survive.

However, the "small" will not be able to make up for the persistent inefficiencies and lack of productivity of China's "large" companies. The latter were to be initially modeled on Korea's chaebol. However, it is thought—and to be hoped—that Zhu Rongji has turned away from this idea, having seen the mess the chaebol have got themselves into in the wake of the Asian crisis. These mammoth companies need the force of competition in order to make themselves productive and valuable assets to the Chinese economy. Yet to do that immediately would certainly risk significant social unrest, given the resulting increase in unemployment which would be necessary in order to turn these companies around. The government, prudently, is not taking this course. At the very least, it is maintaining state control of these large companies in the medium term. It is to be hoped that the ultimate goal is to privatize them.

It comes back to incentives. When you are given something for free, there is no incentive to pay for it—or work for it. The same is the case with state companies. In general, they have no reason to be productive because they do not have to be productive. The lesson of the chaebol should surely be taken onboard. Lack of domestic competition and artificially low credit rates produce overcapacity and lack of productivity. Ultimately the large companies will contribute significantly more to China's economy if they are allowed to deregulate than if they are kept under state control. The longer this does not happen, the greater the cost to the economy.

Deregulation of the corporate base is also essential if the un-employment issue is to be dealt with. While deregulation initially leads to rising unemployment (as we have indeed seen in the case of the tens of thousands of workers from the SOEs who have al-ready been laid off as a result of the reform process), the combina-tion of improved education and more specifically the availability of retraining and technical and graduate education, together with the deregulation process, is ultimately beneficial for the economy. While the U.S. has many social and economic ills, it also has one of the world's most mobile and deregulated workforces, which is a significant fundamental positive in terms of the economy. Given that people are able to retrain, they do so. Thus the "supply" is available, which results in rising "demand." This in turn reduces skill shortages, which reduces rather than increases the compa-nies' overall cost base. When companies are in open competition, if the company benefits then the worker benefits, since he or she could quite easily walk over to the other company and work for it instead. To repeat, people have to be given an incentive, and the two fundamental incentives in life are fear and greed. Granted, of course, there are others. However, when it comes down to busi-ness, to work, these are the two incentives that get things done. If Beijing can get more of the SOEs to be profitable, then a signifi-cant part of its financial problems will be solved.

That in turn could lead to another problem, one of corporate transparency, or the ability of regulators, financial institutions, and the public at large to adequately assess the profit and loss account and the balance sheet of Chinese and Chinese-related companies. As central bankers have noted, corporate trans-parency in both Hong Kong and China is sorely lacking. While China's capital account remains relatively closed and thus the issue of foreign investment is limited, foreign investors are free to trade B- and H-shares and "red chips." Thus the assumption must surely be that Beijing would be happy to see the foreign in-vestor base at least partly finance the restructuring process of the SOEs, therefore reducing the state's own burden. If that is to occur, and particularly in the wake of the Asian crisis which has reopened people's eyes to the twin concepts of overcapacity and unproductive assets, then there must be an attempt by the Chinese authorities to improve corporate balance sheet transparency. Foreign investors are unlikely to participate unless this is significantly improved.

To a certain extent, this is also a case of education, not necessarily of the government officials, but of the public. Until the government has an incentive to change, it is unlikely to do so. That is generally the case, and not just with regard to Chinese corporate transparency. Popular demand for change could be an excellent incentive. China's government also has an incentive for improving the education standard with regard to financial instruments—such as corporate stocks—since its own focus on reducing the role played by the state means that a greater part must be played by individuals in financing the restructuring process. To date, the Chinese stock markets have seen speculative bubbles and ensuing collapses. An understanding of fundamental fair value based on earnings per share, operating profit, and the like remains muted at best. Enforcing improved corporate transparency and encouraging improvements in education with regard to financial instruments such as stocks and bonds will lead to a fundamental shift in the structure of the asset base in China, to the benefit of the restructuring process itself since this would help it be financed.

That said, should this occur, it would not be good news for the banking system. It is widely recognized that at least in Western terms the banking system is bankrupt several times over, as indeed I mentioned before. It relies for liquidity, not to say solvency, on retail deposits. Given that the financial authorities are increasingly placing an emphasis on companies and banks having to fund themselves or go under, those deposits take on crucial importance. Yet if the asset markets in China attract significant outflows from the banking system, that could cause liquidity problems for the banks themselves. To date, the authorities have sought to handle this problem by restricting activity in the stock market, not only because bubbles have resulted in the past but because such flows from the banking system produce strains. Going forward, at least one way to deal with it would be for the

Chinese banks to create mutual funds in order to tap that retail demand and yet maintain sufficient liquidity. This too is some way down the road, but not that long ago, the concept of a private company in China would have been unthinkable.

Ahead of this, the issue of banking system solvency has to be dealt with. China has made advances, but it goes without saying (and is an understatement in the usual way that most things in China are) that much remains to be done. To date, the government's strategy has been to emphasize to the heads of the state banks that restructuring plans need to be drawn up while at the same time issuing RMB270 billion in bonds, which the banks then buy in order to restore at least some semblance of health to their impoverished balance sheets. As with everything else, China has far too much banking capacity, in terms of both branches and workers. The result is a crippling cost base under which no bank could realistically be profitable. That cost base has to be substantially reduced. The government knows this all too well—as indeed do the heads of the banks concerned. However, the trick is to achieve this without disturbing the social fabric of society and overall stability. It is the same problem for the SOEs, and it is not going to go away any time soon. Needless to say, this is the result of lack of competition. If you have no incentive to be competitive, the chances are that you will not be. China introduced a degree of competition to the banking system through the creation of Minsheng Bank, the first private bank in the country not controlled by the state. Even though the bank's activities are limited, it has drawn away substantial retail deposit interest. Like the SEZs, the creation of Minsheng Bank has been a successful one.

The system can work if allowed to do so. It is just a question of the pace. It is noteworthy that in the context of the banking system, the Beijing government asked the U.S. for help in studying how the U.S. Resolution and Trust Corporation worked in restructuring and ultimately saving the U.S. savings and loan industry years before Japan even thought of implementing an RTC-type solution to its problems through the Bridge Bank scheme. While this is an indictment of Japan's lethargy, it is admirable in the case of China that given its relative stages of economic development, the Chinese authorities have such superior foresight. This is not to underestimate the problem. It is, however, good news that the government is serious about doing something about it, which remains to be evident in Japan! Meanwhile, the state banks continue to lend to SOEs, loss-making or otherwise. While one could say that it is only prudent to maintain credit lines to these companies ahead of restructuring so as to preserve labor stability—and this argument has indeed been made officially—what incentive do these SOEs have of ever being efficient, of ever restructuring, if the credit lines remain open to them. Equally, from the banking point of view, what incentive do the banks have of improving credit allocation and credit risk controls if they are still told to keep the taps open for the SOEs?

As for the widening social schisms in China, this is an issue that cannot be put off. It is an issue that demands immediate attention since such differences in economic and social advancement have frequently led to social and political unrest in China—or indeed generally in the world. It is not so much a case of how much do I make, but why is the person next to me making more? Here, the general answer is that in the long run such social schisms—be it between the haves and the have nots in the cities, or between those in the cities and those in the countryside, or between those along the coast and those in middle and western China—can only be dealt with through general improvement in overall economic conditions; in other words, it must be dealt with indirectly by the market rather than directly through government intervention. There will always be those who have to be helped directly, as in any society. However, government intervention for those who should not need help is usually ineffective and certainly inefficient. The infrastructure for the social security system needs to be tightened up, as does the process of tax collection. Yet this alone will not help. Black markets for currencies or assets of any kind do not occur out of thin air. They happen because enough people believe the pricing mechanism in the regular economy is not working for whatever reason. The same is true with regard to tax collection. People will pay taxes if they feel the tax rate is fair and if that tax rate is not so punitive as to damage or even endanger their livelihood. Strict enforceability coupled with low tax rates is usually an excellent way of ensuring payment, but it has to be in line with corporate restructuring that ensures that wages are also paid on time and are proportional to the amount of service and experience given. Needless to say, the same argument could be made for social security. If you get enough social security to live off relative to what you would have got—and been taxed on—working, why work?

Yet the issue of these widening social differences clearly cannot be dealt with in isolation from the economic restructuring process that is going on. The one is to a large extent the result of the other. Economic restructuring cannot be stopped since this would cause even more social dislocation—not to say popular outrage. Yet greater account has to be taken of those who have not benefited from the restructuring process, who have been left behind, not least because it is better to deal with that kind of problem than wait, while it simmers and eventually blows up. Of course, this is easy to say, but what exactly does one do? Here, the West is certainly no model, given that various answers have been tried and for the most part failed to a certain extent. In any case, the Asian model of which China is certainly a part has relied more on strong family structures and self-sufficiency rather than on welfare systems. This is in part because of different stages of economic development. Self-sufficiency is usually a characteristic of the initial stages of economic development, whereas welfare states are usually seen in mature economies. The U.S. is usually thought of outside the U.S. as being in the self-sufficient camp. However, its social security bill represents a massive, potentially crippling burden to the budget and one that Congress has yet to address. Strong corporate structures that rely on profit rather than subsidies, incentives for small businesses, improved education and retraining facilities, and an efficient, compact social security system for those who are truly permanently disadvantaged would seem in order—and more in line with the model that China has followed since the reform process began.

While these environmental and economic problems are being solved—or not—there remains the issue of Party and government legitimacy, something we touched on earlier. It is little exaggeration to say that to the vast majority of the Chinese population, certainly its urban population, the Party and the Communist system have become irrelevant. This is not making a political point; it is just stating what is an undeniable fact. The focus is clearly now on achieving personal wealth. This no doubt shocks previous generations, but it is entirely predictable, not to say understandable, given modern technology and transportation which allow the Chinese people to see the economic prosperity of other countries. The Internet and foreign television stations that are beamed into Chinese living rooms, together with tourism and student exchanges, have quietly revolutionized the landscape of the Chinese political system. This is not to say that this change to a focus on wealth has endangered the Party's hold on the country. It clearly hasn't. It has meant rather that the Party has withdrawn from day-to-day issues, taking a more administrative rather than overtly dictatorial role. While economic prosperity has become the new source of Party legitimacy—and why not?—there clearly remains an issue of finding a support base when the economy turns down. A new covenant is needed between the government and the people which is not just based on money, and we are starting to see the formation of this through the village elections, which theoretically could be expanded to small towns. The goal of the elimination of a PLA presence in commercial activity is a further part of this, as is the Party's goal of stamping out corruption. If the Party is to succeed in this, the elimination of internal corruption— if there is any— is a prerequisite for the ultimate success of this covenant. China will not necessarily become a Western democracy, and indeed there are strong arguments that suggest it should not, given the lack of democratic tradition and the paramount need to maintain stability. However, it does need a base of both social and political infrastructure which provides political as well as economic legitimacy. It would appear that the government, whatever the official rhetoric, is well aware of this and is planning accordingly to develop institutions and processes that will provide stability in the years ahead.

Infrastructure in general is a key issue. Lack of financial infrastructure—in the form of liquid domestic bond markets—was a key reason for the Asian crisis in the first place, given that neither foreign investment nor domestic savings had efficient markets in which capital could be allocated. In the case of China, it needs both institutional and real infrastructure in order to ensure the next phase of growth. All this while the restructuring of the SOEs—without doubt the largest corporate reengineering process (with Chinese characteristics) in history—is taking place, at whatever speed. It is to these subjects that we look to next.

9

Less Is More—Streamlining Capacity and Building Infrastructure

A KEY LESSON for China is that companies have to learn both sides of the supply-demand equation. While the West talks glibly about how the capitalist approach is so much superior in China to that which existed in the former Soviet Union—and tragically remains in parts of Russia and other parts of the CIS to this day—the reality is that the state-owned enterprises, which still make up around 40% of total output, have yet to come to terms with the capitalist ethos. Up until now, they have had little reason to. The four Chinese state banks have been lending them funds far in excess of profitability needs, with the emphasis clearly on expanding the top rather than the bottom line. In addition, up until only recently there was no domestic competition for them, and they were never directed to be profitable—so they weren't. Once again, it is a case of the incentive issue.

Going forward, clearly the model of Chinese capitalism has to change. The government, through its latest batch of reforms and specifically the announcement that the SOEs would have to be restructured and rationalized within 3 years, realizes this. Given the debt levels and inefficiency of the SOEs, the planned restructuring comes not a moment too soon. However, as we saw in the previous chapter, there are impediments to this process, both structural and cyclical, which are an additional cause for concern. In addition, the idea of "grab the large and free the small," along with the implication that the large SOEs will remain in state hands and will face little if any competition, does not necessarily bode well for the likely success of the effort to turn SOEs around. If they don't have to improve, if they don't have to make profits rather than just sales, then why should they?

Then there is the case of the banks. The banking system in China is represented by four main state banks: the Bank of China, the Agricultural Bank of China, the Industrial and Commercial Bank of China, and the China Construction Bank. As I said before, despite efforts to improve it to date, the banking system is without question technically bankrupt several times over. I remember vividly, while I was in Hong Kong, listening to an analyst for an investment bank expound on the merits of a new fund that offered exposure to the Chinese banking system and thinking that anyone who wanted such exposure was either completely off his head or suicidal. The balance sheets of the four state banks are completely rotten, through and through. This is not exactly a secret. It is widely acknowledged in China, which is precisely the reason that the heads of the banks, along with the government, have come up with plans to sack tens of thousands of employees and close down hundreds of branches in order to restore solvency, let alone profitability.

Finally, there is the issue of infrastructure, in terms of the need for both institutional and "real" (bricks and mortar, roads, ports, etc.) infrastructure. Infrastructure, or rather the lack of it, was a crucial aspect of the Asian crisis of 1997. Capital was not allocated efficiently because there were not the transparent, efficient domestic asset markets available to do so. Thus capital was frequently allocated in inefficient—and in many cases corrupt—ways. Equally, Asia, with perhaps the notable exception of Singapore, lacked "real" as opposed to financial infrastructure—ports, roads, bridges, dams, an efficient power system, universities, technical colleges, and so on. Both financial and real infrastructure are fundamental building blocks for bringing an emerging market nation to first-world status. In China's case, they are also crucial in order to save it from financial and economic crisis.

Before looking at the idea of infrastructure, it is necessary to look at more imminent issues such as the SOEs and the banks. The closed capital account allows China at least some time in which to ponder just what types of specific financial infrastructure it needs. There are around 340,000 SOEs of all types currently operating in China, of which some 98,000 or so are industrial SOEs. Having represented over 80% of total national economic output at the start of the reform process, they now make up around two-fifths, a halving in only two decades. Despite this reduction in their output, they still employ around 115 million of the 170 million urban workers, and their debts, at over USD120 billion as of 1996, remain a substantial burden on the economy. Their success, failure, or survival is fundamentally crucial to the ultimate success—or not—of China's economy. Of the 98,000 industrial SOEs, some 4,950 (as of 1996) were considered to be large, according to the *China Statistical Yearbook*, 6,050 medium-sized, and 87,000 small. As of that time, the large SOEs represented 5.6% of the total and had 67% of the fixed assets, 63% of output, 65% of sales, and 82% of pretax profit. Overall profitability has fallen drastically in the last decade despite or to a certain extent because of the reform process. While a more profit-oriented focus has been encouraged, in line with the overall restructuring of the economy along more capitalist— or rather, socialist market—lines, the attempt to wean the SOEs from state debt has damaged their operating capacity. Pretax return on capital at the SOEs fell from an average of 24% in 1981 to around 10% in 1992, while net return on capital fell from 15% to 3%. Along with the reduction in loans—which itself came not a minute too soon for the sake of the state banks!— slack management, inefficiency and waste, rising costs (rising wages and rising costs of raw materials), and a shortage of raw materials were seen as the key reasons for the decline in profitability at the SOEs. By the end of 1997, it was estimated that half the SOEs were operating at a loss, up from 28% in 1990 and 9.6% in 1985. In addition, the average debt-to-equity ratio of

the SOEs at the end of 1995 was around 550%, excluding un-
funded pension liabilities!

The initial SOEs to face the full winds of restructuring have
been the 87,000 small ones. This is in line with the policy of
"grab the large and free the small." In practice that means allowing the small SOEs either to merge, cut costs through reducing
the workforce, and institute other reduction measures or ultimately to go under. There is a clear need to do this. China simply has far too many small SOEs making too many of the same
products at ridiculously unprofitable rates. The result is a sea of
overcapacity and an army of unprofitable companies that should
be merged and rationalized for the long-term benefit of their
managers and employees. In the immediate term, however, as we
have seen through incidents of social unrest, the results have
been extremely painful. They have been so painful in fact that
the PBOC in mid-1998 encouraged the state banks to restart
lending programs to loss-making SOEs just to keep them afloat
and avoid further acceleration of unemployment growth. Many
of the SOEs have become stockholding companies in so far as
they have issued stock to their workers. However, this does not
give the workers voting rights as it would in the West. In addition, the actual issuance of stock on the A-share market by these
SOEs has remained extremely limited. Apart from throwing
workers out of their jobs, or at least making them *"xia gang,"* (literally, "stood down" or sent home with subsistence pay), the approach to financial restructuring at these companies remains
relatively conservative, at least by Western standards. Certainly,
though the aim may be to imitate the reengineering process that
took place in the U.S. from 1992 to 1995, this has not happened
in reality. Just reducing the workforce by itself will not improve
the situation. There have to be improvements in management
techniques, supply availability, and operating efficiency through
mechanisms such as just-in-time and quality. Needless to say,
such aims remain some way off, though the small SOEs that
have been left to fend for themselves are probably closer to that
goal than are the large enterprises. That is because the government intends to keep the larger enterprises firmly in its hands,

seeking to build up large conglomerates that will dominate their respective manufacturing sectors.

For the most part, these larger enterprises are present in sectors deemed strategic to China's interests, such as telecommunications, banking and finance, transportation, natural resources (oil and gas, mining), petrochemicals, and defense. The danger, however, with this approach is that it will simply recreate state monopolies by another name—monopolies that will have at least little immediate incentive to become (more) profitable since they will face little or no competition. Indeed, the government's explicit aim appears to be to create a number of monoliths that will drive forward national growth for the next decade, much as the chaebol did in Korea. At least, that was the explicit aim until the unfolding of the Asian crisis in the second half of 1997 which exposed the fundamental flaws within this idea. And more importantly it exposed the fundamental flaws within the Korean chaebol, such as huge overcapacity, in terms of both the workforce and production, inefficient operations, and massive domestic and external debt burdens. Since then, the Chinese government has apparently been mulling an alternative plan to this for its own large SOEs, though no details are as yet available. China's government has a distinguished history of flexibility, and there is little doubt that Zhu Rongji and his government subordinates will have learned from the economic and financial woes of the chaebol. In regard to the chaebol, having become unproductive, inefficient, and indebted, the answer must surely be to reengineer their financial structure by selling off assets, refinancing short-term domestic and external debts through long-dated debt and through further issuance of stock, and having specific debt-to-equity targets. Such a model of financial restructuring would also benefit China's SOEs, though the government as ever will remain cautious given the need to maintain social stability.

While many Western commentators see the SOEs solely as a financial burden to China's economy, the Chinese government sees them very differently—as greatly alleviating the fiscal burden given that they, not the state, provide for welfare benefits. In addition, the government, while seeking to modernize its economy through what are perceived as Western-style capital methods, does not necessarily see anything wrong with a persistently strong statist hand in the economy. The state's role in the economy is to be reduced; it is not to be eliminated, nor indeed can it be otherwise or it could also threaten anarchy. That is how Beijing sees the situation. Hence, there are no plans to privatize the cream of the large SOEs, nor to reduce the role of the state in them through any other means. While the state is to increasingly be an administrator rather than a dictator of economic policy, the maintenance of its domination over the large SOEs will be a key lever of power. While this is understandable, it too threatens to result in inertia within these large SOEs. As with many other things, it all comes back to incentive. Granted, there are many people who are going *"xia hai,"* "jumping into the sea" of private commerce. The benefits of that process, as well as the negative consequences, are already highly visible. However, the managers and workers of these large SOEs are unlikely to change until they face the threat of elimination through competition. Reducing their benefits will not be enough by itself to stop inefficient and unproductive business practices.

It is clear that given the resumption of state bank lending, along with the relative lack of stock offerings on the A-share market in 1998 and equal lack of corporate bond issuance to finance necessary financial restructuring of the SOEs, the government is taking a slightly more cautious approach than it first adopted at the 15th Party Congress. While this is in line with the government's approach all along, which is to proceed cautiously with strategic and economic reform, there is an argument to be made to the effect that the government has to accelerate the process rather than seek to slow it down, even at the threat of social unrest. Granted, every effort must be made to reduce the latter since economic reforms and progress cannot happen if instability is the result. However, if the SOEs are allowed to any major extent to carry on with the old unproductive practices, which as we saw above have already caused substantial deterioration of all profitability measures, one of two things could occur: a Soviet-style collapse of the state sector or a rising and intolerable burden on the state budget if the government seeks to avoid the former. Theoretically, the PBOC could go back on its principles and print money to support the state banks, which would in turn support the SOEs, but this would merely be to exchange an SOE and banking crisis for a fiscal and ultimately a current account crisis in the future. Time is of the essence. The SOE problem has to be dealt with now, however much pain it causes, for the alternative will surely be even more painful. There are ways to alleviate that pain, which the government is presently looking at, namely, setting up a safety net to support and retrain those who have become victims of the SOE restructuring process. Most estimates put the creation of a sufficient safety net for these needs at 5–10 years away. Again, China does not have the time to wait for this to occur, so in the meantime it will have to muddle through.

One way of doing this is to increase the burden on existing workers by having them pay substantially more of the cost of pensions, medical insurance, employment insurance, and housing so as to reduce the burden on the SOEs themselves, thus helping the SOEs to cut costs and at the same time providing at least part of the financing; the government would have to pick up the rest of the bill for at least a preliminary safety net. Experiments along these lines are being attempted in several Chinese cities, with the plan clearly to broaden these across the country if the results prove satisfactory. Needless to say, this process is not without social and political hazards. It is vital, however. The message from the Chinese government has been unequivocally for the state to reduce its role in the economy and for an increasing number of companies—and thus workers—to look after their own needs rather than be supported. A safety net, however temporary, still has to be provided to reduce the suffering. It would be particularly effective if it were combined with technical training to improve the skill-sets of unemployed workers.

There is no doubt that problems remain, however. Chronically unprofitable medium-sized SOEs cannot effectively liquidate tens of thousands of jobs, sell off assets, merge, or form joint ventures without creating new welfare schemes to support their new social burdens. But they are unable to finance those schemes precisely because of their precarious financial state. At some point, ironically, the government has to step in and help at least a specific number of these companies stay on their feet while attempting the restructuring process. The challenge will be to maintain national fiscal discipline while attempting this, an exceptionally tricky balance. Meanwhile, people cannot move because they would lose their welfare benefits. In addition, major fiscal changes are needed to improve tax revenue collection, surely a fundamental weakness of all emerging markets. Regarding this last, it is notable that the 11,000 large and medium-sized SOEs pay around 65% of the tax revenue of the industrial SOEs. Yet without fundamental reform, which can be achieved most effectively only through the introduction of competition, surely this will fall as the profitability of the companies falls further.

Of course, if China does indeed achieve a full restructuring of its SOE sector with an accompanying social safety net, it will have achieved something no other country has done—the transformation of a socialist economy to a capitalist economy (albeit one with some degree of state guidance) in a single generation. It goes without saying that there remain substantial obstacles to overcome before this can be achieved. Whether now or later, the bottom line is that the SOEs that do not perform, starting with but not ending at the small and medium-sized SOEs, must be allowed to fail. In addition, the *"guanxi,"* the connections between the top management of the SOEs and the ministries and government offices at the national level, and provincial bureaucrats at the local level, must be severed. As long as the SOEs are still able to rely on government aid or support, they will not have to obey the rules of the market, and thus they will have little incentive to become operationally profitable. Of course, achieving this will not be easy given that *"guanxi"* is fundamental to Chinese capitalism, whether in the mainland, Hong Kong, or Taiwan.

Nowhere is the idea of *"guanxi"* more prevalent and nowhere more necessary to reduce if not eliminate it than is the relationship between the SOEs and the banking system, and more specifically with the four state banks. As a direct result of those links, enforced through decades of explicitly government-targeted credit policies, the profitability, indeed the solvency, of the banking system has been decimated. It is no exaggeration to say that the fundamentals of the Chinese banking system, taken as a whole, are probably worse than any other country in Asia, including Thailand and South Korea. The meltdown that occurred in Indonesia would have to be viewed separately from this comparison, as it is a unique tragedy in Asia's history of the past 2 years. Still, this does not detract from what is otherwise a truly dismal financial picture. By just about any measure—the share of nonperforming loans, capital adequacy, profitability, and loan loss provisions—three of the four main state banks come out among the worst if not the worst in Asia (the exception being the Bank of China, which through superior management and greater exposure to foreign banking practices and demands is on a decidedly sounder footing). Taken together, the four have a workforce of 1.7 million people, 153,000 branches, and deposits of RMB4.5 trillion. They have bad loans amounting to around RMB1.3 trillion, or 30% of the total loan book. Government and PBOC estimates put the figure much lower, at around 6–7%. However, official estimates of nonperforming loans only include nonpayment of principal. A debtor could have long ago defaulted on interest payments and the loan would not officially be declared nonperforming until the principal itself was defaulted on. Even since the start of the reform process in 1978, the role of the state banks has been to suck in retail deposits and funnel them to the SOEs. To this day, 80% of state bank lending is still to the SOEs, though the government's intent is clearly to reduce this. As reforms have spread through the SOE sector, profitability has declined for the reasons stated above—part of which was indeed due to a reduction in state bank lending. Thus, state bank NPLs have increased dramatically in this period, in return reducing the return on assets, which has fallen from an average of 1.4% to under 0.3% by 1996. Loan loss reserves as a percentage of total loans are also dangerously low at 0.85%. These two figures compare with an average of 1.70 and 1.60 for banks in Hong Kong. Note that this collapse in return of assets for Chinese state banks took place in a period when absolute lending soared, implying that the profitability of the lending collapsed exponentially. Even these official data are probably overoptimistic in any case, as, given the official definition of NPLs, they allow the state banks to overstate their interest income. In late 1996, an analysis of the intrinsic safety and soundness of the four state banks by Moody's ratings agency resulted in a dismal E+ grade for three out of the four.

In light of this appalling situation, how do the four state banks and China's banking system as a whole stay afloat? The main answer is that depositors in China have little real choice of putting their deposits in banks—and thus adding to the liquidity of the banks—apart from putting their money in the stock market or under their pillows. They cannot easily change their deposits into foreign currency, and in a deflationary environment there is no incentive to change their deposits into hard assets. As for the stock market, while the PBOC and the China Securities Regulatory Commission, through their measures to curb what they perceive as excessive speculative activity, have no doubt made a concerted effort to avoid the asset bubbles of the past, a more fundamental purpose has been to curb retail activity in the stock market in general so as to avoid putting the banking system under strain through drainage of deposits. Incidentally, this is a further reason why the PBOC has been cautious in its monetary easing in 1998 despite real interest rates being 9% or more at one point, as a too aggressive easing might have caused a flood of deposits being withdrawn and moved into stocks. In addition, with the capital account all but fully closed (foreign investment is allowed into the B-share market, and of course foreign direct investment is positively encouraged, let alone allowed) and the renminbi thus not convertible on the capital account, Chinese depositors have not been able to take their money out of the country. Naturally, these two issues are interlinked. Both have given the government much needed time to restructure the banking system. However, once again that time is not limitless. As we have seen in the ASEAN, Korea, and Japan (above all!), the problem of nonperforming loans has a way of feeding on itself, on expanding of its own volition if left unchecked. Non-performing loans of necessity reduce overall banking system liquidity, which thus reduces availability of loans to the corporate base, which in turn reduces corporate profitability at the least and in some cases causes small and medium-sized companies to go under. The workers in those companies and others who see this happening spend less and save more because of resulting job insecurity, which in turn reduces bank liquidity, which causes banks to cut back further on their loans—a truly vicious circle. The lack of convertibility of the currency is a window of opportunity, and yet it is one that has to be exploited given the credit profligacy that most of the state banks remain guilty of. In addition, the PBOC's decision to reverse its edict and encourage the state banks to resume lending to loss-making SOEs will hardly help banking system solvency, whatever the benefits to the SOEs concerned.

As with the SOEs, the restructuring of the state banks is being pursued aggressively in public, yet cautiously in reality. The Commercial Banking Law in 1995 defined for the first time a set of business guidelines for commercial banks in China, dictating that the ratio of outstanding loans to deposits be set at no more than 75% and equally that liquid assets to liquid liabilities be set at no less than 25%. Since then, nothing as bold as this has as yet been put into practice, however bold the rhetoric and the plans. This is not to say that the plans do not exist. All four state banks have publicly acknowledged very aggressive plans to cut costs, through the reduction of both the workforce and the number of branches. But there has been little evidence of this actually happening despite the PBOC itself taking the lead by detailing and acting on its own plan to cut costs and centralize operations. What is needed to speed up this restructuring process is clearly a centralized payments, clearing, and settlement system between all the banks in China. The reality is that they are still some way from achieving this. It would be unfair to say that the authorities have not been pursuing reform in the banking system. Yet the application of that reform has undoubtedly been marked by a degree of caution similar to that concerning the SOEs. The last thing the government wants to do is to risk creating a banking crisis as a direct result of the reform process! That said, caution can easily turn into inertia.

Time is running out. China's state banks are of course dependent on retail deposits for their solvency given the government's insistence that it reduce the PBOC's role in propping up the banking system. Yet those retail deposits are themselves dependent on ordinary Chinese citizens' retaining confidence in their banking system. Some USD20 billion left China in 1997, and in the January–September 1998 period, that figure was around USD90 billion, as measured by the net omissions and errors column in the Chinese official balance of payments data. To a certain extent, this is a chicken and egg scenario. Retail and corporate confidence in the stability of the renminbi is waning, hence money either is being translated into foreign exchange onshore (illegally since this is not being done directly for trade purposes) or is being taken out of the country. This in turn puts pressure not only on the currency but the banking system itself, hence the vigorous nature of the efforts by the PBOC and the State Administration of Foreign Exchange to crack down on black market foreign exchange activity. While this link may seem exaggerated, the Chinese authorities remember well that in the ASEAN and North Asian economies that are now in recession, a currency crisis turned into a banking crisis, and not just because there were large external debts but because the currency crisis caused bank runs. China cannot afford that to happen, not only because it would critically injure the banking system but because it could potentially cause major social instability. Confidence is key, but so is improving the level of competition in the banking industry while at the same time seeking to recapitalize it through bond issuance.

China's four state banks dominate the banking industry. However, the authorities 2 years ago tried a further experiment. They permitted the creation of the country's first truly private bank,

Minsheng Bank. In just 2 years in operation, Minsheng Bank has built up around USD2.4 billion in assets, with a staff of only 800. A loan there takes only 7–10 days for approval, compared with months at a state bank. It is an experiment that has been an unqualified success. China's financial authorities may remain nervous that further competition in the same way to Minsheng Bank may strain the state banks and thus the banking system as a whole. But nothing is likely to cause them to become efficient themselves except competition, however cautiously or gradually imposed. Just as with the SOEs, it is the case for the banks that there is no greater incentive to improve than survival. The lack of competition that the state banks faced, in addition to direct government orders to make loans to the SOE sector, was a key reason for the insolvency of the state banks. Chinese state banks need to act, rather than talk about acting. They need to cut costs, and they need to change their approach to credit allocation, becoming more commercially sound in the process. It is difficult to enforce commercial behavior on what are for the most part insolvent banks. Private and semistate banks need to be allowed to develop further in order to enforce the laws of the market on the state banks, again however gradually. That is the most likely way of ensuring that the processes that caused the insolvency in the first place—credit targeting—are changed.

Of course, the government should not stand idly by, nor is the government likely to do so. There are things that it can do to speed up the situation, and it was thus a positive when the Ministry of Finance announced on February 28, 1998, that RMB270 billion (around USD32.5 billion) would be raised through special bond issuance for the sole purpose of raising additional capital for the state banks and recapitalizing the banking system as a whole. In addition, this was thought to have aimed at boosting capital adequacy ratios to the 8% level required by international banking standards (as set down by the BIS) ahead of the March 31 end of the fiscal year. At the time and subsequently, some Western commentators have wondered whether this special bond issue was just a cosmetic exercise to reshuffle the state banks' balance sheets given that the state banks themselves were among the buyers. In addition, it was noted that huge as the RMB270 billion sum was, it remains paltry relative to the total nonperforming loans of the state banks, which amount to around RMB1.3 trillion. Clearly, further massive special bond issues will be needed if this is the route to be taken. Recapitalizing the banks alone, just pumping money into them, is not enough. They need to change the way they do business at the same time, the way they allocate credit. Hence, further competition needs to be simultaneously encouraged, albeit cautiously so as not to endanger the system itself. As noted above, it is difficult, if not impossible, to successfully encourage commercial behavior on what are mostly insolvent banks. The most effective way of doing it is to increase competition so as to force the state banks to improve themselves. The role of the semistate and private banks has to be increased, cautiously and gradually, thus providing adequate incentive—survival—for the heads of the state banks to reform their previously errant ways. A further way of helping turn the situation around would be to create an RTC-type organization that would take some of the nonperforming loans off the books of the state banks, thus freeing them up again to resume lending, though on a more commercially driven basis.

China's banking system has a window of opportunity as a direct result of the lack of convertibility of its currency on the capital account and the lack of alternatives for retail depositors. Because of China's extremely high savings rate, huge sums of public money continue to pour into the coffers of the state banks, thus keeping them afloat. Some within the Chinese government make the argument, as with the SOEs, that this itself will allow the banks the time to restructure. Yet as I argued above, the greatest incentive for them to restructure, and quickly, is for the semistate and private banking sector to be increased, at however gradual a pace, to provide competition. A final element that would help in this process is that of developed stock and bond markets. China's A- and B-share markets, despite experiencing stellar growth since their inception, remain paltry as a percentage of GDP. And the corporate bond market has been all but dormant since 1993 despite sporadic bursts of issuance. As a result, China's SOEs have no alternatives for funding except loans from the state banks and the occasional semistate and private bank. Just as a cartel or a monopoly, by its very nature, distorts the pricing mechanism within an industry, so the lack of alternatives to the loan market (to a large extent from the state banks themselves) distorts its own pricing mechanism. This in turn makes raising funds more expensive for the corporate base, thus reducing investment and ultimately profitability, which in turn can reduce the ability of the SOEs to pay back those initial loans.

Deep and liquid asset markets, and particularly a well-developed government and corporate bond market, would reduce corporate dependency on the loan market, thus making loan pricing more efficient and at the same time allowing the SOEs greater access to cheaper and longer-dated funding through corporate bonds. This type of financial infrastructure is crucial if China is to avoid the mistakes of its Asian counterparts. They opened up their economies to trade and their markets to investment without developing adequate institutions and markets to cope with the resulting massive capital inflows. China, of course, has the benefit of having witnessed this and learned the appropriate lessons. Financial infrastructure is crucial before one can allow the capital account of an emerging market country—or any country—to be fully opened. In addition, it is fundamental to the long-term growth and prosperity of the country concerned.

Allowing and creating efficient funding alternatives to the corporate base reduces funding costs, which in turn feeds through to greater profitability, helping in part to reduce the banks' own nonperforming loans. Of course, further types of financial infrastructure are needed. China has no private pension schemes, relying on the state version. Private pension funds would reduce the burden on the state to provide state pensions. At the same time, they would help to finance the development of the domestic asset markets since they would seek to invest in the domestic stock and bond markets, whichever offered the better returns at the time. Domestic savings would thus be channeled into funding the SOEs at efficient rates, which would in turn help the profitability of the corporate base, in turn helping to boost wages, thus boosting savings—a virtuous, rather than a vicious, circle. Fund management remains in its infancy in China though the government is showing signs of trying to develop it. Again the purpose would be to create the necessary financial infrastructure both to finance the immediate financial needs of the system and to help reduce the state's role, and further out to prepare the way for the opening up of China's markets. Foreign banks could help in the development of the bond market, given their undoubted superior knowledge. Yet the government is likely to remain cautious in allowing this, for two major reasons. First, to allow foreign banks to take part in equity and bond offerings to the market would be to allow them to dominate such offerings, thus hurting the state banks. Second, such domination would be politically unacceptable to a government that remains extremely sensitive to perceived foreign domination of any sector of its economy.

Of course, all this is fine in theory, but the practice could well be different. China's experience with the stock market, for instance, has been extremely volatile, involving bubbles and crashes. Given a lack of education about corporate fundamentals, China's A-share market was perceived as a casino, or as some viewed it, an elevator, where the public rode it up and down! Transparency remains a major problem, not just with regard to foreign investment in the B- and H-share markets, but with regard to enforcing a more rigorous domestic analysis of corporate profitability, which would in turn cause more efficient domestic pricing. The government's goal of increasing the domestic markets' burden of raising necessary funding for the state banks and the SOEs is a sound one, though more strenuous regulation is needed if both markets are to prosper. In the past, the stock market was often the subject of scandals involving corrupt practices, with equity underwriters using bribes to land new deals. If the Chinese public, which to a certain extent has been traumatized, as well as thrilled, by its experience with the stock market, is to trust the markets as a source of investment rather than speculation, education and stricter regulation will be needed. China is proceeding along these lines. It just needs another Deng Xiaoping to walk about in the south again (the "*nanxun*" mentioned previously) to accelerate the process! Developing a government bond yield curve off which the corporate base could price issues would be an excellent way of reducing corporate costs and at the same time allowing companies access to long-term funding. This would reduce their vulnerability to short-term loans and allow them necessary capital to boost investment. A bond market is fundamental to long-term growth and prosperity. As I pointed out in *Asia Falling*, one of the key lessons of the Asian crisis was that Asian countries relied too much on external funding and had not done enough to develop their domestic bond market, resulting in vulnerability to foreign exchange risk. Going forward, it remains inevitable that Asian countries will seek to change this disparity, developing yield curves and creating the financial infrastructure that will allow the return of foreign investors, as well as an alternative for the domestic investor base. Watching this, can China do less?

Many Western commentators, frustrated with the apparent lack of progress in China in this regard, publicly call for a "big bang" of securities deregulation, of the type that occurred in the U.K. and the U.S. This seems extremely unlikely. Beijing continues to favor a more incremental approach to economic policy in general and is particularly likely to do so in the case of the development of securities markets given the volatility that it has already seen in its A-share market. Developing and expanding the government bond market must therefore be the main priority. At present, the size of the Chinese government debt market is around 7.5% of GDP, reasonable for an emerging market country but paltry in comparison to the industrialized world. One reason for this is that the government has up until now been reluctant to issue sizable amounts of debt since this would not be in line with its focus on fiscal prudence. The present huge trade and current balances, however, give the government some leeway in this. And in any case if the aim is to use fiscal stimulus in order to turn around domestic demand, those budget numbers are going to have to deteriorate—however temporarily. Why not at the same time develop and deepen the government bond market and kill two birds with one stone?

Currently, the Ministry of Finance issues Treasury bills and notes primarily for budgetary purposes and only to local (rather than foreign) institutions. The government also issues savings bonds that are in the same form as the Treasury bills and notes but targeted to individual investors via the banking branch network. A key issue is secondary market liquidity. Treasury bills of the voucher type are nontradable securities. In addition, secondary market liquidity in the Treasury bill and note market is relatively limited in general. There are various other types, including fiscal bonds, special-purchase bonds, and book-entry T-bonds. Taken together, the total size of the government bond market is around RMB550 billion outstanding. Government debt can only be bought by local investors, and the interest from government bonds and most financial bonds is not taxable. Corporate bond interest payments are, however, liable for a tax of 33%, a key reason why the corporate bond market remains extremely small, with outstandings of under RMB40 billion as of the end of 1996. While the authorities have sought to limit the size of the corporate bond market in order to avoid corporations building up too much bond debt—an irony since their loan debt would easily be enough on its own to cause insolvency under any normal accounting practices—a further reason is to avoid Treasury issues being crowded out by their corporate counterparts. Hence, the regulatory authorities have put ceilings on the coupons of enterprise bonds in order to reduce their ability to draw away investor capital from Treasury notes and bonds.

Corporate bonds are also issued under a quota system, thus slowing up the process of issuance. Again, these would be prudent limitations on total debt issuance were it not for the fact that the SOEs have been profligate in their loan borrowing from state banks. Since June 1997, all interbank Treasury bonds and repos have had to be traded through the China National Interbank Money Market system. All Treasury bonds and financial debentures can now be traded in the repo market, a major positive in terms of liquidity. Going forward, in order to develop secondary market liquidity, the financial authorities will have to more efficiently pool the retail and institutional savings base by creating domestic institutional investors, pension funds, and asset management companies that can invest in and trade government and ultimately corporate debt. In addition, the tax on corporate debt interest payments should be cut in order to make it less punitive for companies to issue debt and for investors to buy it. In sum, what is needed is strong regulatory and supervisory bodies (which China has already set up), an institutional investor base, a developed yield curve (the government debt yield curve is 2–10 years), incentives for companies to issue domestic debt through a reduction in the corporate bond interest tax, and finally guidance from the authorities that companies can use the bond market as a further means of refinancing their balance sheets through borrowing at the long end in order to reduce short-term loan debt and free up needed cash flow. The bond market can also be a useful tool in monetary policy, not only in setting nominal interest rates but in soaking up surplus funds from the population which would otherwise be used for consumption, thus driving prices higher. The Chinese authorities have long ago learned this lesson and used the bond market for exactly this reason in the early 1990s during the time when inflationary pressures were on the rise. Nowadays, however, this is clearly not the case. Deflation, not inflation, is the threat. While theoretically one could argue that government and corporate bond issuance could in such circumstances act the other way, taking needed consumption power out of the economy and thus hurting it, the economy's real problems are overcapacity and lack of liquidity resulting from a massive debt overhang. Expanding the development of the debt markets in China would help alleviate, rather than exacerbate, those problems, as it would allow the economy to refinance itself.

Of course, not just financial infrastructure is needed. "Real" infrastructure is also very much needed. It is a key problem, with emerging markets eventually reaching a choke point beyond which it is difficult to pass without the necessary infrastructure to allow a broadening and extrapolation of the growth potential. Hindsight is of course 20/20, and in the current economic circumstances in Asia one could conceivably use just about any analogy to justify one's thesis. However, a cursory examination of the traffic problems in Bangkok, Jakarta, or Hong Kong could have told anyone at the time that those economies would be heading for trouble if the necessary infrastructure were not developed to free up those clogged arteries and allow more blood to flow to more parts of the body. The example has repeatedly been made of the highway and railway systems in the U.S., which contributed more to the growth of the U.S. than any other economic factor. Highways alone will of course not grow an economy. However, if you try and grow an economy without them, eventually you will create traffic jams, real ones and metaphorical ones. Slowing growth will be the result, followed by stagnation, with ensuing social and political consequences if nothing is done. In government circles in Beijing, there have been mutterings about the need to invest up to RMB1 trillion in infrastructure projects over the next 3 years. As staggering as such a figure is, it is not beyond the realm of possibility since the government has already earmarked RMB200 billion this year for such projects, financed through bond issues. Power plants are needed, as are highways, railways, and effective telecommunications across the country. As we saw when looking at the issues of the environment and the ecology in China, lack of infrastructure is already starting to hurt growth through pollution, wastage, and shortages in energy.

This is not unique to China. It is quite a common feature of Asian and generally emerging market economies. One of the key reasons why Singapore is an emerged rather than an emerging economy is that it, unlike much of the rest of Asia, possesses infrastructure in abundance. In China's case, energy shortages are a direct result of inefficient pricing mechanisms and lack of transportation infrastructure. Although China is the third largest power producer in the world, substantial shortfalls still exist. What is needed is a commercially driven pricing mechanism, with minimum government interference and a national power grid. The government aims to develop the latter by the year 2009. It is an awesome task—one of many such—but it is fundamental not only to the development of efficient energy pricing but to the further development of the economy as a whole. The slowdown in the economy has temporarily reduced the need for power, but such a breathing space will be fleeting and should be used as an opportunity to speed up rather than slow down reforms in power generating, pricing, and transportation. The government has sought to progress along these lines by enacting legislation to structure tariffs in such a way as to allow power plants to make profits. While this is positive, more and better progress would be achieved through the injection—yet again—of competition into the power industry. Certain industries are by their nature deemed sensitive in China. However, just as in banking, a little competition can go a long way in encouraging more productive use of existing power resources.

In terms of the highways, the last 5 years have seen phenomenal growth in the number of highways being built in China, particularly in the south and east, linking industrial factories with cities. As a result, highways now make up over 50% of domestic passenger traffic and around 15% of freight traffic. Yet, clearly, major problems still exist in terms of road transportation. For a start, many areas in middle and northwestern China have little or no road transportation, and what is available is of poor quality, which means that traffic usage is inefficient. At the start of the 1990s, a Ministry of Transportation study suggested that if all the third-class roads were upgraded to second class, this could increase the total transportation capacity by 40%. Lack of roads, let alone highways, still means that goods do not get transported, even at the end of the twentieth century. As for those highways with their toll booths, while their creation is a positive development in terms of China's future growth, many are ill-placed, some bypassing major cities by hundreds of miles. In addition, you can frequently travel along a Chinese highway and be the only car on the road—and thus subject to hijacking attempts by criminals! What does that tell you? For one thing, obviously, the economy is slowing down and therefore road transportation is not needed, as in good times. More fundamentally, it suggests that China continues to rely overly on rail and river transportation. For relatively short distances—and in China, distances are indeed relative—road transportation via highways is much more efficient. Reliance on rail transportation is a classic characteristic of an emerging economy, which is why the now industrialized world started with rail transportation and then moved on to place a greater emphasis on roads. This is not to say that China should not use its railway system. In outlying areas, which by themselves make a substantial portion of the Chinese landmass, railway transportation has to be increased, not decreased, as a preliminary stage of economic development before such areas can then pass on to highways and first- and second-class road systems. In the more developed areas, more and better roads, for freight as well as passenger traffic, have to be the emphasis. The great corporate visionaries in Hong Kong, such as Gordon Wu, see the need for such "real" infrastructure and are attempting to do something about it. The task, though, is a mammoth one that requires government financing help, not just market forces, to ensure it takes place.

So where is all this money going to come from? After all, the government will need extra funding for a safety net to provide for those who become victims of the restructuring of the SOEs and the banks, funding to recapitalize the banking system, and a multiple of funding to develop sufficient infrastructure in order to support what is an extremely burdensome population size. In 1997, China officially had a budget deficit of 0.7% of GDP, and most estimates for the 1998 figure put it at around 1.5%. Yet this figure is potentially deceptive since it does not include subsidies to the SOEs or the state banks. If you include those, the budget deficit of China could be as high as 6%. This is of course a major reason why the government wants to reduce that burden by making the SOEs and the state banks stand on their own feet without government support.

With state bank nonperforming loans at around RMB1.3 trillion and planned infrastructure spending at RMB1 trillion—let alone the costs of building a safety net for the unemployed and "*xia gang*" resulting from the restructuring of the SOEs—the fiscal burden can only increase. How is this to be financed? Clearly, there is a limit to government participation—unless of course the government resorts to printing money, which would be disastrous and which it is not likely to do. More than ever, the government needs to speed up the development of the institutional investor base so as to create available buyers for the flood of government (and probably corporate) bond issuance that is likely to appear in the next few years. At present, RMB4.5 trillion in retail deposits is sitting in the state banks, earning miserable returns. If but a small portion of this were channeled into the government and corporate bond market via a "buy side" (which is in the process of being created), this would more efficiently allocate capital where it is needed and reduce the overall government financing burden.

That still leaves a need for fiscal reform. While the government will have to ease the overall fiscal burden in order to take account of the restructuring process and at the same time cope with the economic slowdown and the need to fund infrastructure, a more efficient tax collection and assessment system is needed. As part of the move to deregulate in Beijing, the portion of tax revenue available to the national government has fallen from around 35% in 1978 to 12% as of 1996, while that available to provincial governments has risen to 40%. Beijing has talked about slowing or reversing this process, but unsurprisingly such talk has been met with fierce opposition from the provinces. Such a substantial portion of tax revenue in provincial hands is potentially dangerous for China—and indeed has been dangerous in the past—given that it could encourage the provinces, not to secede altogether, but at the least to increase their independence from central coordination and authority. From the tax perspective alone, such independence can be a temptation to corruption, allowing for inefficient local services.

New national taxes have to be thought up in order to restore the balance somewhat and also to help finance investment initiatives. One way of doing this would be to take another look at the housing market. Granted, the property market is yet another example of a classic boom/bust scenario. Too much property was built, and now there are not enough buyers, resulting in a collapse in prices. Meanwhile, the government earlier in 1998 announced the intention of scrapping the housing subsidy on July 1, which would have in effect forced people to buy their homes rather than merely rely on state subsidies. A positive you would think, not only in terms of financing the deficit but in terms of establishing a home-owning ethos and therefore further developing capitalistic (or socialist market) tendencies in the economy as a whole. However, July 1 came and went and the subsidy remained. Given the economic conditions at the time, with thousands of people being made unemployed every day and the economy as a whole slowing down, this was not particularly surprising. To have kicked away the support of housing subsidies might have resulted in a nasty social backlash. While the wholesale scrapping of the housing subsidy may seem draconian, not to say imprudent in such circumstances, a more cautious approach could be to create mortgage departments within banks, to provide tax relief on mortgages, and to reduce rather than completely eliminate housing subsidies. Such an approach would appear more in tune with the idea of "feeling for rocks underfoot while crossing the river." That said, as harsh as a total scrapping of the housing subsidies might appear, speed is needed given the fiscal burdens that will be placed on the government as part of its unfinished revolution, its effort to revitalize and modernize China's economy for the twenty-first century.

China stands on the brink of greatness—on the edge of a resumption of its rightful place in the world, of achieving in three decades (1978–2008) what it took the industrialized world 150 years to achieve, on the edge of economic, military, and political superpower status—or on the brink of an abyss. The restructuring of the SOEs and the turning around of the state banks are must-win battles. They cannot afford to be lost, for if China's economy were to fall into the kind of slump that is currently afflicting most of Asia and a growing part of other emerging and emerged countries, the results could be devastating, not just in the economic sense and not just for China. So what will the future be for the Middle Kingdom? The ideas that we have looked at so far in this book will, it is hoped, give us a framework with which to anticipate and forecast China's future in the next decade. It is to this that we turn to in the next, and last, chapter.

10

China in the Future — Myths, Realities, and Forecasting

THERE IS NO question that China will be a "great power" rather than just a powerful country. It is just a question of the extent of that greatness and from what will it originate. China's economy, in historical terms, has clearly changed at light speed. It has gone from being a largely agrarian-based economy, when the reforms began, to a growing emerging economy at the least and one that people talk openly about as surpassing the U.S. in absolute GNP and GDP terms over the next two decades. The progress made to date is outstanding, greater than anything that has ever happened before, even than the industrial revolutions of the U.S. and Europe, in terms of elevating people out of poverty, in terms of modernizing the most populated country in the world at a speed that has never been seen before. There is no doubt whatsoever that Deng Xiaoping, who is largely responsible for this, will go down as one of the truly great men of the twentieth century, whatever his misdeeds or otherwise with regard to Tiananmen Square.

At the end of the twentieth century and the dawn of the twenty-first, the new millennium is seen by many as being China's. It is not my contention that this definitely will not be the case. It may well be, particularly given the progress made to date. I would suggest, however, that it is far from the certainty that many anticipate. Indeed that is the central tenet of this book. People who have actually been to Beijing, Shanghai, and even Guangzhou marvel at the changes that have taken place in only the last 5 years. Quite often forgotten or missed, however, are the victims of "progress"—the environment, the unemployed. National economic elevation brings with it negative consequences as well as positive ones, the growing social schisms between the haves and the have-nots, between the coast and the provinces, between the cities and the countryside. Many who saw the Asian model of economic growth as almost self-perpetuating, as never ending, now in their ideological disillusionment regard China's persistently high growth rates as proof that the Asian model remains sound, despite the apparent evidence that it contained serious faults, despite similar evidence of fundamental flaws in China. A lesson of the Asian crisis is surely that growth driven solely by inputs is eventually unsustainable, even if it lasts for decades. With countries breaking down trade and capital market regulations, the game of global competition continues to heat up. Countries ultimately have to bring something special to the table, creativity, innovation, not just low product prices or cheap labor.

Here China's growth in the last two decades is of a better quality than that of many of its Asian counterparts, based profoundly on a revolutionary ideological change to become a mercantilist rather than a collectivist society. Unfettered competition, as well as having nefarious side effects, breeds creativity and innovation, the types of activity that lead to total factor productivity, the residual of growth *after* all the inputs are removed. China's consumer market is a classic example of this. Having been barely in existence at the start of the reform process, China's consumer market has grown in only two decades to become one of the most ferociously competitive markets in the world. The dream of many Western companies of unlimited wealth resulting from being able to tap the world's largest market without restriction has, however, been severely curtailed. The price of entry into China's market is high, the margins thin, and the competition frenzied. Still, companies continue to repeat the mantra that they have to be in China precisely because it is the world's largest, most populated market, as if that were the be-all and end-all, as if the business necessities and demands in other markets are somehow not applicable or should not be in China. This is not to say that China is not different. Of course it is, and companies need to adopt specific strategies that are targeted toward the Chinese market if they are to have any hope of succeeding, and rightly so. However, companies have to make profits. That is why they exist—and few Western companies in China today are making money. It is an uncomfortable fact that few are willing to admit openly, the excuse always being that they are there for the long haul, that they cannot afford not to be there, and that eventually the investment will more than pay for itself as profits roll in. This brings us to the idea of what is Western theory with regard to how China works, what are its strengths and weaknesses, and what is the reality. To my mind, there are five key issues, five key myths, about China which need debunking.

Myth 1. The Chinese consumer market is a gold mine that is a relatively untapped resource and has unlimited potential for Western manufacturers.

Reality. Few Western companies are as yet making a profit in China, having had to support oversized domestic workforces that are relatively unskilled in second- and third-generation technology and whose welfare benefits usually cost more than their salaries. Such companies are effectively blackmailed into handing over technology in return for access to the local market and have in many cases had to buy locally made parts whatever the cost or the quality. Many Western companies no doubt viewed the China market as a new Klondike, a new gold rush. In many cases, it is they that have been panned! This is not necessarily a deliberate policy on the part of Beijing. The very nature of the economic decentralization policy that Beijing has pushed risks provincial abuses, and there is little question that we have seen these in abundance, at least by Western standards, in terms of economic abuses on both their own provincial populations (official corruption, overpricing, waste) and Western companies.

Yet Beijing is clearly determined to avoid the situation where Western corporate exploitation of China's markets merely becomes the modern economic version of the imperialist domination and humiliation of the nineteenth century. This is entirely justified of course; yet it would seem hypocritical for a national government to remain extremely defensive about exploitation that happened a hundred years ago while at the same time at the very least turning a blind eye to the exploitation of Western companies. The latter are of course not there for the common good—though no doubt their advertising would claim as much! Western companies are there to make money, but they are there to do that under conditions of fair competition. The bottom line, however, is "if you don't like it, get out." That is made abundantly clear.

This all sounds pretty gloomy, and local Chinese may even see it as a Westerner whining in defense of huge Western companies which can easily look after themselves and in many cases dominate their markets. It is not all gloomy, and Western companies can and should look after themselves. Competition should be fair, however, because when it is not, it risks a protectionist backlash in the parent country of the company. In addition, protectionism in almost every case robs the consumers that it is officially protecting. Finally, in the past 6 months we have seen the unthinkable. The first Western companies that have been in China for years, but that have not made any money and that have amassed huge losses, are reducing operations or actually getting out. If China can say no, so can the West. This is not a threat, nor an attempt at Western belligerence. It is to say that if the global economy is to prosper and all within it, including China, then there have to be rules that all sides abide by, standards. Needless to say, the West—and more specifically the U.S.—thinks that it sets the standards for the world. Many in the emerging markets and notably China might beg to differ. China is becoming more confident as a result of its economic successes. Given these and given the increasingly important role it is playing in the global economy and in global politics, the issue of standards and rules could potentially become one of different and clashing civilizations. A potential clash of cultures, of civilizations, looms. However, I am optimistic. I think that the Chinese government, having watched the rise of Japan and the rise of the ASEAN and their subsequent fall, is keen on not making the same mistakes. One of these is that vested economic interests should not be protected at the expense of either the economy or any sense of mutual standards that can be developed. Economic transparency remains woefully limited in China, however the path has been set. China is developing its consumer and financial markets and its economy, and will do so in a pragmatic way that will seek to enable it and its government to regain long-term economic prosperity and political self-esteem on a global scale. Issues over transparency, technology appropriation, intellectual property protection, and fair competition will be agreed on. Compromises will be made. The Western side might argue (in private) that it is not there primarily to help China, it is there to make money—which should indirectly help China. The Chinese side might retort that the price of entry is to help in building China's industries. To a certain extent both are right. An agreement will be reached, and it will be one not based on politicians or high diplomacy but on the most fundamental of economic factors—supply and demand. China has a long history of assimilation, of absorbing other cultures and customs and turning them into a Chinese version. Both sides should approach the issue from this foundation.

As for the consumer market, it does hold tremendous, unparalleled potential. To date, China's reforms have elevated over 200 million people from a state of poverty. China's per capita savings rate is one of the highest in the world, and it is conservatively estimated that by the end of the decade and the century 450 million people in China will have annual household incomes exceeding USD3,000, in 1995 U.S. dollar price terms, and 100 million will have annual household income exceeding USD9,000.[1] For manufacturers, these are decidedly more useful figures than the pipe dream of what would happen to automotive profits if the same proportion of Chinese bought a car as in the U.S. This is of course not to guarantee that this will occur, but it is to give an idea, a framework of potential purchasing power. Obviously, market potential is not enough. Manufacturers, domestic or foreign, have to fit their products to local tastes and fads. The Chinese consumer has clearly "awoken" and having bought immediate household goods has become much more discriminating. Technology and product quality are having to shift with this change. The consumer market has become ferociously competitive, initially on price, but product quality and technology competition clearly are the way forward.

Myth 2. All global companies "cannot afford not to be in China."

Reality. Sure they can. This is clearly not to say they shouldn't be in China, but if they are amassing significant losses due to an uncompetitive and unproductive workforce and ferocious competition which is killing their margins, a rethink is in order as to why exactly they are there and for how long. Those who simply enter with dreams of untold riches available for little effort will get their capitalist heads handed to them. On the other hand, if they have a well-focused business strategy, targeted to local needs, then the potential of the China market would suggest that it would be the height of folly not to be present. Western manufacturer penetration of the China market has, I would suggest, gone through a number of phases, albeit in the stunningly short time it has taken to grow the consumer market from almost nothing. The first phase was clearly the gold rush, or Klondike, phase where, if the manufacturers were honest, they would say that hopes were high for unparalleled exploitation. The last untapped market had become available, and it also just happened to be the largest market in the world! This phase has clearly come and gone, and more sober analysis and projections are the result. Perhaps the next phase could be called the "regrouping" phase, where Western companies sought to reanalyze the situation and in the case of many see where they went wrong. The third phase will be one characterized by those who are in China for the long haul, focusing on domestically oriented strategies rather than simply attempting to force global strategies on the China market which are frequently inappropriate. In addition, there will be those who, experiencing mounting losses and witnessing the local Chinese asset markets in a major downturn, decide it is time to reduce their exposure to China or cut it entirely. During this phase, we are likely to see the continuation of the slowdown in foreign direct investment into China which began in the second half of 1997. Clearly, from the point of view of foreign direct investors who are looking to set up plants in China, the declines in local asset markets are symptomatic of the significant overhang of domestic overcapacity which exists in the economy. From the point of view of tapping the local market, this implicit prospect of diminishing returns, in the near term at least, makes the idea less attractive. FDI will, however, continue to pour into China in order to use it as a low-cost exporting platform for other parts of the world, though even this will be reduced given the devaluations in Asian currencies which have now made those countries much more competitive vis-à-vis China.

Myth 3. China's socialist market economy is relatively unsophisticated, its government persistently authoritarian and determined to hold power at any cost.

Reality. The first part of this is easy to dismiss. The best way to look at this issue is to examine the consumer market in China which has achieved growth and advancement levels in the last 10 years which took the rest of Asia three decades to achieve. I distinguish between growth and advancement because the former concerns quantity and the latter quality. In the major centers such as Beijing and Shanghai, the major consumer brands that Westerners take for granted—whether or not they can afford them!—are equally available. If sophistication is defined by product quality and speed to market, then China's consumer market is rapidly becoming one of the most sophisticated in the world. Price competition is so frenzied that domestic manufacturers recently called for an armistice on price cutting so that at least some degree of margin could be maintained! To a certain extent, this is due to the fact that while household incomes have grown tremendously since the start of the reform process, even this significant rise did not keep pace with the initial product increases in the late 1980s and early 1990s, before the government's fiscal austerity measures finally managed to tame inflation.

In addition, production overhang still exists relative to demand. If the socialist market economy is to be judged by the growth and advancement of its consumer market, then clearly it is unjustified to call it unsophisticated. Product quality and availability have grown phenomenally. Indeed, product quality and the concept of value-added will be the key focus for product differentiation going forward. When Western manufacturers first entered the China market in the wake of the start of the reform process, product novelty, status, and pricing power were the key determinants of those who managed to attain initial market gains. Going forward, top-line P&L success will be determined by perceived value-added. With price competition so intense, those who rely alone on price will see their margins eliminated. In addition, even those Western multinationals that have substantial brand-name advantage will have to be nimble on their feet given the fast-changing nature of Chinese consumer tastes and trends. What was trendy to drink, eat, or wear yesterday may not be tomorrow—and literally tomorrow because the pace of change in China is considerably faster than in the developed world. The need to be flexible and able to change product lines quickly is essential when considering the current economic downturn that is affecting the country.

If Western economic cycles are anything to go by, Chinese consumers will adopt more defensive buying patterns, reducing purchases of perceived luxuries and putting greater emphasis on basic necessities and saving. Despite the advances made, the development of the consumer market and indeed the socialist market economy as a whole clearly has some way to go. Beijing itself acknowledges this, professing that China remains a developing economy, and it will take some time—20–30 years at the least—to catch up with the developed world, let alone think of surpassing it. Institutional infrastructure has to be developed not only in terms of China's financial markets but with regard to its consumer market, ensuring that standards are upheld. Social safety net, environmental, hygiene, and medical issues have to be examined and dealt with. Progress will be made because the Chinese people will demand it. Such demands have plenty of historical precedents, the most notable of which in Asia was the case of Japan. While a mature society, Japan could have been deemed an emerging economy after the war given how devastated it was. Like emerging Asia, Japan experienced stellar growth from the late 1950s on; yet environmental standards were appalling relative to today's Japan. Eventually the Japanese people stood up and said "no more!" And things changed. The same will be the case with China. When economies become mature, following their initial phase of growth (however long that lasts), individuals place a greater emphasis on free time and on social activity. Needless to say, environmental abuses and rampant pollution can often be inconsistent with these pursuits; hence a showdown will indeed happen on this issue in China.

As for the government being authoritarian, by Western standards this certainly was the case, and there are instances with regard to prisoners specifically imprisoned for their dissenting viewpoints where this remains the case. Yet the government is changing rapidly—to a certain extent trying to keep up with the changes its economic reforms have unleashed. China's political and economic leaders are, above all, pragmatists. The need for stability remains paramount, and this will always be the case given the country's history of social unrest and even civil war whenever the central power base has been sufficiently eroded. However, the government, as I suggested earlier in this book, is keenly aware that with economic advancement and reform must eventually come political reform. It is a case of when and by how much, not if. The village elections are thus a crucial litmus test of the willingness of the Chinese population to take up the challenge of greater participation and responsibility in their country's future. Given its apparent success, this test could well be extrapolated to towns, in much the same way that the experiment of the special economic zones was carried out. The Party will remain dominant. That is not an issue. Yet the Party's nature will undoubtedly change in order to be more flexible and responsive to its people. This process is already happening. The Party is changing itself into a national administrator, driving and responding to the economic necessities of its population while simultaneously emphasizing the ideological grounding that is the foundation of the "socialist" nature of its market economy.

To any Westerner visiting China, this may only seem apparent by the presence of the PLA and the Public Security Bureau on the street. Yet there are elements of Chinese society which remain fundamentally at odds with the economic practice of laissez faire. It will take a considerable time for China to become a Western-style democracy, if indeed that ever occurs. The basic elements of the family, of the Confucian belief system that necessitates the idea of a benevolent dictator, and most importantly of the need to avoid instability (which as the events of the Cultural Revolution and Tiananmen Square demonstrated benefit no one) would seem to suggest that a strong power base must be maintained in order to keep the disparate elements of society together. For Western politicians to call on the Chinese people to rise up and take power (this used to be frequent but thankfully nowadays is rare) is simply irresponsible. Progress toward universal suffrage and popular participation at the political level can only be given from above and that will only happen when the government and the Party feel secure. Of course, being in the West it is easy to say this, but this is nothing other than pragmatism. What do we in the West mean by democracy anyway? What is the role of government? Surely, its role is first and foremost to ensure economic stability and progress. You can't eat ideology, and this is true of both communism and liberal democratic ideology. Deng Xiaoping put it brilliantly—as ever—in two quotes when he said, "poverty is not socialism" and "whether it is a black cat or a white cat, it is a good cat if it catches mice."

Ideology is, quite frankly, not the prime concern. The prime concern is to continue to raise the economic standards of the Chinese people. That said, it seems inevitable that the nature of the Party will continue to change and that such change will have a profound effect on policy, both political and economic. Some commentators have forecast that the Party will become like the Liberal Democrat Party in Japan, which maintained an effective one-party state for 40 years, albeit in a supposed liberal democracy. Deng himself admired the Singaporean form of government. The bottom line is that the nature of government in China is changing, at both the local and national levels, and the Party is changing to adapt itself to a more responsive role. Government and Party legitimacy cannot only be founded upon making people wealthy, as this approach is fraught with danger when the economy inevitably turns down, as economic cycles dictate. It will increasingly have to experiment with allowing a greater amount of popular participation, while at the same time maintaining central control.

Myth 4. China seeks to dominate Asia, if necessary by the use of military force.

Reality. As incredible as it seems, this myth continues in some Western circles. I say incredible because it shows an astounding level of ignorance about the necessities, motives, and historical demands of the Chinese government—a level of ignorance which is potentially dangerous. No Chinese government that relinquished its claim to Taiwan could survive. It is as simple as that. It is a historical imperative that the Chinese government regain Taiwan, just as it was an imperative that Hong Kong and Macao be regained. The idea of national territorial integrity, of regaining control over all of the motherland, particularly those elements that were taken by imperialist adventurism, is central to the view from Beijing. It is nonnegotiable, and it is indeed something that Beijing is theoretically prepared to go to war over, though it has shown considerable restraint to date, relative to what it could have done. The history of China is one of alternating periods of retreat and advancement *within its own historical national boundaries.* China has not sought and does not seek to be, as it terms it, a "hegemonistic" nation. Instead, it seeks to regain national territorial integrity over lands that were previously its own. As an emerging great power, it also seeks respect, partly because of a bruised pride due to those imperialist adventurers of old and the territories that were lost as a result, and also due to the huge economic gains that it has made in the past 20 years. It is not much to ask for when you think about it. China also has economic interests that it intends to defend, most notably the oil-shipping lanes in the South China Sea which are becoming increasingly important because of its increasing dependency on imported oil. Its motivation is defensive rather than aggressive. At a time when its economy is gaining it a greater importance in global economic and political affairs than at any time since 1840, it is only natural that it seeks to attain defensive capabilities that ensure that that happy situation remains. China has no history of military projection beyond its own perceived historical borders. One can of course argue about Tibet and Xinjiang. However, whatever one's own belief, the Chinese government believes these to be inexorably and historically part of China.

There are two elements to the idea of a "China threat." The first is the reaction within China to a Western notion of China being a regional or even a global threat. I would strongly suggest that were Western governments to pursue a line that China represents a threat, this would become a self-fulfilling prophecy. Constructive engagement should be emphasized, stressing the pragmatic needs and expectations of both sides. China seeks what many in China believe is its rightful place in history, namely, that of a great power that represents a force of stability and harmony, of noninterference and of cooperation. Attempts to contain China's expansion of its domestic interests could well result in China being a threat and should be avoided at all costs. There is no reason why China cannot be a force for stability in the Asian region, alongside the U.S.

Equally, China should realize that those within who call for the U.S. to leave Asia are being unrealistic. The U.S. has important national security interests in Asia which it will not and cannot abandon. Realism and pragmatism have to come from both sides. A U.S. presence in Asia does not of necessity mean a containment policy aimed at China. Instead, it can potentially represent a new and groundbreaking degree of cooperation between it and China.

A second element of this concerns Japan. There is little question that China's growth has been viewed with concern as much as admiration or expectations for economic potential in Japanese government circles. Indeed, comments from Japanese officials have noted this expansion, not only in economic but in military terms, one even suggesting that Japanese national security can only be ensured through China remaining domestically unstable and thus focused on domestic stability rather than regional expansion. While such a view is clearly hysterical, not to say profoundly misguided (since nothing would potentially represent a greater threat to regional stability than domestic instability in China), China should be sensitive to the concerns of other nations, even ones that invaded it only 60 years ago, in seeking to allay fears of economic or military projection. China is not the only country that can be defensive. The political ineptitude of the existing Japanese government along with rising popular discontent at the economy, coupled with the perception of a rising threat from China, could be a potent combination, potentially causing instability in Japan—which would not be in China's interests, let alone anything else. While such thoughts may seem unrealistic, it should not be forgotten that Japan's military adventurism of the 1930s happened as a direct result not only of Chinese weakness but of the social and economic crisis that brought the military to the forefront of Japanese politics. Right now, Japan is close to, if not in a state of, economic and financial crisis. It is not a time for misunderstandings.

Myth 5. China's replacement of the U.S. as the world's leading economic superpower is inevitable.

Reality. There are many reasons why this could occur, but it remains far from inevitable. This is the heart and soul of this book. What goes up, can—let us not forget!—come down. It was not that long ago that Western analysts watched with awe the seemingly inexorable rise of the Chinese A-, B-, and H-share markets, only to see them plummet to earth. Equally, it was thought inevitable that China would continue growing at double-digit rates, just as it was considered inevitable that the economic rise of the ASEAN and North Asia would continue ad infinitum. The current economic slowdown in China, which started in 1992, is proof that fundamental economic weaknesses have yet to be solved—if such proof were needed. When you look at the consumer market in China, with its latest fashions (Chinese and Western), the Internet, illegal watching of foreign satellite channels, and growing demands from the public for quality and value-added, it is clear that China is well on the way to becoming a leading economic powerhouse, and thus given its population at least one of the economic superpowers. Even this, however, remains far from inevitable. If you just walk around Beijing itself, you see that poverty and backwardness live hand in hand with that modern, thriving consumer market we looked at earlier—and this is Beijing, not the countryside. One could of course counter by saying that one could see the same thing in any U.S. city. However, by backwardness I mean areas where the processes of modernization appear to have been missed or forgotten. For the most part, the poor areas in U.S. cities are victims of the nefarious aspects of modernization—drugs, for instance— rather than having missed the process entirely. China remains a developing country, a developing economy, albeit the biggest one in the world! In today's context, a mature economy is characterized by possessing leading-edge technology so as to be part of the "information age" (of which much has been talked about—much of it entirely spurious), developed institutional and "real" infrastructure, a developed service sector that is responsive to both the economic and social needs of the population, a strong education system, and finally the architecture for popular political participation and government responsiveness.

In the meantime, China has to continue to deal with the current slowdown. To date, its policies for dealing with this have not had their usual success. Fiscal expansion has yet to reignite domestic demand the way it did in the past. In any case, it remains risky because of the existing debt burden of the SOEs—which the government is of course seeking to offload via the restructuring process. Monetary easing has also yet to see any notable results. Deflation remains the key economic determinant, given the extent of overcapacity that exists in almost all product segments, from food to property. This overcapacity can be worked out by a continuation of the deflationary trend and/or a currency devaluation. In addition, the property glut needs to be reduced by a fire sale of assets. This, along with reducing state bank nonperforming loans, is the only way of getting liquidity back into the system short of the PBOC printing money (which, as noted before, ultimately would be detrimental to the system and could cause a banking and/or a current account crisis). The immediate issue is not whether China can become the leading superpower, but whether or not it can avoid economic and social crisis.

So, where do we go from here? What will the future be for China? With the transition of leadership from Deng to Jiang having been smoothly achieved—the first such peaceful transition in China's history—the president and the government are sufficiently secure to focus their attention on tackling the economic slowdown, improving economic and political relations further worldwide, boosting the institutional and real infrastructure, and in general doing what is necessary to achieve developed country status. What holds China together, aside from a unifying or ethnic or racial identity, is the idea of the "Chinese dream," of achieving previously unimagined economic status and prosperity. For this dream, people are prepared to work exceptionally hard, but the genie is out of the bottle. It cannot be put back. This remains the main focus, and it is this focus that the government will thus have to respond to first.

China also wants to be a nation that can no longer be bullied, a nation with a strong sense of self-worth, a nation that takes its rightful place on a global scale. The key focus for the government will remain on improving the domestic economic architecture, for this now is the source not only of domestic aspiration but of political legitimacy, particularly at a time when the engines of economic growth are sputtering. Power no longer comes out of the barrel of a gun; it comes out of the economy. Despite its achievements to date, the government continues to face daunting challenges. There remains a need to continue the restructuring of the economy along the lines of the targeted socialist market economy, and yet there also remains a paramount need to maintain stability. This is an exceptionally fine balance. History teaches that whenever stability is threatened, restructuring stops or at the least is slowed down—thus risking stagnation. Then there is the issue of succession. In the West, there is a widely used system of dividing postwar Chinese leaders into generations, with Mao representing the first generation, Deng Xiaoping the second, and Jiang the third. As secure as Jiang Zemin is, the man is 71 years of age. So there is a need for choosing a fourth generation of leaders to drive China forward from some time in the first or second decades of the next century. At the 15th Party Congress and subsequently in public statements, it has been made clear that Jiang's chosen successor—at least for now!—is Hu Jintao. As we saw with Deng, being a chosen successor does not necessarily mean that you will get the job, given what happened to Hu Yaobang and Zhao Ziyang. Hu Jintao does start from an advantage, however, relative to previous chosen successors, which is that the factional disputes have largely been solved one way or another. There is now no ideological dispute over which direction the economy and the country should take. In addition, previous disputes about the desired speed of economic restructuring have also largely been ironed out, though these could potentially resurface in light of the extended economic slowdown that we are seeing. Given this relatively stable political backdrop, the question remains: What will the future be for China? Forecasting is always dangerous— as one person famously put it, "particularly of the future"—but the following is an attempt at a framework by which to anticipate Chinese economic, social, and political progress over the next two decades, having witnessed the past two. I stress that it is a framework. It is not aimed at anticipating specific events per se. In addition, much depends on the outside world, for whether the Chinese government likes it or not, China remains greatly influenced by the outside world with regard to its domestic policies. Having made all those qualifications, let us *"xia hai,"* or "plunge into the sea" of forecasting, in the hope that an anticipatory framework of China's future will provide value.

Politics

- China remains politically stable in the near term, with the 16th Party Congress in 2002 seen as the benchmark for political emancipation going forward, expanding the village election experiment to SPZs—special political zones—where village, town, and city local elections and a much greater voice are allowed. The Party ensures that it will remain the dominant political force. However, it allows greater expression for the existing "other" political parties. No party is openly allowed to be in opposition. All work toward the "common good," but the Party's consultations with these parties become increasingly meaningful.
- Jiang Zemin, while emphasizing the paramount need for stability, increasingly disassociates himself from the crackdown at Tiananmen. The process of "de-Dengification," disassociating oneself from elements of Deng Xiaoping's policies while simultaneously relegating the great man to mythical status—much as was the case with Mao—continues. Jiang officially nominates Hu Jintao as vice chairman of the Central Military Commission after nominating him as vice state president, thus officially making him the chosen successor. The target for succession is the 17th Party Congress in 2007.
- The National Peoples' Congress gains in influence and is able to make official and independent recommendations to the executive, the State Council.
- Li Peng dies and is publicly vilified for his alleged involvement in the events of Tiananmen Square.
- Zhao Ziyang dies, and China holds its breath as students and workers take to the streets to mourn his passing. The events are brief, the relationship with the police is relatively

friendly, and the whole affair passes off peacefully. The world breathes a sigh of relief.

- China and Taiwan hold direct talks with regard to the notion of "one country, three systems," with the Hong Kong Special Administrative Region playing a consultative role. Though popular discontent within Taiwan at the thought of reunification with the mainland will remain, the example of the HKSAR and increasing political reform in China itself will bring about a groundbreaking deal, allowing for the "return to Chinese national sovereignty of the territory of Chinese Taipei" by 2010.

- The Party continues to alter its nature to one of an administrator, modeling itself along the lines of other dominating Asian parties and governments. Its role continues to be to foster the economic rather than ideological advancement of the nation, though it places an emphasis on helping the disadvantaged in order to avoid incurring a backlash from those remaining elements of the left.

The Economy

- By 2020, China, if it remains peaceful, has the biggest share of world manufacturing production. This causes protectionist backlashes in the political U.S. and Europe, though their corporate counterparts are firmly ensconced in the Chinese mainland with developed bases, hub-and-spoke operations, both to serve the China market and to use China as an exporting base. Increasingly, China is too expensive for the latter, and such exporting operations are being moved to India and to Africa.

- The property glut in China continues to depress prices for the next 3–4 years, though further efforts to deregulate the housing market spur demand.

- By 2000, the renminbi is devalued by 30%, allowing exporters to regain lost competitiveness to their Asian counterparts. Given that Asia has by this time stabilized and is on the mend, the event passes without much incident.

- By the 17th Party Congress in 2007, the renminbi has become fully convertible; China has open capital markets, merging the A- and B-share markets, having previously restructured its banking system; and it has joined the WTO. Many within China question the prudence of joining the WTO since China already has many of the benefits while seemingly gaining little out of joining.
- By 2005, before that happens, the Shanghai Stock Exchange has the largest market capitalization in Asia. The HKSAR has made valiant efforts to reengineer itself, placing more emphasis on multimedia and being a hub for information technology and an international financial center. However, it is increasingly clear that Shanghai *is* in competition with Hong Kong, contrary to Zhu Rongji's comments before the handover in 1997—and that Shanghai has already won. By 2010, Shanghai is the most important international financial center outside London, Tokyo, and New York. Some Japanese corporations move their headquarters to Shanghai, resulting in a press backlash in China that this is the 1930s all over again.
- The generation of "little emperors" fuels a recovery by 2000. However, this is at the expense of the trade balance, which sees its surplus shrink dramatically due to booming imports.
- The Chinese government and the PBOC, in consultation with other Asian nations, including Singapore and the U.S., create a national provident fund scheme that is a decided improvement on any existing pension benefits, necessitating individual and corporate payments.

The Environment, Society, Food, and Oil

- By the year 2005, China is officially the most polluted country in the world, and it is widely recognized locally that pollution is an important factor in the economic slowdown. This is coupled with public demands, notably from the generation that has contributed to the economic successes of the 1990s, for "something to be done." The Chinese environmental agencies get real teeth and are allowed to fine and even imprison corporate and factory heads who breach Chinese environmental laws.

- By 2005, one-tenth of the land area of China is desert due to overforestation, logging, and herding.
- China is increasingly dependent on food and oil imports. Much of the arable and cultivated land has been destroyed by pollution. The resulting acceleration of the move by farmers into the cities causes social unrest.
- By 2010, the Chinese government is promoting a campaign of recycling in order to preserve the environment.
- The family structure starts to disintegrate, with the generation of the "little emperors" paying little attention to the moral tenets of their elders, preferring to focus instead on economic betterment. Drugs become a major problem in China, and there is a national crime campaign against the triads, which openly flout provincial and national laws. Several triad leaders are caught and are executed.
- Much greater emphasis is placed on service industries, with the generation that caused the economic advances of the 1980s and 1990s wanting to enjoy their retirement.
- China is increasingly defensive about its oil imports in the South China Sea and the need to protect such imports. Japan becomes equally defensive, having failed to achieve the necessary levels of oil exploitation in Russia. The first major military tensions since the military exercises in the Taiwan Straits in 1996 take place between China, Japan, and the U.S. in the South China Sea. Cool heads prevail—this time—and the three sign a treaty to protect the shipping lanes and one another's rights.

Conclusion

THE START OF 1999 is a better time than most to review the economic, social, and political fundamentals of China. In terms of Hong Kong, it is now more than a year after the Handover. The initial, somewhat hysterical, fears in the West that the return of the territory to Chinese sovereignty would result in rising authoritarianism have given way to a more sober assessment of the subsequent economic recession that has befallen the former crown colony. The idea of "one country, two systems" has proved itself—and proved yet again what a remarkable man Deng Xiaoping was. Were it not for the economic downturn in Hong Kong, the residents, locals and expats, would for the most part be expounding on the virtues of the system, and it would be held up as a realistic model for the eventual return of Taiwan to Chinese sovereignty, if indeed the Taiwanese people should choose that.

Meanwhile, in the mainland, the economy continues to grind lower, weighed down by the twin burdens of massive overcapacity on the domestic economic front and regional recession and currency devaluations against the renminbi externally. There is little doubt that people in China itself are worried. Drop in at the average bar or restaurant in Beijing or Shanghai, or Hong Kong for that matter, and you will inevitably hear nervous talk about the economy, and more specifically about what could amount to the largest property glut yet in Asia. In 8 or 9 years, Shanghai is said to have built the same number of buildings as it took Hong Kong four decades to build. At one time, some 20% of the world's cranes were in Shanghai. A sea of half-empty residential and commercial buildings is the result, which has in turn—inevitably—led to asset price deflation as property prices correct lower to levels that would be attractive to buyers. Equally inevitably, markets overshoot, which will mean that the downturn in property asset prices in China will be exceptionally painful. Needless to say, China's economic exposure is nothing as a percentage of GDP compared with that of Hong Kong. Yet this is a further burden to an already severely strained banking system.

To a large extent, booming economies are particularly forgiving of fundamental weaknesses, just as at the microeconomic level few people worry about the weaknesses of an individual company's balance if the entire stock market is rocketing higher. The Asian economic model that was so successful for so long is now seen to have been flawed. This does not make Asia particularly unique. Most economic models at some time become flawed since most models are not flexible enough to react to critical changes in internal and regional dynamics. The Asian model was founded on providing the base for attracting significant short- and long-term foreign capital, using cheap, hardworking, and relatively well-educated workforces. That capital was then recycled domestically to produce further investment, accelerating the growth pattern. In other words, the model was entirely dependent on inputs. If inputs slowed as they inevitably must, then so would growth, so went the argument of those who saw the Asian "miracle" as a myth.

China comes into this equation because its own economic model is similar to that used in the rest of Asia (not including Japan) over the last decades, *similar* but not an exact duplicate in a number of key respects. Like the rest of Asia, growth was led by domestic investment; yet crucially the Chinese government also focused on fundamental deregulation of the economy, encouraging competition and transferring the onus for personal success from the government to the individual. While the national government—and thus the Chinese Communist Party—still plays the determining role in economic matters, the Chinese consumer is an increasingly important factor in the direction and strength of the economy going forward. The transfer of responsibility for welfare from the state to the individual, as incomplete as that is, has resulted in major changes in general economic patterns. In terms of consumption, it has meant that the individual now plays a greater role in the economy than at any time in China's recent history. Consumption is now half of China's GDP. China's leading bureaucrats, while no doubt rejoicing at this since it represents a significant success on their part, must have thought that they would have at least some breathing space, despite the breakneck speed of reform in China, before such crucial issues as restructuring the banking system and improving total factor productivity-type activities would have to be addressed. The Asian financial and economic crisis and the ongoing economic slowdown in China permit no breathing space. Time is of the essence. Just as booming economies are forgiving of fundamental weaknesses, slowing economies are particularly merciless in exposing them. To repeat: In China itself, the talk, for now, is no longer of China being the world's leading economic superpower but of how to avoid an Asian-style crisis.

As bizarre as it may sound, this is no bad thing. China starts from an advantage in that its economy is slowing (GDP growth will still come in this year at around 6–7%), rather than booming and then collapsing. China's leaders have seen what has happened in Asia and have learned the relevant lessons. What are those lessons? That short-term capital flows are potentially dangerous if not effectively managed. That institutional infrastructure is necessary to manage them. That "crony capitalism" is essentially economically inefficient and will inevitably result in diminishing returns. It is no coincidence that the economies of Indonesia and Russia lie in ruins and that they were also the most corrupt of countries. Crony capitalism results in distortion of the pricing mechanism, which in turn leads to distortion in production. Unproductive manufacturing and investment are the inevitable consequence. It will also not have escaped the attention of the more astute Chinese leaders that authoritarianism is eventually economically inefficient, that popular participation, just like increasing microeconomic competition, allows for greater economic efficiency, transparency, and ultimately long-term prosperity. Whatever the moral arguments, authoritarianism will inevitably result in economic deterioration. As one visionary analyst in Hong Kong put it, "At the end of the day, someone has to be there to blow the whistle. There have to be checks and balances, both to the economy and to the political system."

Needless to say, given the extent of the economic catastrophe that has befallen Asia, easy answers could be sought and found: namely, that short-term capital is bad and that foreigners are bad. Throughout its history, China has been prone to bouts of xenophobia and could well be so again. Indeed, economic downturns are perfect breeding grounds for nationalism and racism, as the 1930s in Europe confirmed. When it comes down to it, the Chinese leaders are pragmatists as well as patriots and nationalists and Communists (are there any real ones left?). They are there to survive, to change the role of the government and the Party so as to be responsive to the changing domestic and external conditions. Allowing for rising nationalist and xenophobic sentiment, unless under the most desperate of economic conditions, would be counterproductive and, more to the point, could not be controlled. Equally, on the economic front, the lesson is not that short-term capital is bad but that short-term capital poorly allocated and poorly managed through effective institutional infrastructure can indeed be harmful. Saying short-term capital is inherently bad is like saying stock markets are inherently bad. It is childish nonsense. Yet no doubt there will be some who find it politically expedient to go down this line. My view is that this will not be the case in China. China needs capital, both short and long term, in order to continue its economic expansion, much of which will have to come from abroad. While the Asian crisis will provide a further incentive in the short term not to open up the capital account or make the renminbi fully convertible, it should also encourage the government to accelerate the development of the appropriate institutional infrastructure to cope with capital flows when that capital account is finally opened up—for it is inevitable that it will be opened up, and indeed the Chinese government has pledged that this will be the case.

A more realistic danger is that in its implementation of economic policy, the national government will become more statist-oriented in the wake of rising unemployment, slowing exports, and falling asset prices. Indeed, the move by the PBOC to reverse its previous edict, and instead encourage the state banks to resume lending to loss-making SOEs, is a potential concern. Equally, the focus on improving performance at the state banks while limiting competition would seem a contradiction in terms. While the present economic emphasis remains focused on *"jie gui,"* on "connecting" the Chinese economy to the global economy, China's history teaches us that periodically it goes through times of turning inward. The Great Wall is as much a mental as a physical thing in China. Again, it is my profound belief that pragmatism will rule the day, that a combination of continuing on with economic reform and attempting to ensure social and economic stability will prevail in the next couple of years.

The danger with this strategy, however, is that time is not necessarily on the government's side. The Asian crisis and the ongoing slowdown in China necessitate that the fundamental weaknesses within China, notably the SOEs and the banking system, need to be dealt with now. They cannot be put off despite the risk of instability, for to do will simply aggravate the crisis that will occur. While the injection of RMB270 billion in government bonds into the banking system will allow the state banks to meet international standards in terms of capital adequacy, one should not be fooled into thinking that solves the problem. The lesson of Japan in particular is that if you put off a banking bad-debt problem, you create a banking crisis down the road. For the Chinese government, this must of necessity be an unacceptable trade-off. At 20–30% of total, systemic nonperforming loans are intolerably high. The result will be a collapse of the banking system, or the need for the PBOC to print money, thus threatening inflation and a current account and balance of payments crisis if they are not dealt with in short order. Further capital injections are necessary to provide a more solid foundation for these banks so that they can start to offload their non-performing loans, either writing them off or selling them to an RTC-type institution. Yet money alone cannot solve the issue. Commercial banking practices and standards have to be encouraged, and this can only be done through the increased introduction of competition into banking (gradually so as not to threaten the system itself) and through the creation and enforcement of international banking standards in China. People frequently do not change unless they are forced to change. This is the case for both the state banks and the SOEs.

To a certain extent, the very fact that the SOEs now represent less than 40% of total production makes the job of turning them around somewhat easier. Despite hiccups and the temptation to slow down the restructuring process, the SOEs continue (for the moment) to reform, cutting benefits and workers and seeking to operate along more commercial lines. Note that between 1995 and 1997, the total number of industrial SOE employees fell by almost 4 million. During that same period, private-sector employment grew by over 10 million workers. The key will be not in simply throwing money at the SOEs to try and prop them up but in creating the proper regulatory and institutional infrastructure to encourage the continuation of private-sector growth, thus providing the opportunity for the private sector to take up the employment "slack" of the SOE sector. In addition, a sophisticated bankruptcy code, which China admittedly has made initial attempts at, needs to be created in order to ensure that the incentive to avoid the inability to repay loans is sufficient to further encourage prudent business practices. I mentioned the possibility of setting up an RTC-type institution before, and indeed the Chinese government has consulted with its U.S. counterpart about how the Resolution Trust Corp. did in fact solve the savings and loans crisis in the U.S. and how this can be applied to China. The most obvious way is through debt-to-equity swaps whereby a Chinese RTC takes on some of the nonperforming loans of the SOEs in return for equity stakes, as a precursor to privatization on the A-share stock market. Needless to say, capital injection in the state banks and the encouragement of increased competition therein must go hand in hand with this; otherwise there is a risk of substantial capital being drained out of the banking system and into the stock market—if of course Chinese investors view the SOEs as attractive. That said, as the Chinese RTC takes NPLs off the balance sheets of the SOEs, so it does for the state banks as well—since the problems of the state banks and the SOEs are inherently interlinked—potentially allowing the banks to lend new liquidity to the system, it is hoped, in a more profitable manner for all concerned.

The task of recapitalizing the banking system, restructuring the SOEs, and providing a social safety net for the victims of the restructuring process will, needless to say, be extremely costly. In the past, the SOEs, through the benefits of the iron rice bowl, provided most of the welfare benefits for their workers, thus releasing the government from the task. While the government is naturally loath to take this up now, given how immense that burden is, it must and will administer alternatives, notably a national pension system and welfare benefits, provided for through employee and employer contributions. In addition, the government itself has to provide for the unemployed and the disadvantaged, particularly when it appears inevitable that the socialist market economy in China will have the same effect in weakening the solidity of the family unit as free-market capitalism has done in the West. The July 1, 1998, deadline of the wholesale restructuring of the housing market came and went, with the government seemingly unwilling to scrap the household subsidies, an act that would burden a public already concerned by economic slowdown at home and a regional crisis that is unfolding on their TV sets. As I noted before, however, a private housing market is a crucial element of an efficient economy, whether of the socialist market type or more laissez faire. Not only does it provide a greater sense of personal worth, but more importantly in an economy like China it allows for greater labor mobility. This is particularly the case with regard to the employees of small and medium-sized businesses, such enterprises usually being unable to provide housing for their employees. An efficient housing market not only is important per se but also is important in the context of corporate restructuring. A key positive aspect of China's reforms to date is that the government has provided incentives for change—and thus change has occurred. Yet we know that whenever change is seen to potentially threaten stability, then change, not stability, will be sacrificed. In the short term, this may seem prudent, but the current economic backdrop is not one of a booming economy that might otherwise support economic flaws. Rather, it is of an economy that continues to slow, burdened by the mistakes of the past, by a property glut, by massive overcapacity, and by an overvalued currency. Only if the SOEs and the state banks are given the appropriate incentive— change or die—through competition as well as government mandate, will they change the inefficient business and banking practices that were responsible for their present lamentable state. The Chinese people too will have to take up their share of the task of restructuring China's economy. This will necessitate better use of public savings through a more efficient national tax system, a pension scheme, and the further development of the government and corporate bond markets, which can simultaneously help in the economic restructuring process while giving better returns than are available on banking deposits.

While the world is currently focused on thoughts of global economic downturn and possible recession, subsequent to the Asian crisis which began in 1997, it should keep an eye on China, both in the immediate and in the long term. Put simply, the world cannot afford for China's economy, the third largest in the world, to collapse. Indeed, in some respects China's economy is even more important than the second largest, Japan's, given the size of China's population and what a collapse could mean, not only in economic, but in political and even military terms. On the economic front, the transition from economic slowdown to recession in China, coupled with currency devaluation, would represent a further massive deflationary impulse in the global economic (dis)order, which would be devastating for global financial markets. As great as the economic achievements of China's government have been to date, the ability of the government to avoid that scenario remains to be seen.

I am not saying economic collapse *will* happen in China. What I am saying, at the risk of repetition, is that the issue in the immediate term is whether or not its economic successes will survive the current downturn. This may seem overly melodramatic, but we live in a world where the parallel successes of the rest of Asia, including Japan, have been devastated, not by short-term capital flows, but by governmental economic mismanagement and the resulting withdrawal of those short-term capital flows due to deteriorating returns. I am a fundamental believer in the market, in the validity of a pricing mechanism based on free and unfettered competition which dictates the efficient creation and allocation of capital. China's government appears to have gone down the path toward this type of economic system, whether it is called a "socialist market" or overtly a "laissez faire" or "free-market" economy. Whatever it does now, it seems certain that the government cannot turn back the clock to a more state-oriented system that did not give its population economic choices. Indeed, it must know well that the Chinese public, having tasted the initial fruits of the reform process, would not tolerate such a reversal. The trick is therefore to go forward, to traverse that river while feeling for rocks underfoot at an even quicker pace, given the necessity of avoiding the economic calamities that have befallen much of the rest of Asia. Granted, China benefits from the economic "Great Wall," which is the fact that its capital account is for the most part closed. However, this will not protect it indefinitely and is certainly no substitute for accelerated reform. This is no substitute for a sound economic foundation. Whatever the artificial barriers to capital, history teaches that the market will always find a way to get around them if there are sufficient doubts about the strength of that foundation. China may crack down on illegal foreign exchange trading, but to do only that is to attack the symptoms, not the disease. The danger remains, as always, to resort to easy answers, to slow rather than accelerate reform, thus aggravating a set of crucial economic problems that have merely been delayed, a ticking bomb that if allowed to go off will be heard in Moscow, in Washington, in London, and in Buenos Aires.

Of course, this need not be the case, and if the past is anything to go by, China's government will indeed solve its problems and in record time. If the state banks are recapitalized, if the SOEs are further restructured to implement more profitable practices, if the private sector is encouraged to take up more of the slack, and if the institutional and investment infrastructure is developed to pay for all of this, then China will indeed be a global economic force to be reckoned with, potentially even *the preeminent* global economic superpower that some have, somewhat prematurely, anticipated. In that context, China could be a force for Asian economic rebirth. It hangs in the balance. China is on the brink either of unparalleled success, even by the exceptional standards of its recent achievements, or of continued economic slowdown at best, collapse at worst. If the world isn't holding its breath, it should be. Meanwhile, that paradox that I mentioned in the introduction remains—the lack of political reform relative to economic reform. The government has realized the inherent contradiction and is, in its usual gradualist style, seeking to tackle the issue through both allowing elections at the village level and allowing the NPC a slightly greater voice. This is another headache for the government, but as the Chinese character *"weiji"* describes, it is both a "danger" and an "opportunity." If economic conditions are to worsen further in the near term in China, which remains a strong possibility, you want the people on your side, and you do that by giving them a greater voice and responsibility in their own affairs. That's so if things get really bad, they don't turn round and blame you!

This should all be seen against the backdrop of the current global economic downturn and potentially global economic and financial crisis. The risk is recession worldwide. It is that prospect that we are staring at right now. Asset markets have collapsed, and real wealth has been destroyed. We are in the midst of a global margin call after years of profligate monetary growth. From behind its Great Wall, China watches these developments nervously, and it is indeed right to be nervous. Its increasing involvement in the global economy means that slowdown elsewhere, not just in Asia but in the U.S. and Europe, will impact China's economy, closed capital account or not. That impact, which will not be positive, could incite domestic elements to call for more protectionist rather than looser trade and capital market regulations in China. Similar calls are entirely possible in the West—which would represent the repetition of the lunatic irresponsibility we saw at the end of the 1920s and early 1930s which led to the Depression. If the government of China manages to navigate successfully all these hurdles—a very big "if"—the world should not forget.

Notes and Sources

Chapter 1

1. *Asian Development Outlook, 1996 and 1997,* Asian Development Bank, Oxford University Press, 1997, p. 242.
2. "IMF Direction of Trade Statistics," as cited in John Fernald, Hali Edison, and Prakash Lougani, "Was China the First Domino? Assessing Links between China and the Rest of Emerging Asia," Board of Governors of the Federal Reserve System, International Finance Discussion Paper No. 604, March 1998.

Chapter 2

1. *Asian Development Outlook, 1997 and 1998,* Asian Development Bank, Oxford University Press, 1997, p. 223.

Chapter 3

1. *Hong Kong Economic Journal,* January 21, 1997.
2. Ibid.
3. *South China Morning Post,* November 28, 1996.
4. *The Globe and Mail,* July 18, 1997.

5. *The Sydney Morning Herald*, May 15, 1997.
6. Wang Shaogang and Hu Angang, "The Decline in the Extractive Capacity of the Chinese Government and Its Results," *Twenty First Century*, No. 21, February 1994.
7. "Hainan Island: Communal Politics and the Struggle for Identity," Feng Chongyi and David S. G. Goodman, in David Goodman (ed.), *China's Provinces in Reform: Class, Community and Political Culture*, p. 76.

Chapter 5

1. Laurence J. Brahm, *China as No. 1: The New Superpower Takes Center Stage*, Butterworth-Heinemann Asia, 1996, p. 120.
2. Ibid., p. 123.
3. Ibid., p. 125.
4. Paul Krugman, "The East Is in the Red, a Balanced View of China's Trade," *The Dismal Science*, July 17, 1997.
5. Rudiger Dornbusch, "Next, China? Reform Not Devaluation Is the Way Forward," *Financial Times*, August 6, 1998.

Chapter 6

1. IMF and Hong Kong government data.
2. "Recent Economic Developments," Dubravko Mihaljek, Aasim Husain, and Valerie Cerra, *IMF Report on the People's Republic of China Hong Kong Special Administrative Region*, April 13, 1998, p. 23.
3. Ibid.

Chapter 7

1. As mentioned in an article by Zheng Yongnian, "Comprehensive National Power, an Expression of China's New Nationalism," in Wang Gungwu and John Wong (eds.), *China's Political Economy*, East Asian Institute, National University of Singapore, Singapore University Press, World Scientific Publishing, 1998.

Chapter 8

1. He Bochuan, *China on the Edge: The Crisis of Ecology and Development*, China Books & Periodicals Inc., 1991, p. 159.
2. Ibid.
3. Ibid., p. 9.
4. Ibid.
5. Hu Angang, *Existence and Development*, National Situation Analysis Group, Academica Sinica, Scientific Press, Beijing, 1989. As cited in Susumu Yabuki, *China's New Political Economy: The Giant Awakes*, Westview Press, 1995, pp. 15–16.
6. Ibid.
7. *Statistical Yearbook of China 1993*, State Statistical Bureau, Beijing, p. 480.
8. He Bochuan, op. cit., p. 69.
9. Ibid., p. 71.
10. Yabuki, op. cit., p. 91.
11. Ibid., p. 93.
12. IIe Bochuan, op. cit., p. 31.

Chapter 10

1. Conghua Li, *China: The Consumer Revolution*, Deloitte & Touche Consulting Group, John Wiley & Sons, 1998, p. 4.

Bibliography

Books

Brahm, Laurence J., *China as No. 1: The New Superpower Takes Center Stage*, Butterworth-Heinemann Asia, 1996.

Conghua Li, *China: The Consumer Revolution*, Deloitte & Touche Consulting Group, John Wiley & Sons, 1998.

Goodman, David (ed.), *China's Provinces in Reform: Class, Community and Political Culture*, Routledge, 1997.

He Bochuan, *China on the Edge: The Crisis of Ecology and Development*, China Books and Periodicals Inc., 1991, now Pacific View Press.

Wang Gungwu and John Wong (eds.), *China's Political Economy*, East Asian Institute, National University of Singapore University, Singapore University Press, World Scientific Publishing, 1998.

Yabuki, Susumu, *China's New Political Economy: The Giant Awakes*, Westview Press, 1995.

Official Publications

Asian Development Bank, *Asian Development Outlook, 1996 and 1997*, Oxford University Press, 1996.

Asian Development Bank, *Asian Development Outlook, 1997 and 1998*, Oxford University Press, 1997.

Fernald, John, Hali Edison, and Prakash Loungani, "Was China the First Domino? Assessing Links Between China, and the Rest of Emerging Asia," Board of Governors of the Federal Reserve System, International Finance Discussion Paper No. 604, March 1998.

Mihaljek, Dubravko, Aasim Husain, and Valerie Cerra, *Recent Economic Developments*, IMF Report on the People's Republic of China Hong Kong Special Administrative Region, April 13, 1998.

Newspapers

The Financial Times, August 6, 1998.
Hong Kong Economic Journal, January 21, 1997.
South China Morning Post, November 26, 1996.
The Sydney Morning Herald, May 15, 1997.

Index

About the Author

Callum Henderson is an Emerging Market Currency Strategist at a global investment bank in London. He previously spent 6 years in New York and Hong Kong analyzing global currency markets, with a particular emphasis on developments in Asia. A widely quoted authority on currency markets, with particular emphasis on currency crises, he has given lectures and seminars around the world on the current, spreading emerging market crisis.

Prior to his 9 years writing about and analyzing the financial markets, he earned a B.A. Honors in politics, economics, and French from Sunderland Polytechnic, a DEF III (Diplôme D'Etudes Françaises) from L'Université de Tours in Tours, France, and an M.A., in Middle East politics and economics from Exeter University in the U.K.